THE RITES OF BRIGID

Seán Ó Duinn OSB

The Rites of Brigid,
Goddess and Saint

the columba press

First published in 2005 by
the columba press
55A Spruce Avenue, Stillorgan Industrial Park,
Blackrock, Co Dublin

Cover by Bill Bolger
Origination by The Columba Press
Printed in Ireland by ColourBooks Ltd, Dublin

ISBN 1 85607 483 8

Table of Contents

Foreword

In a flight of imagination, the author of *Beatha Bhrighdi* (The Life of Brigid) in the *Leabhar Breac* sees the soul of Brigid as the blazing sun illuminating the Heavenly City. There are the angels and archangels, cherubim and seraphim, accompanying Mary's Son and there is the Holy Trinity, the Father, Son and Holy Spirit. Inspired by this vision, the author prays:

I ask for the Lord's mercy
through the intercession of blessed Brigid.
May we reach that unity
which exists for ever and ever (Stokes, 1877, 86).

This mystical effusion is concerned above all with the otherworld and the last times.

On the otherhand, there is in *Beatha Bhrighdi* a message of hope and consolation for those who in this world make their way painfully to God amidst trials and afflictions:

It is she who helps everyone in trouble and affliction.
It is she who cures diseases.
It is she who mitigates anger and calms the stormy sea.
She is the prophesied one of Christ.
She is the Queen of the South.
She is the Mary of the Gael. (*Beatha Bhrighdi,* 1703-1705)

In Brigid, two elements come together – the eternal and the temporal – and she is seen as a female warrior trampling on demons and on the forces of evil in her efforts to lead a person over the dangerous bridge of this present life to the gleaming country of heaven.

After a short summary of the life of Brigid as it is presented in various biographies, we proceed to the principal object of this work, that is, to discuss the rites and ceremonies with which the Feast of Brigid is celebrated.

Since Brigid is, as it were, a bridge between this world and the world beyond, it is no wonder that her fame extended far and near. As the poem says:

Gabhaim molta Bhríde,
Ionmhain í le hÉirinn;
Ionmhain le gach tír í,
Molaimís go léir í. (Mac Giolla Chomhaill, 1984, 29)
(I proclaim the praises of Brigid; she is dear to Ireland; she is dear to every country; let us all join in her praises.)

The object of this work is to examine the ways in which the people of Ireland praised Brigid in the traditional rituals pertaining to her Feastday.

In the biography of Brigid as contained in the *Leabhar Breac* (Stokes, 1877, 50-87), a very full account is given of her life. Moreover, some elements of pre-Christian practice may be discerned in the narrative. While this version is not as old as that of Cogitosus (*JRSAI*, Vol 117, 5), nevertheless its ethos is close to that of the folk-cult of the people who revered Brigid. For this reason, the *Leabhar Breac* version is the one used as a basis for the following shortened account of her life:

Brigid was the daughter of Dubhthach mac Dreimne. Dubhthach had purchased a slave-girl named Broicseach, a daughter of Dall-bhronach of Dal Chonchuir in the southern area of Breagha. Dubhthach married the girl and she became pregnant. Dubhthach's wife, Breachnat, was furious and threatened to leave him if he did not sell Broicseach to somebody living far away. But Dubhthach didn't want to sell her.

One day, while Dubhthach and the slave-girl were going past the house of a certain druid, the druid heard the noise of the chariot and he came out to greet them.

The druid made a foretelling that they would have a wonderful daughter whose fame would spread far and wide because of her power and virtue.

After this, God sent two bishops – Mel and Melchu – to Dubhthach and when Mel learned of Breachnat's anger he informed her that her own descendants would serve the descendants of the slave-girl. Nevertheless, she would be of assistance to them.

Then, another druid happened to come that way and the bishops advised Dubhthach to sell the slave-girl to him but not to hand over the infant in her womb. Dubhthach agreed to this and the druid took Broicseach to his home.

Shortly after this, another *file* or druid from the territory of Conaill purchased the slave-girl. This man prepared a great banquet for the king of Conaill and it so happened that the queen at that moment was on the point of giving birth. A *fáidh* of the learned class, who happened to be present, was asked if this were a lucky time for a royal birth. The *fáidh* said that the child born next morning with the rising of the sun would have an outstanding destiny. However, the queen's child was born in advance of this point and he was born dead.

The *file*, then, asked the *fáidh* about the slave-girl's child. The *fáidh* answered: 'The child born tomorrow at the rising of the sun, and who is born without being inside or outside a house – that child will surpass every other child in Ireland'

It happened then, at the break of day, that the slave-girl,Broicseach, was going into a house, holding a bucket of buttermilk in her hand.

She had one foot inside the threshold and the other outside the threshold when Brigid was born. The servant-girls washed the baby and the mother with the buttermilk which was in the vessel. Brigid was born on a Wednesday, on the eighth day of the moon, at Fochairt Mhuirthemhne.

Brigid was taken then to the place where the queen's baby lay dead. When Brigid's breath reached him he became alive and well. The druid and Broicseach and Brigid then went to the Province of Connacht where they settled down.

One day, the people of the area saw that the house in which the child Brigid lived was on fire. They rushed to the house to extinguish the flames but found on arrival that there was no fire at all. The people concluded that the child was filled with the grace of the Holy Spirit.

Once, while asleep, the druid saw three clerics , that is to say three angels, coming and pouring oil on Brigid's head to complete the rite of baptism. The three clerics instructed the druid to give the name Brigid to the child.

Brigid was not accustomed to take the ordinary food available to her. For this reason the druid obtained a white cow with red ears and she used to drink the milk of this cow.

As Brigid began to come of age everything under her care increased and flourished. She took care of the sheep,of blind people and of the poor.

The druid gave Brigid back to Dubhthach, her father, and they returned to the area of Uíbh Fhailí. It happened that her nurse was ill at that time. Brigid prepared a potion for her from water, having the taste of beer, and the nurse was cured of her disease.

Some guests arrived at Dubhthach's house. Brigid prepared five portions of meat for them. It happened that a hungry hound was passing by and Brigid gave him one of the portions. When he had eaten that, she gave him another portion. 'Have you all the portions?', asked Dubhthach. 'Count them,' said she. He did so and all the portions were there. 'That girl works many wonders', said her father.

On one occasion, Brigid attended a Synod of Leinster. It happened that a holy man who was present had had a vision in which he saw Mary coming to the meeting. When Brigid entered, this man said: 'This is the Mary I saw in a vision,' and from that time on, she was called *Muire na nGael* – Mary of the Irish.

Without her father's permission, Brigid went to her mother who was poor and ill and still a slave-girl in Connacht. She took over her mother's duties and it was her custom at the time of butter-making to divide the butter into twelve divisions in honour of the twelve apostles and a large lump in honour of the Son of God. Although she used to give away butter to the poor, there was no reduction in the amount manufactured. 'It was Christ and his twelve apostles who proclaimed the gospel to the peoples of the world,' said Brigid, 'It is in their name that I look after the poor, for Christ is to be found in the person of every faithful poor person.' Finally, Brigid's miracles so impressed the druid and his wife that the druid became a Christian. The druid gave Brigid a herd of cows and made her mother a free-woman. Brigid and her mother Broicseach returned to Dubhthach.

Dubhthach, however, was not over-satisfied with this arrangement as he saw his wealth diminish while Brigid handed over his goods to the poor. He decided to sell Brigid to Dunlaing Mac Enda, king of Leinster, as a servant, to grind corn.

Brigid and her father went to the king's fort by chariot. When they arrived, Dubhthach went inside to meet the king, leaving Brigid and his sword in the chariot. While Dubhthach was inside, a leper happened to pass by and Brigid gave him her father's sword.

Dubhthach was furious at the loss of his sword and he took Brigid into the fort to meet the king. The king asked her if she intended to give his property away to the poor also. Brigid gave the king no satisfactory answer. She answered that if all the wealth of Leinster were at her disposal she would give it all away to the King of the Elements. The king said that Brigid's status was higher in the eyes of God than among men. He gave a sword with an ivory hilt to Dubhthach on Brigid's behalf and he made her a free-woman.

Brigid went, along with other virgins, to Telcha Mide, to receive a nun's veil from Bishop Mel. It happened that through the bounty of the Holy Spirit, the rite of Ordination of a Bishop was read over Brigid. Mac Caille said that it was not right to confer the status of a bishop on a woman. Bishop Mel, said, however: 'We have no power over it, because it is from God himself that this honour came to her – an honour beyond that of any other woman.' For this reason, the men of Ireland, bestow the honour due to a bishop on Brigid's successor.

It was on the eighth day of the moon that Brigid was born; she took the veil on the eighteenth day; she went to heaven on the twenty-eighth day; she was consecrated along with eight virgins and she lived her life in accordange with the eight Beatitudes

With one sack of malt, Brigid succeeded in providing beer for the seven churches of Tulach for Holy Thursday and the eight days of Easter.

On one occasion, Brigid went to a church in Teathbha for the celebration of Easter. On Holy Thursday she washed the feet of the people in the church. Among them were four who were very ill. Brigid cured the four of them.

Brigid went to Dunlaing, king of Leinster, with two requests. She promised him the kingdom of heaven for himself as a reward. The king, however, took little notice of this promise. 'I can't see the kingdom of heaven,' he said, 'and nobody knows anything about it. For that reason, I don't bother about it at all. As for granting the kingdom to my son, I don't bother about that either, for I myself won't be around. But give me a long life in my kingdom and give me victory over the Uí Néill in battle, and above all make me win the first battle against them to give me courage for those to follow.' This was granted, and the king won a great victory over the Uí Néill in the battle of Lochar (70).

Brigid's fame spread throughout Ireland because of the miracles she performed especially those of curing the sick.

Brigid travelled to the territory of Fir Ros and she asked the king of the area to set a certain prisoner free. The king refused her request but he handed over the custody of the prisoner to her for one night. Brigid appeared to him and she instructed him to recite the hymn 'Nunc populus' when the chain which bound him was loosed. He was then to turn right-handwise and flee as fast as he could. The prisoner followed these instructions and escaped from prison.

One day when Brigid was travelling in Maigh Laighean (the Plain of Leinster) she met a student and he was running. 'Where are you rushing to?' Brigid asked him. 'I'm going to heaven,' he

answered. Brigid recited the 'Our Father' with him. He was
Ninnid Lámh-Idan who at a later stage was to give Holy
Communion to Brigid.

Brigid went to Bishop Íobhar to mark out her city for her.
They arrived at the place where Cill Dara now stands. It happened, just then, that Ailill Mac Dunlainge was going through
Cill Dara with a hundred horse-loads of wooden posts. Two of
Brigid's women came and asked Ailill to give them some of the
posts. Ailill refused. With that, the horses were glued to the
ground and were unable to move. Ailill was forced to give
Brigid all the posts and it was with these that she built her
monastery in Cill Dara. As a reward, she said that Ailill's heirs
would have the sovereignty of Leinster for ever.

On one occasion, Brigid gave a cow to each of two lepers.
One of them was a proud man and he began to insult her. As
they were crossing the Bearbha the river rose up against them.
The humble leper and his cow managed to cross in safety while
the proud leper was drowned.

The Queen of Leinster came to Brigid and gave her a silver
chain as an offering. Brigid gave the chain to her nuns and they
hid it away without telling her, as she was always giving things
away to the poor. A leper came along and Brigid gave him the
silver chain. The nuns were furious when they heard that the
chain was gone. 'Your mercy to everybody is of little use to us,'
they complained, 'while we ourselves are in need of food and
clothes.' 'You are a bad lot,' said Brigid, 'go to the church, to the
place where I pray, and you will find your chain.' They did so
and there was the chain even though it had been given to the
leper.

On another occasion, seven bishops came to Brigid, and she
had no food for them. She had the cows milked for the third time
that day and they had plenty of milk (80).

Another time, he had a large number of workers gathered together cutting the corn. It began to rain in Maigh Life but because of Brigid's prayers not a drop fell on her own farm.

Brendan, in the western area of the country, heard of Brigid's miracles and he came to talk to her. Brigid came in from herding her sheep to welcome him. She took off her cloak and hung it on a sunbeam coming in the window. It hung there as if suspended from a crook. Brendan instructed his servant to hang up his own cloak in the same way but it fell down twice. Brendan's anger rose and he hung up the cloak on the sunbeam for the third time and this time he was successful. After this, each of them confessed the state of their souls to each other. 'It is not usual for me,' said Brendan, to travel over seven ridges without my mind being directed to God.' 'From the time I first directed my mind on God,' said Brigid, 'I have never taken it away from him'.

After Brigid had founded many monasteries and having performed miracles more numerous than the sands on the seashore or the stars in the sky, Brigid came to the end of her holy life. She was ascetic, she was generous, she was patient. She was joyful in the service of God. She was steadfast, she was humble, she was forgiving, she was loving. She was a consecrated vessel to contain the Body of Christ, she was a temple of God, her heart and mind formed an enduring throne for the Holy Spirit. She is like a dove among birds, like the vine among trees, like the sun among the stars of heaven.

Ninnid Lámh-Idan arrived from Rome and he gave her the Holy Viaticum. Then her spirit ascended to heaven. Her relics are preserved on earth with great honour and reverence.

* * *

It cannot be said that the Life of Brigid, as it is contained in the *Leabhar Breac*, corresponds to our understanding of a modern biography, with its wealth of historically correct details. Many of the *Lives* of Brigid emphasise the amount of miracles she performed during her lifetime and it appears that the various writers had in mind the promotion of devotion to Brigid among the faithful as their primary object.

From the searching analysis of the *Life of Brigid* by Cogitosus made by Dr Seán Connolly, it is clear that Brigid's faith/belief was of high significance. Jesus declared: 'All things are possible to him who believes' (Mark 9:23). Cogitosus lists a large number of miracles and these wonders are an expression of the power of God. But it is through Brigid's outstanding faith that God's power becomes effective in this world and revealed to the people.

Many of Brigid's miracles dealt with the multiplication of food and drink for the benefit of the poor and for ecclesiastics. Domestic affairs and hospitality are prominent and it is easy to imagine her as a female Christian Hospitaller (*Brughaidh*).

In the *Poems of Bláthmac* a special importance is given to hospitality and to the mercy of Christ, and these same virtues are discerneable also in the *Lives* of Brigid. It is said in the *Life* in the *Book of Lismore*, that Brigid chose the phrase: 'Blessed are the merciful for mercy shall be shown unto them' (Mt 5:7) from the Eight Beatitudes as a motto for herself (Macdonald, 1992, 27).

It appears that these particular virtues were emphasised in early Christianity in Ireland. It is clear that the mind of Christ and the mind of Brigid were closely united and that episodes in her life reflected the gospels.

On the otherhand, Brigid's life was bound up with contemporary Celtic life in Ireland, and so differed greatly from the lifestyle portrayed in the New Testament. Brigid was trying to follow Christ and to put the precepts of the gospel into practice while operating within the native Irish tradition. While the cult of Brigid extended throught the country as a whole, the various *Lives* of St Brigid, and place-names such as Cill Bhríde, indicate that it was concentrated around the centre of the country and especially in the area of Uíbh Fhaillí. Even today, it is in the Barony of Uíbh Fhaillí that Cill Dara (Kildare) is situated (McCone, 1982, 83).

Brigid belonged to the tribe of the Fothairt of Uíbh Fhaillí (Smyth, 1982, 19). Perhaps this influenced the tradition which holds that she was connected to Fothairt Mhuirtheimhne (Faughart) near Dún Dealgán (Dundalk) in Co Louth.

Broicseach, Brigid's mother, was the daughter of Dallbhrónach of the Dál Chonchúir, in south Breagha, according to the *Leabhar*

Breac. Brigid's genealogy, from her father Dubhthach's side is given there also:

'Brigid,daughter of Dubhthach son of Deimhne, son of Breasal, son of Den, son of Conla, son of Artrach, son of Art Corb, son of Cairbre Nia, son of Cormac, son of Aongus, son of Eochaidh Fionn Fuathnairt, son of Feidhlimidh Reachtaire', and so forth.

Brigid's *Genealogy* was used in Cúil Aodha in West Cork by people emmigrating. It was believed that there was no danger of drowning if they had this *rann* or poetic text. Consequently, they learned it by heart from the old people (IFC 900;85-86). However, a certain unevenness may be discerned between Brigid as presented in the *Lives* and Brigid as the object of the people's rituals.

As has been said already, from the literary point of view, Brigid is especially associated with Leinster, although she is seen to travel beyond that area on occasion.

On the otherhand, the folklore accounts will show that her cult belongs to the whole country. This gives rise to the question as to why the cult of Brigid is countrywide while the cult of other Irish saints is confined to their own areas.

From the historical point of view, Kildare was particularly important:

Although Kildare lay on the fringes of Uí Failge territory in the north-western region, its association with the Curragh and its domination by the Uí Dunlainge kings of Leinster from the seventh to the twelfth centuries, made it one of the most important centres in northern Leinster. After the Anglo-Norman invasion, it was here, almost certainly, that Strongbow established his headquarters. Kildare began life in the prehistoric Celtic past as a cult centre of the goddess Brigit, beside a sacred oak, which in the sixth century was taken over by a Christian virgin and her community of nuns – hence Cill Dara. The ritual fires which were kept continuously burning here in the thirteenth century testify to the origin of Kildare as a pagan sanctuary (Smyth, 1982, 41).

Within this context, the importance of Kildare is readily understood, as politics and religion were contained in one centre.

Professor McCone discusses this question and, on the one hand, lays bare the historical weaknesses of the *Lives* of Brigid the saint while, on the other hand, pointing to the considerable evidence for a Celtic Goddess of the same name. As a result of this confusion, a trace of paganism can be discerned in the cult of the saint:

> Fiú má bhí bunús staire le corrshonra faoi shaol Bhríde sna beathaí éagsúla seo, níl muide in ann é seo a dhéanamh amach go cinnte anois, agus caithfear admháil mar sin nach bhfuil aon eolas iontaofa faoi Bhríd mar bhean stairiúil le baint amach astu. Ar an láimh eile, tá neart fianaise le fáil faoi bhandia pagánta na gCeilteach i gcoitinne, agus na nGael go háirithe, darbh ainm Bríd, agus níl aon amhras ná gur fhág an cultus pagánta seo lorg ar an gceann Críostaí' (1982, 82).

> ('Even if there were a historical foundation for some detail concerning the life of Brigid, we are unable now to distinguish it with certainty, and we are forced to admit that it is impossible to draw any reliable information on Brigid as a historical personage from the *Lives*. On the otherhand, there is a wealth of evidence regarding a pagan goddess of the Celts in general, and of the Irish in particular, whose name was Brigid, and there is no doubt but that this pagan cult left its mark on the Christian cult.)

At a later stage, we will see the account given by Giraldus Cambrensis (Gerald of Wales) of the perpetual fire kept by Brigid's nuns in Kildare, and this carries certain pre-Christian overtones. In a similar vein, a statement in *Sanas Chormaic* concerning Brigid, daughter of An Daghdha, describes her as Lady of Ironwork, Lady of Medicine and Lady of Poetry.

Imbolc is her feastday. Apart from the literature, however, little remains in the actual site in Kildare to indicate that a pre-Christian sanctuary ever existed there, although a Holy Well and the site of the Perpetual Fire are still in evidence.

It will be seen, nevertheless, that if Cill Dara itself is included along with Cnoc Almhaine (Hill of Allen), Nás na Rí (Naas) and

Dún Ailinne (Dunawlin) that a square is formed on the landscape with these sites forming the corners, and perhaps Aonach
Carmain – the great Fair of Carman – was celebrated within this
square in Cuirreach Life.

This means that Brigid of Kildare lived within an area that
was steeped in history, prehistory, politics and mythology and
that a lively way of life was going on around her during her lifetime.

CHAPTER ONE

Brigid and Springtime

St Brigid's Feastday – Lá Fhéile Bríde – occurs on the first day of February, the beginning of spring and the period of the rebirth of nature after the long death of winter. The turning of the sun at the winter solstice occurred six weeks ago, and the lengthening day speaks of new life and fresh beginnings, as the poet Raifteirí expressed it:

Anois teacht an Earraigh,
beidh an lá dul chun síneadh,
is tar éis na Féile Bríde ardóidh mé mo sheol.
(Now that the spring has come, the days will grow longer, and after St Brigid's feastday I will hoist my sail.)

The sun's new power is energising the vegetation. A dark green colour spreads over the grey grass. Buds appear on the trees and bushes as heralds of new life. The herbs of spring arise from the earth. The song of birds proclaims that the winter is past and a new era beginning.

The farmer is aware that the earth is calling him to a new period of care. This is the lambing season and the time of preparation for the sowing of corn. The evils of the winter season must be banished to allow the fertile energy of spring to enter.

The month of February marks a dynamic change of season, and in ancient pre-Christian Ireland, the Feast of Imbolc/Oimelc on the first of February stood out as the signal for the beginning of spring.

The exact meaning of 'Imbolc' or 'Oimelc' presents considerable difficulty, and Pamela Berger suggests gently that cleansing of the fields after the winter and preparing them for sowing the grain in the spring may be a fundamental idea underlying the term. She refers to the theory which separates the term 'Imbolc/Imbolg' into two words: *im* and *bolg*, *im* meaning 'around,' and *bolg* 'belly' – the belly of that goddess – that is the land, the farm. This would refer then, to a traditional ritual procession around the farm, at the beginning of spring, to create a cleansing boundary, so that this particular area of land would be safe from any evil forces threatening the growth of the new corn. Perhaps there is a remnant of this to be found in the 'Brídeog' procession of today on St Brigid's Feast (1988, 71).

The idea can certainly be compared to that of the *Litaniae Minores*, or Rogation Processions, in which, in Catholic countries, the priest and people processed around the boundaries of the parish on the three days before the Feast of the Ascension of Our Lord into Heaven, praying and sprinkling Holy Water as a means of safeguarding the growing crops from disease.

While this etymology may be uncertain, nevertheless, examples occur of processions through the fields in which an image of the goddess is carried so that her blessing may fall on them.

While the Feast of St Brigid is on the first of February, the next day – the second of February – is the Feast of the Presentation of the Lord in the Temple. However, from the ninth century onwards, north of the Alps, there is a tendency in the church's books of ritual to call the Feast *Purificatio Beatae Mariae Virginis* and this custom prevailed until the Second Vatican Council (Stevenson, 1988, 346). By this time the church had moved out from the cities to the country areas and was, no doubt, coming under the influence of the farming population with its preoccupation with cleansing and protecting the farms at this time of the year. In the light of this phenomenon, one can expect a certain similarity between the Feast of Brigid and that of the Purification of the Blessed Virgin Mary, also called Candlemas.

Mary's Feast of the Purification, moreover, may have a pre-Christian model in the custom of Greek women running through the fields in February with lighted torches to simulate the goddess Demeter's search for her daughter Persephone who was taken to the underworld by Pluto, and in consequence the fields were barren. This torchbearing ritual may well have influenced the Candlemas of the western church (Berger, 1988,115).

Professor Berger gives a useful summary account of the month of February in so far as it is connected with purification and fertility:

Throughout the Middle Ages and into modern times February was considered a month of purification. It was the time of the ceremonial purification of the fields before the seed could be placed in the ground. And it was also the time of purification of women who had given birth during the preceding year. Until the last century, women would come to the church on February 2 for a postchildbirth blessing and would take home with them their blessed candles. Since the pagan torch or candle procession had been assimilated into Christian ritual, an originally pagan seasonal practice was to endure, transformed, until the twentieth century (1988, 115).

With the arrival of St Brigid's Day, a remarkable change is perceptable in nature:

'Tá sé ráite go dtosnaíonn an fhuiseog ar sheinim Lá 'le Bríde agus an londubh leis, agus deirtear go dtosnaíonn éanlaith an aeir go léir ar chúpláil ó Lá 'le Bríde amach' (IFC 900; 39; Ciarán Ó Síothcháin, Cléire, Co Chorcaí)

(It is said that the lark begins to sing on St Brigid's Day and the blackbird also, and that all the birds of the air begin to mate from St Brigid's Day onwards.)

The growth of vegetation in springtime is described very effectively in the folklore of Cúil Aodha. It begins with the week beginning on St Brigid's Day and progresses into April, but it is remarkable that three goddesses ar held responsible for this development of the crops during the spring period. One is naturally reminded of the the triple goddess of the Celts or the *Matres* (Mothers) depicted on plaques of the Gallo-Romans on the Continent or in Britain. The three are pictured clearly, for instance, on a plaque found in Cirencester, Gloucestershire. The three goddesses are shown sitting down with baskets on their laps holding loaves of bread and fruits of the earth (Bord, J. and C., 1982, 24).

Perhaps an echo of this ancient tradition is found in folklore: 'Deireadh na seandaoine go mbíodh nithe ag cuimhneamh ar bheith ag fás Lá 'le Bríde, go mbíodh cailleach a' cur aníos agus beirt chailleach ag a gcur síos, agus nuair a thagadh Lá 'le Pádraig bhíodh beirt chailleach ag cur aníos agus cailleach ag cur síos. Ach nuair a thagadh an chéad lá d'Abran bhíodh an triúr cailleach d'aobhuíon chun bheith ag cur neithe aníos. Deir na feirmeoirithe gur mithid cuimhneamh ar obair an earraigh nuair a thagann Lá 'le Bríde agus 'sé ceol na n-éun a chuireann so i n-iúl dóibh' (IFC 900;89-90; Amhlaoibh Ó Loingsigh, Cúil Aodha, Contae Chorcaí, Narrator, Cáit Uí Liatháin, Cúil Aodha, Scribe)

(The old people used to say that things would be thinking of growing on St Brigid's Day; that one 'Veiled One'/hag would be pushing the vegetation upwards while two hags would be keeping it down. Then, when St Patrick's Day would come round, two hags would be pushing it upwards. But when the first of April arrived, the three hags would join forces to push the vegetation upwards. The farmers say that it is time to think of the spring work when St Brigid's Day arrives and it is the music of the birds that reminds them of this.)

The fishing season on the River Barrow in Wexford begins on St Brigid's Day and it continues to October (IFC 907;179). This conforms to the general pattern throughout the country except for the Garbhóg River in Co Sligo:

'Salmon fishing opens in all Ireland that day with the exception of the Garvogue in Sligo, for it is said that St Brigid blessed it when passing and fishing opens in it on the first of January.' (IFC 902;242; Mícheál Ó Gallchobhair, Cill Fhearga, Druim Átha Thiar, Contae Liatroma, Scribe.)

From the literary point of view, Brigid's connection with fishing is not as pronounced as her connection with cows. However, it is not entirely absent, as is evident from the story of St Brendan the Navigator and St Brigid:

One day, Brendan was standing on a high cliff looking out to sea. Suddenly, two whales leaped out of the ocean and began to fight. The fight went on and on and it was evident that the smaller whale was getting progressively weaker. It was only a matter of time before he would be killed. However, at the last moment, the smaller whale shouted out with a human voice calling on Brigid to save him. With that, the larger whale seemed suddenly to lose all interest in the fight. He turned around and went off, leaving the smaller whale unharmed.

When Brendan saw what had happened he became very upset. He said, 'Why did the whale call on Brigid to save him and not on me?' He said to himself that the fish all knew him from seeing him constantly sailing the ocean and they would have known that he was a holy man and any request of his would be immediately answered by God. And yet, the whale had ignored him, and instead, called on the land-lubber Brigid who knew nothing of the sea. He was very disturbed to discover that the fish preferred Brigid to himself.

Brendan decided to return to Ireland and consult Brigid herself to find an explantaion for this strange phenomenon.

Brendan, however, was often distracted and his mind preoccupied with various worldly matters. The fish knew Brendan well from his many years living among them but they also recognised that his awareness of God was not up to Brigid's standard and this was the reason, that in his hour of need, the whale ignored Brendan and called on Brigid to save him (Plummer, 1922, 85-86).

Among the fishermen of the coast of Galway, a custom prevailed called *An tIasc Beo* (The Living Fish). An account of it comes from Cill Rónáin, Inis Mór, Árainn:

'Lá 'le Bríde bheireann cuid de na daoine isteach an t-iasc beo (an bairneach). Itheann siad cuid díobh agus caitheann siad cuid eile díobh i gcúinne sa teach. Iascairí a dhéanas é seo le

go mbeadh rath ar an iascach' (IFC 902; 3; Seán Ó Maoldomhnaigh, Scribe).

(On St Brigid's Day, some of the people bring in the living
fish – the limpet. They eat some of them and the throw some
of them into a corner of the house. It is fishermen who do this
so that there may be luck on the fishing)

This custom is difficult to interpret. It seems that it was mostly
small fish enclosed in a shell that were involved. Those thrown
into a corner of the house were not killed though they would
have died quickly from lack of water.

A similar account comes for Co Clare and this mentions four-
corners of the house:

'On St Brigid's Eve, people near the sea collect pennywinkles
(periwinkles?) and put them in the four corners of the house'
(IFC 901; 64; Pádraig Mag Fhloinn, Cill Fhionnabhrach,
Scribe).

In this account it seems that, again, small fish enclosed in shells
are involved.

Fundamentally, the custom was associated with the luck of
the year, with fertility and with a plentiful supply of food. This
is the conclusion to be reached from at least some of the acounts.
This, however, is only part of the problem, for any kind of fish
would have sufficed for this purpose.

We have seen, however, that it was shellfish which were put
in the corner or four corners. There is a parallel usage in the
sprinkling of a sacrificed cock's blood on St Martin's Feast (11th
November) on the four corners of the house and, undoubtedly,
this rite was connected with the luck of the year, protection and
fertility, for this is really the celebration of the Celtic Feast of
Samhain (1st November) which, through a dislocation in the calendar, became the 11th November (Cooper and Sullivan,1994,
VI).

A similar dislocation of ten days is seen when St Brigid's
Day, the first of February is compared to that of St Gobnat of
Baile Bhoirne, Co Cork, on the eleventh of February.

This however, does not explain the use of shellfish. But the explanation may lie in the shell itself.

According to the research undertaken by Marija Gimbutas on the goddesses of Old Europe, it is clear that the hedgehog and the snake were connected with the Great Queen, with the Goddess of Fertility. In this country, perhaps, the distinction between the hedgehog and the badger was not emphasised, as both of them appeared at the beginning of spring to coincide with the return of the goddess herself. However, the question of the snail and of the periwinkle remains.

The snake is a constant companion of the goddess in archaic sculpture and, undoubtedly, the serpent's habit of casting off his old skin and emerging as a new being impressed ancient peoples hugely, transmitting the idea of the snake having the secret of perpetual renewal and immortality (Campbell, 1965, 9).

Since the goddess personifies the death and resurrection of nature in the cycle of the year, her connection with the serpent was easy to recognise.

The snail and the *iasc beo* (periwinkle) are parallel in so far as a shell is involved in both cases. However, it is not the shell itself that is in question but rather the figure on the shell – that is to say the Spiral – a figure that is found so frequently in megalithic sites such as Newgrange and on pottery associated with the goddess.

The Spiral stands, apparently, for the thread of life emerging from the goddess and again returning within her for renewal. Like the snake, the Spiral is another form of presentation of the eternal cycle of life and so it is a valid symbol of the goddess herself as Mistress of Life (cf. Streit, 1984, 51).

This is not to say that there is any strict proof that the custom of the *Iasc Beo* derived directly from this source. Rather, an effort is made to explain a ritual whose origin was probably unknown even to those who practised it. The explanation is contained within the mentality of 'Old Europe'.

Before potatoes were introduced, corn was the major crop and this in various ways has left its mark on the celebration of the Feast of Brigid.

Firstly, one of the chief materials used in the making of St
Brigid's Cross is straw. Straw suits and hats are often used by
those taking part in the Brídeog procession from house to house.
A ritual which emphasised corn as the great source of food for
the people was that of placing a sheaf of corn on the doorstep on
St Brigid's Eve:

'Seo nós a bhíodh ag na seandaoine fadó. Nuair a bhíodh
Féile naomh Bríd ann do théadh fear an tí amach san oíche
agus d'fhaigheadh sé punann choirce agus d'fhágadh sé ar
leac an dorais í. 'Sé an fáth a dhéantaí é sin ná nuair a thagadh Naomh Bríd chuig an doras an oíche sin agus nuair a
fheiceadh sí an phunann go gcuireadh sí rath ar an gcoirce
sin an bhliain sin' (IFC 902; 108; Seán Ó Conaire, Druim
Snámh, Mám, Contae na Gaillimhe, Narrator; Cáit Ní
Chonaire, Scribe).

(Here is a custom which the old people had long ago. When
the Feast of Brigid arrived, the man of the house used to go
out on that night and get a sheaf of oats and set it down at the
doorstep. The reason for doing this was, that when St Brigid
arrived at the door that night, and when she saw the sheaf,
she would put her blessing on this year's crop of oats.)

What is expressed here, is a belief fundamental to the cult of
Brigid in Ireland – the belief that Brigid returns from the
Otherworld on this night, that she visits the houses of those who
venerate her, and that she bestows her blessing on various objects placed outside the door, notably 'Brat Bhríde' – a piece of
cloth called 'St Brigid's Cloak' used for cures and protection.

These objects, placed outside the door on St Brigid's Eve, acquire special powers because Brigid has touched them. For an
understanding of the rites, it is necessary to accept the visit of
Brigid to the various houses as the cornerstone of the cult.

In Castleisland, Co Kerry, the custom of the sheaf, sometimes
accompanied by a cake, was in vogue, to keep out hunger during the year (IFC 899; 196). In an account from Co Donegal, emphasis is placed on the reason for the practice and also the pre-
Christian element is indicated:

'A sheaf of corn and an oaten cake used to be placed on the doorstep on St Brigid's Eve for the 'wee' folk (fairies) and also as a thanksgiving for the plenteous grain-crop and for good luck during the following year' (IFC 904; 178; William Gallagher, Socker, Narrator; Mrs Mary Starrit, Ednacarnon N.S., Letterkenny, Scribe).

This account belongs to the district around Cill Mhic Réanáin and the sheaf ritual is associated with the Old Religion. In this offering, it is acknowledged that the ancient deities, the Tuatha Dé Danann (Peoples of the Goddess Dana) have control over the fertility of the earth. In another part of the country, Cnoc Fírinne in Co Limerick, the sanctuary of Donn Fírinne, the Irish God of the Dead, similar offerings were made:

'On May Eve and Halloween girls lay gifts on the high fields, or at the foot of the Stricín ... this was done probably on St Martin's Eve' (Béal. 18, 155).

Other 'gifts' laid on the hill are mentioned by Thomas Ball:

'They bury eggs in hay, in crops of corn, and also parts of dead animals.' 'All these customs prevail in all the districts within view of the remarkable hill' (Béal. 18, 156).

This account shows also the importance of Imbolc within the Irish Ritual Calendar.

Proceeding northwards from Cill Mhic Réanáin to Ros Goill, we find another description of the rite of the the sheaf and the cake:

'Roimhe seo chuirtí císte trí-choirnéal agus punann coirce ar leac an dorais Oíche 'le Bríde. Deirtear go gcoisriceadh Naomh Bríd and phunann coirce agus an císte. Faoi am luí nó mar sin, thugtaí isteach iad agus roinntí thart ar an líon tí an císte agus thugtaí an phunann coirce don eallach. Deirtear go sábhalfadh Naomh Bríd na daoine is an teaghlach ó gach uile dháinséar ar feadh na bliana' (IFC 904; 190; Seán Ó Siadhail, Cnoc Dumhaigh, Narrator; Tomás Mac Fhionghaile, Carraig Áirt, Leifear, Contae Dhún na nGall, Scribe).

(Formerly, a three-cornered cake and a sheaf of oats used to

be placed on the doorstep on St Brigid's Eve. It is said that St
Brigid would consecrate the sheaf of oats and the cake. When
it was time to go to bed or around that time, they used to be
brought in and the cake divided among the family and the
sheaf of oats given to the cattle. It is said that St Brigid would
protect the people and the household from every single danger throughout the year)

Rather than being merely a sign of the harvest to come, the sheaf
of corn on the doorstep on the holy night, would have been a
true symbol – bringing about effectivly the product it represented
– a plentiful harvest.

In some of the accounts, it appears that a plentiful harvest
would result from the sheaf being at the door, through the
power of the sheaf itself operating within the ritual frame of this
holy night of a supernatural order. In other texts, however, a
more personal approach occurs and the sheaf reminds Brigid, as
she visits the house, of the needs of the people. Making use of
her own power, she guarantees a good harvet.

Until now, we have been considering the large sheaf left outside the door, but in one case – Johnstown in Co Kilkenny – it is
mentioned that the St Brigid's Cross, hanging on the wall on the
inside of the house, was made from an unthreshed sheaf (from
which the grain was not removed) and that the remainder of the
sheaf was put in the cowhouse and stables (IFC 907; 225-226).

This is close to the custom found in certain areas in Co
Galway and, apparently, in Co Roscommon also:

'A small sheaf of oats and a potato used to be left on the doorstep until bed-time and stuck on a 'scolb' (wooden spike) and
put up behind a rafter at bed-time on St Brigid's Eve.

When the Spring came, the oats would be rubbed between
the hands and the seed would be put with the oats for sowing. The potato used to be cut and sown with the rest of the
'slits'. While this was being done St Brigid was invoked to
protect the crops from all diseases' (IFC 902; 182; Anne
Tuohy, Ballygreaney, Ballymacward, Woodlawn; Narrator;
Theresa M. Hurley, Colemanstown, Ballinasloe, Scribe)

In this case a small sheaf of oats with the grain still on it is placed outside the door on the holy night as with the large sheaf in other areas. It is accompanied by a single potato – a symbol of the new type of food side by side with the ancient foodcrop of the people.

At bed-time, after Brigid had visited and left her blessing on the sheaf and on the potato, they were brought inside and hung up on the rafters just as was done in the case of St Brigid's Cross. They were left there until sowing time – usually in the interval between St Brigid's Day (1st February) and St Patrick's Day (17th March).

When the ground was ready for sowing the crops, the grain still hanging on the little sheaf on the wall, was taken off and mixed with the seed-grain to be sown in the field. Similarly, the 'slit' or piece of potato hanging on the wall or rafters was taken and mixed with the other 'slits' or seed-potatoes about to be sown. In other words, the seed blessed by Brigid mingled with the ordinary seed to be sown in the ground and by the touch of the blessed seed all the other seed was sanctified. In this way, as a result of Brigid's return from the Otherworld on the holy night, a prosperous harvest was assured. An intervention of the Otherworld had taken place, something had been added to the normal rhythm of the seasons.

This rite belongs to Brigid as Lady of Fertility and it illustrates Brigid's central role in what belongs to a basic element of human existence – the provision of food.

In this context, it may be well to glance briefly at the case of St Blaise. His feastday on the third of February is very close to that of St Brigid and to that of the Purification of the Blessed Virgin Mary. On St Blaise's day, there is the blessing of throats in the Catholic Church with a prayer that, through the intercession of St Blaise, we may be protected from ailments of the throat and from every other evil. In many parts of Europe, the Feast of St Blaise was associated not only with throats – a legend said that Bishop Blaise cured a young boy who was choking on a fishbone – but with agriculture and spring sowing of crops.

It may be that the similarity of the name 'Blaise' to 'Ble' (wheat) in French influenced popular thinking, and it is clear that this male saint had ascribed to him something of the characteristics of the goddess of fertility (Berger, 1988, 81).

In many villages of southeast France, a great carnival took place on St Blaise's Day. The statue of St Blaise was carried in an ornamental carriage accompanied by four caravans in which villagers illustrated the agricultural work proper to the seasons of the year. The women used to take a container of grain to the church to be blessed by the priest. This was the *Benedictio seminum granarum* (The Blessing of Corn Seed) and, although the actual blessing was widespread, it was not to be found in the church's official ritual books. The women used to give half the grain to the priest and the rest was mixed with the seed-grain to to be sown that spring (Berger, 1988, 81-82).

In Ireland, however, the church was not involved in this way and the blessing of the grain came from Brigid herself.

CHAPTER TWO

Foretelling the Future

Although St Brigid's Day is not the beginning of the year according to the traditional calendar, it is nevertheless, regarded as the
first day of spring and the beginning of the agricultural year, as
well as the start of the fishing season. This idea of 'beginnings'
has left its mark on the celebration of the feast, particularly as regards predicting the future.

At the beginning of a year people are anxious to know what
will befall them and if the new year will bring them luck and
prosperity. This phenomenon is very evident at Samhain
(Halloween), the start of the Insular Celtic Year, where prediction rites such as looking for the ring concealed in the *Báirín
Breac* cake, to see if one will be married within the year, are well
known and widely practised.

Similarly, prediction rites occur in St Brigid's Feast, or
Imbolc, in certain areas of Ireland and Scotland.

It would seem that the custom of prediction linked to St
Brigid's Feast arose, among the people, from the fact that this
was the beginning of the new season of spring and a dramatic
break with the old season of winter. There was also some foundation for it within the literary sources. As we have seen, according to one of the *Lives* of Brigid, a druid made predictions regarding Brigid before her birth.

Brigid herself predicted that it would be from the hand of
Ninneadh that she would receive Holy Communion on her
deathbed. On this account, he kept his hand covered throughout
his life. For this reason, he was known as Ninneadh Lámhghlan
(of the pure hand) (Stokes, 1877, 85).

Another story concerning Brigid and prediction is contained

in the *Leabhar Breac* and different versions of the episode have come down to us in folklore.

Accordingto the story, Brigid fell asleep while St Patrick was preaching and in her sleep she had a vision. In the vision she saw four ploughs in the southwest and they ploughed the whole country. Before the sowing was completed the harvest arrived, and beautiful wells and lovely streams came from the furrows, and the workmen wore white garments.

After this, she was shown four other ploughs, in the north of the country, and the oats grew at once and ripened, but on this occasion, it was black streams that came out of the furrows and the workmen wore black clothing. Brigid told the vision to Patrick and he interpreted it for her.

At first, it is Brigid and Patrick themselves who are involved. They are preaching the four gospels and their work meets with success. Later, however, false teachers will arrive who will destroy their labours. But by the time this happens Brigid and Patrick will both be in the presence of the Creator.

In the folklore version from Co Cork, white sheep appear first, and later, grey spots appear on them; then pigs, wolves and wild dogs appear on the scene. The interpretation of the vision is the same – the Golden Age will disappear (IFC 900; 199).

In certain areas of Munster it was a common custom to make a prediction by making use of a piece of cord or a piece of cloth. On St Brigid's Eve (31st January) the cord or cloth was measured carefully and its length noted. Then it was left outside the house all night and in the morning it was brought in and measured again. If it were longer than when measured previously, then luck would follow the family during the course of the year. But if it had grown shorter during the night, then bad luck would follow, and there would be a death in the family (IFC 901;136; Co Clare).

In Co Leitrim there is an account of a different method of prediction in which fire was used. Candles were made from rushes remaining over from the making of St Brigid's Crosses and one of these lighted candles was given to each member of the family.

The person whose candle went out first would be the first of the family to die (IFC 902; 239).

Although many of the prediction-customs of St Brigid's Feast are about life and death, good luck and bad luck, the fertility or barrenness of the soil, there are some customs to be found connected with marriage.

An account from Carraig Mhór, Co Tyrone, describes the custom concerning engagement and marriage. A very small girl would make a little spinning-wheel from rushes and she would give it to a young man to put under his pillow on St Brigid's Eve. In a dream he would see the woman he would marry.

In the same way, a man would make a small ladder from rushes and give it to a young woman and she would put it under her pillow on St Brigid's Eve and she would see her future husband (IFC 905; 146-147).

The custom of prediction is found in Scotland also and in it Brigid features prominently.

The women used to make a basket in the form of a cradle and this was called 'Leaba Bhríde' (Brigid's Bed). A figure of Brigid made from a clothed sheaf of corn was put into it. A small stick (Slatag Bríde – Brigid's Staff) was put near the image. After this was done, ashes was arranged around the fire. The people hoped that Brigid would visit the house during the night and if the marks of the staff, or better still, her footprints, were on the ashes, then they would be filled with delight as this was a sign that Brigid would bring luck to the family duringthe year. On the otherhand, if the ashes remained unmarked in the morning, this would mean that Brigid was displeased with them. To rectify this situation, they performed *tabhar agus túis* (Offering and Incense), that is to say that they sacrificed a cock or chicken by burying him alive in a *Neimheadh* or Sanctuary – a place where three streems meet. Then, incense was burned in the fire. All of this was done to regain Brigid's favour (CG, I, 167-168).

These practices of prediction make it clear that the Feast of Brigid was regarded as one of the hinges of the year, as a starting point for a new era. From the point of view of the rationalist, some of these customs appear odd, but this was not so to a people steeped in a mytholigical tradition, integrated into the patterns of nature, and conscious of the everpresent reality of the divine.

At Samhain (Halloween), the boundaries between this world and the supernatural world of the Tuatha Dé Danann break down; it is neither day nor night, neither winter nor summer; it is a brief interval of chaos before cosmic order is again established. The division between past and future is destroyed to give a basis for rites of prediction (Rees, 1976, 91). As the beginning of the spring and the agricultural year, Imbolc shares with Samhain this particular practice of prediction.

CHAPTER THREE

The Annual Return of Brigid from the Otherworld

We have seen that the people believed in the return of Brigid from the Otherworld on the holy night; she visited the houses in which she received a welcome; certain objects were placed outside the door for her to bless as she passed by.

This idea of the annual return of Brigid was firmly rooted and widespread among the people. It was this return, along with the blessing which accompanied it which gave power to the objects laid on the doorstep such as St Brigid's Cross, *Brat Bhríde*, the Sheaf, the Cake and so forth. Brigid's supernatural power had touched them and communicated its healing and protecting virtue to them. Moreover, it is likely that the Brídeog procession, in which an image of Brigid is carried from house to house, is a ritualisation of her invisible visit. We will see more of this later.

In an account from Co Kilkenny, it is said that a ribbon or handkerchief (*Brat Bhríde*) was left outside the window during the night:

'People believe that St Brigid comes at night time and blesses the ribbon or handkerchief' (IFC 907; 211; Séamus Ó Duibhir, Bearna na Gaoithe, Ros an Aonaigh, Narrator; Seán Ua hAonghusa, Scribe)

'Tá áiteanna sa cheantar seo agus ní dhúntar doirse an oíche sin mar creidtear go mbíonn Naomh Bríd ag gabháil timpeall an oíche sin agus go ndéanfadh sí an rath agus beannacht ar an teach agus ar mhuintir an tí' (IFC 900; 234; Tomás Ó Faoláin, Baile Mhic Áirt, An Rinn, Dun Garbhán, Contae Phort Láirge, Scribe).

(There are places in this district in which the doors are not

closed on that night as it is believed that St Brigid goes
around on that night and that she brings blessings and prosperity to the house and household)

A striking account of Brigid's visit comes from Kilbehenny on
the borders of Co Limerick and Co Cork:

'On the Eve of St Brigid a sheaf of rushes (green) was placed
on the doorstep or flagstone of the door on the outside on
which St Brigid would kneel when she and St Brigid's Cow
visited each house during the night. St Brigid would kneel on
the rushes and pray that God might bless the house and its
occupants. Also it was a custom to tie the St Brigid's ribbon
on the latch of the door outside and this also she blessed
when she blessed the house, the people in it and especially
the dairy and cattle. No house was locked on the night of St
Brigid's Eve but the door was kept on the latch. When St
Brigid came along she drove with her a white cow which was
known as St Brigid's Cow but had a special name in Irish
(forgotten by the narrator). There is also an insect much like
the shape of a black beetle but red in colour and with a black
spot on its back and about as big as a larlge fly called St
Brigid's Cow. The old people used to say: "St Brigid and her
cow will come around tonight." Usually milk is very scarce
in January, but the old people used to say during the month
when they heard anyone complaining of the scarcity of milk:
"It won't be scarce very long now as St Brigid and her white
cow will be coming around soon." The people also placed a
sheaf of rushes on the doorstep of the dairy, i.e. the house in
which the churn as made and in which the cream was kept in
large wide-open coolers, so that she might bless the dairy, the
milk and the herd and that the cows would give more milk
during the year and produce more butter' (IFC 899; 259-265;
Áine bean Uí Chléirigh, Gleann na gCreabhar, Narrator;
Pádraig Seosamh Ó Cadhla, O.S., Gleann na gCreabhar, Baile
Mhistéala, Contae Chorcaí, Scribe).

As regards this marvellous description of Brigid's visit on the

holy night, it may be remarked that, according to the writer
(Scribe), Mrs Ó Cléirigh was 71 years of age when she supplied
this information in 1942. She had heard this account 60 years
earlier (1882) from her grandmother then aged 70. The transmis-
sion, then, went back to the beginning of the nineteenth century.

Another account shows that the same belief in Brigid's visit
was held in Connacht as it was in Munster and Leinster:

'Nós eile a bhí acu. Nuair a bhíodh gach duine sa teach
imithe a chodladh, thógfadh fear an tí ball éadaigh ó gach
duine sa teach, leagadh sé taobh amuigh iad, ionas dá
mbeadh Naomh Bríd ag dul thart go mbeadh éadach aici le í
a choinneáil te nuair a bhíos sí a' tabhairt cuairt ar na tithe a
thugas onóir di. D'fhágtaí na doirse oscailte freisin agus tine
bhrea thíos ionas go bhféadfadh Bríd a theacht isteach agus í
féin a théamh' (IFC 902; 71; Máire Ní Cheanndubháin, na
hÁille, An Cnoc, An Spidéal, Contae na Gaillimhe, Scribe,
from her father's narration)

(They had another custom. When everybody in the house
had gone to bed, the man of the house would take some article of clothing belonging to each member of the family , and
place it outside, so that if St Brigid were passing by she
would have clothing to keep her warm while visiting the
houses that honoured her. The doors used to be kept open,
also, and a fine fire burning, so that Brigid could come in and
warm herself.)

Co Antrim seems to be particularly rich in its accounts of the return of Brigid. The folklore accounts describe the *Leaba Bhríde*
(Brigid's Bed) and how it was made ready so that she would
have lodgings for the night. The dispositions of the local people
seem to be akin to those of Co Kilkenny with regard to Brigid's
travels, and we have seen already that Brigid's visit was of great
importance in areas of Gaelic Scotland. The following passage
gives a vivid description of the preparations made on the Eve of
the Feast and shows also that a new mentality was coming to the
fore which was inimical to the traditional way of thinking:

'This is an old custom which some of the old people in our

district still practise. On the eve of St Brigid's Feastday, they sweep the hearth and draw a little table over to the fire and place a chair near it. A meal is then prepared for one person and placed on the table. If any person comes seeking help on the eve of St Brigid's feast, it is believed by these people to be St Brigid in disguise and they think that it is unlucky to refuse alms on the eve of St Brigid's feast. Some of the other villagers think that it is unlucky to believe such things and that it would be impossible for St Brigid to come down to earth again' (IFC 904; 305; May Kearney, Castle St, Antrim, Narrator; T. Marrion, Creeve, Randalstown, Co Antrim, Scribe)

We have seen the evidence, then, for the belief in Brigid's return from the Otherworld on the holy night. There is no doubt but that this was a firm belief among the people and it was under threat by the growth of a more rationalistic mentality among the younger generation. We must, then, endeavour to trace the foundation for this strange belief.

Firstly, it must be asked, if it is the normal practice for a Christian saint to return to earth on his or her feastday. The answer is quite clear – it is not the custom for a saint to come back on this occasion. The annual return of a saint is not part of the tradition of the Catholic Church. Generally speaking, saints have had a hard time in this world, they have had their fill of it, and display no great desire to return to it. The annual return of a saint is not part of the Christian inheritance. There are stories, however, of saints who manifested themselves to people on certain occasions.

In the Roman Rite, for instance, the Feast of Our Lady of Lourdes (11th February) is celebrated as the occasion when the Blessed Virgin Mary appeared to Bernadette at the Lourdes Grotto. Similarly, in the case of Joan of Arc. She maintained that St Katherine and St Margaret appeared to her on certain occasions (Lang, 1908, 44).

These are occasional appearances of saints to a person still living in this world and there is no question of the saint returning regularly on an annual basis on his/her feastday. Perhaps, the nearest thing to the annual return of a saint is the case of the liquefaction of the blood of St Januarius in Naples. It is believed that St Januarius was a martyr of the fourth century, and his blood is preserved in a glass vessel in the cathedral. The blood is normally dried up but liquifies on 18 occasions during the year:

1. On his feastday (19th September) and every day for another seven days after it.

2. On the Saturday before the first Sunday in May and on the eight days after.

3. On the 16th day of December.

This strange phenomenon is mentioned as early as the 14th century. On these particular occasions, the saint's head is placed on the altar in the church. The priest brings the vessel of blood near the head and keeps turning the container up and down. Meanwhile, the people in the church are praying fervently. Soon, the blood liquifies and the priest announces: 'The miracle has occurred.' Priests and people then sing the *Te Deum* as a sign of thanksgiving (Ryan, 1966, Art. Januarius, 7, 827-828).

The Saturday before the first Sunday of May is connected to the transfer of the saint's relics from the monastery of Monte Vergine to Naples in the year 1497, and the date 16th December recalls the avoidance of the eruption of Vesuvius in the year 1631 (Butler, 1956, 594-595).

While this is a strange phenomenon, it is also odd that it takes place around significant calendrical dates – the winter solstice (21st December), Bealtaine (1st May) and the autumn equinox (21st September).

While it fosters the devotion of the faithful who experience it, this remarkable occurance, like that of Brigid which it resembles, is an exception to the general tradition of the Catholic Church. In a certain sense, Januarius returns from the Otherworld as Brigid does.

The ordinary attitude of the official Roman Church is to be found in the Prayers of the Roman Missal. Usually, the number of ideas contained in the *Oratio* is quite limited – we are now celebrating the feast of this particular saint; he/she performed great acts of holiness during his/her time on earth; now that he/she is in heaven may he/she intercede with God on our behalf; so that we may receive divine help in our troubles; may his/her example be an inspiration to us in our daily lives.

As an example, we may take the Collect for the Common of Doctors of the Church:

'O God, you gave blessed (Name) to be a minister of eternal salvation to your people; grant, we beseech you, that we who have had him for our teacher on earth, may also be worthy to have him for our advocate in heaven.'

(St Lucy) 'Graciously hear us, O God of our salvation, that even as we rejoice on the festival o blessed Lucy, Virgin and Martyr, we may learn to be loving and devout towards you.'

(Sts Cyprian and Justina) 'Lord, let your blessed Martyrs Cyprian and Justina ever lead us to strength and protection; for you never cease to look with mercy upon those to whom you give the help of your saints.'

(St Januarius) 'God, our Father, enable us, who honour the memory of Saint Januarius to share with him the joy of eternal life.'

(St Brigid) Lord, you inspired in St Brigid such whole-hearted dedication to your work that she is known as the Mary of the Gael; through her intercession bless our country; may we follow the example of her life and be united with her and the Virgin Mary in your presence.'

In this ecclesiastical tradition, the saints, while they intercede for us who are on earth, remain firmly established in heaven.

We now look at a different tradition, in which a supernatural personage visits this world yearly, on a regular basis.

We take, firstly, the case of Áine Chliach, the great and popular goddess associated especially with Cnoc Áine and Loch Ghair in Co Limerick, her principal cult area, but also associated with Cnoc Áine, Teileann, Co Donegal, and Dún Áine, Co Louth where she is connected to the Festival of Lughnasa (Ó hÓgáin, 1991, 21).

'Aine is sometimes to be seen, half her body above the waters, on the bosom of Loch Guirr, combing her hair, as the Earl of Desmond beheld her by the bank of the Camog (river). The commoner account is that she dwells within the hill which bears her name, and on which she has often been seen. Every Saint John's Night, the men used to gather on the hill from all quarters. They were formed in ranks by an old man called Quinlan, whose family yet (1876) live on the hill; and "cliars" bunches, that is, of straw and hay tied upon poles, and lit, were carried in procession round the hill and the little moat on the summit, *Mullach- Crocháin lámh le leab' an Triúir* (the top of the hillock near the grave of the Three). Afterwards people ran through the cultivated fields, and among the cattle, waving these "cliars", which brought luck to crops and beasts for the following year.

One Saint John's Night (23rd June) it happened that one of the neighbours lay dead, and on this account the usual "cliars" were not lit. Not lit, I should say, by the hands of living men; for that night such a procession of "cliars" marched round Cnoc Áine as never was seen before, and Áine was seen in the front, directing and ordering everything. On another Saint John's Night a number of girls had stayed late on the hill, watchng the "cliars" and joining in the games. Suddenly Áine appeared among them, "thanked them for the honour they had done her" but said that now she wished them to go home, as "They wanted the hill to themselves." She let them understand whom she meant by "they", for calling some of the girls she made them look through a ring, when behold, the hill appeared crowded with people before invisible. Áine is spoken of as "the best-hearted woman that ever lived" and the oldest families about Knockainy are proud to claim descent from her. These *Sliocht Áine* (descendants of Aine) include the O'Briens, Dillanes, Creeds, Laffins, O'Deas. We must add Fitzgeralds, what few remain thereabouts. The meadow-sweet, or queen of the meadow, is thought to be Áine's plant, and to owe to her its fragrant odour' (RC, IV, 189-190).

The usual Gaelic tradition connects *Oíche Bhealtaine* (May Eve) and *Oíche Shamhna* (Halloween) with the entrance of the *Aos Sí/Tuatha Dé Danann* (the ancient divine beings) into this world. The *Bruíon* or *Sí* (Sacred Hill or underground dwelling place of the gods) in each area is opened on these occasions and the normal barriers between the human and divine worlds break down. This intrusion of Otherworld beings into our human world is symbolised by the masked figures which go from house to house looking for gifts at Halloween (*Samhain*). Traditionally, the *Púca* (a supernatural horse) gallops around on this night and the dead were thought to return to their old homes for a short visit on this night also (Rees, 1976, 89-90).

The two Otherworldly parties, the Tuatha Dé Danann / Aos Sí and the Dead are brought together neatly in the the ancient story *Echtra Nerai* where on *Oíche Shamhna*, the *Tuatha Dé Danann* emerge from the Sí and the Hanged Man visits the houses of the living (RC 1889, 212-228).

The significance of St John's Eve is that this is the summer solstice when the sun, having reached its highest point in the sky with the longest day of the year, now begins its steady decline until the winter solstice at Christmas.

While *Samhain* (1st November) is the usual time for the visit of supernaturals, in the case of Brigid it is Imbolc and in the case of Áine, it is the summer solstice. We can distinguish two different calendrical systems in operation – firstly, a strictly solar calendar with four stations of the sun, namely, winter solstice (21 December); spring equinox (21st March); summer solstice (21 June) and autumn equinox (21 September) This is the calendar used by Áine.

We have also, the Insular Celtic Calendar which appears to be a modification of the 'Four Stations of the Sun' calendar. This calendar has four great feasts also – one at the beginning of each-season. These are: *Samhain* (1st November); *Imbolc* (St Brigid's Day, 1st February); Bealtaine (1st May) and Lughnasa (1st August).

This latter system may be an adaptation of the former for

agricultural purposes, as it corresponds closely to the seasons and the type of weather expected. It will be noticed, that the Celtic feasts come half way between the solar stations. *Samhain* is half way between the autumn equinox and the winter solstice; *Imbolc* is half way between the winter solstice and the spring equinox; *Bealtaine* is half way between the spring equinox and the summer solstice, and *Lughnasa* is half way between the summer solstice and the autumn equinox.

In Gaelic tradition there is considerable variation in the date on which a supernatural being returns.

Like their neighbour Áine, the goddesses Clíodhna and Aoibheall in the folklore of Cork, hold their convivial feasts at the time of the summer solstice, and at this time Aoibheall, who has been transformed into a white cat and occupies a cave in Castlecor, regains her human form for a week (*JCHAS*, 1897, 86).

On the other hand it is at *Samhain*, in common with the *Aos Sí* in general, that Aillean Mac Midhna emerges from Sí Charn Fionnachaidh to burn down Tara, with fire coming from his breath as he plays his sleep-inducing harp (Acall. 1661-1670).

Similarly, the Bean Sí Rothniamh emerges from Sí Chliach on Cnoc Áine every *Samhain* to instruct the local king, Fingen Mac Luchta, on what is to happen during the course of the coming year. This story, *Áirne Fingein*, is much preoccupied with matters of prediction (Ed.Vendryes, 1953).

Pádraig Ó Fionúsa, of the Decies, speaks of the tradition concerning Parthanán and the very practical matter of saving the harvest:

'Tagann Lá Pharthanáin gairid do dheire an Fhoghmhair, agus bíonn gach aoinne ag iarraidh a chuid arbhair a bheith bainte aige fé (faoi) dtiocfadh an lá sin. Mar deirtear go ngabhann sé timpeall (sé sin Parthanán) ag bualadh an arbhair, agus ná fágfadh sé gráinne síl ar aon arbhar ná beadh bainte. Aoinne ná beadh sé ar a chumas an t-arbhar a bheith bainte aige rithidis bata air sa tslí ná faigheadh Parthanán teacht air chun é bhualadh. Is gnách stoirm timpall an lae sin a mhilleann arbhar a bhíonn 'na sheasamh. Is dócha gurab é

seo a cuireadh i gcomparáid le fear ag bualadh agus ag
briseadh an arbhair' (Béal. 3, 1932, 284).

(Parthanán's Day comes near the end of the harvest, and
everybody tries to have his corn cut that day for it is said that
Parthanán goes around beating the corn, and he wouldn't
leave a grain of corn (seed) on any corn that was standing.
Anybody who was not able to cut the corn in time used to
beat it down with a stick so that Parthanán couldn't get at it.
It is usual to have a storm around that day– a storm which
will destroy standing corn – and it is likely that this was compared to a man beating and breaking corn)

Undoubtedly, Pádraig Ó Fionúsa is correct in suggesting that
Parthanán is a personification of the storm which frequently occurs towards the end of August.

But, perhaps, there is a connection here between Parthanán
and St Bartholomew, the Apostle, whose Feast occurs on the
24th August (25th August in *Féilire Aonghusa*). In the manuscripts his name takes various forms: Bartholom, Parthalon, and
Partholan (Stokes, 1905, 178). This last name is close to
'Parthanán'. Perhaps, also, there is an echo of the Parthalon
mentioned in the *Leabhar Gabhála Éireann*. He reached Ireland on
a Tuesday, the 17th day of the moon, on the kalends of May
(Macalister, 1940,3, 4). In folklore, he is called *Beartla na Gaoithe* -
Beartla of the Wind (Ó Súilleabháin, 1942, 343).

At present, it is on the Saturday nearest to St Bartholomew's
Feastday that the rite known as 'Burning Bartle' take place in
West Witton, Yorkshire, England. In this ceremony, a large effigy
of Bartle is paraded through the town with stops at various stations accompanied by the Chanter's Proclamations:

'On Penhill Crags, he (Bartle) tore his rags.'

'At Hunter's Thorn, he blew his horn.'

'Shout, lads, shout!'

Crowd: 'Hooray.'
Chanter: 'Hip, hip.'
Crowd: 'Hooray.'

Bartle is finally given over to the flames with great jubilation on the part of villagers and tourists (Taylor, 1987, 32-33).

This marvellous piece of folk-liturgy is obviously the celebration of the Festival of Lughnasa at the beginning of the corn harvest, coinciding more or less with the Feast of St Bartholomew.

In his brilliant study of this ritual ('The Giant of Penhill'), Ian Taylor discusses the myth behind the ritual in which a knight-hermit overcomes the oppressive giant Bartle. Similarly, in Ireland, the stingy autocratic harvest god *Crom Dubh/Crom Cruaich* is defeated by the generous god *Lugh Lámhfhada* who make a plentiful harvest available to the people.

The return of Brigid from the Otherworld at Imbolc may be situated within this context of the breakdown of barriers and the visitation of pre-Christian deities at sacred seasons of the agricultural year.

Within this same context we have the cult of the Santa Klaus, popular among children. This is St Nicholas whose feastday is on the 6th Deceember – again very close to the winter solstice. It is uncertain how this Bishop of Myra (in modern Turkey) arrived in Northern Europe and became endowed with furs and reindeer. He was renowned for his assistance of young women who wished to marry but were unable to do so as they lacked the necessary bride-price. In such cases, Bishop Nicholas went around to the girl's house and threw a bag of money in the window. A re-interpretation of the legend brings him back from heaven annually to distribute presents to children. In parts of Germany, but especially in Holland and Belgium, groups of people dressed as St Nicholas (with mitre and crozier) and his companions go from house to house and ask about the behaviour of the children. If good, they promise presents next morning and the children put their shoes aside to receive the presents, and also some hay for straw or St Nicholas' white horse when he returns. He may travel by donkey, however, and children prepare red carrots as, in popular belief, donkeys love carrots (Miles, 1976, 219).

Certain scholars who have examined this question maintain,

however, that it is a christianisation of the cult of the northern
god Woden (Miles, 1976, 208). In other words, it is not the
Christian saint who returns annually but the god.

One can see a distinct similarity between features of the cult
of St Nicholas and that of St Brigid. In both cases, there is a visitation ritual in which an effigy or an actor representing the supernatural figure, accompanied by attendants go from house to
house. We will see more of the *Brídeog* procession later.
Secondly, this human, visible, visit is a prelude to an invisible
visit of the supernatural figure which will take place later that
night. Thirdly, the supernatural visitor will distribute various
gifts or 'the luck of the year'. Fourthly, the visit takes place annually at a significant calendrical point, near the winter solstice in
the case of Nicholas and at the spring quarter day in Brigid's
case. Even the singular detail of leaving hay or carrots for St
Nicholas' horse or donkey resembles the custom sometimes
found in Ireland of leaving a sheaf of corn outside the door for St
Brigid's white cow (Danaher, 1972, 15).

In the actual processional rite a strange ambivalence is experienced. The supernatural visitor is present here and now, but
nevertheless, he/she is yet to come. An oft-quoted example of
this type of thinking is to be found in the 'Cherubikon Hymn' of
The Divine Liturgy (Mass) in the Byzantine Rite: 'We who mystically represent the Cherubim, who sing to the life-giving
Trinity the thrice-holy hymn, let us now lay aside all earthly
cares that we may receive the King of the Universe, borne aloft
by armies of unseen angels. Alleluia, Alleluia, Alleluia' (Raya,
1958, 82-85).

This ancient hymn is sung very slowly to a very elaborate
melody while the priest and deacon carry the veiled Offerings of
bread and wine to the altar. The people kneel or prostrate exactly
as they would do if it were Christ himself in the Blessed
Sacrament that was being borne in their midst. The ritual and
the awesome atmosphere which it engenders expresses the presence of the divine, even though the Eucharitic Prayer which
makes Christ present has not yet been said. The great liturgist

Adrian Fortesque discusses this phenomenon: 'This reference to the 'King of all things' long before the consecrtion, is a conspicuous case of what is common to all rites (especially this one), namely a dramatic representation that does not correspond to the real order of time. There are instances of this in the 'Proskomide' where the bread is called the 'Lamb' and treated as if already consecrated at the very beginning' (1908, 85-86, footnote).

There is another example of a saint who returns annualy in the case of St Thomas, the Apostle, whose feast was formerly on the 21st of December – the winter solstice. This is the 'Doubting Thomas' of the gospel (John 20:24-29) who wouldn't believe that Christ had risen until he had seen his wounded hands and side. Perhaps a subtle irony had dictated the choice of this date, for the winter solstice is hard to pinpoint and for some days after the 21st December there seems little evidence for the lengthening of the day and some people may doubt if the solstice has occurred at all.

In certain villages in Bohemia, the people believed that Thomas returned regularly each year to this world on the eve of his feastday (20th December) Again, it is thought that the god Odin or Woden stands behind this phenomenon. Thomas was a noisy and terrifying visitor. He would drive a fiery chariot around the village and finally stop at the graveyard. Here, all the dead men whose name in life had been Thomas, had risen from their graves and helped him to alight from his chariot. He would then pray before the great graveyard cross which lit up with a red mysterious light. He would then give his blessing to every dead Thomas and they would all return to their graves until the same time next year. The terrified villagers listened with relief to Thomas' noisy departure and prayed that he would deliver them from the evils of the year. They would sprinkle salt on the head of each cow with the words: May St Thomas preserve you from all diseases' (Miles, 1976, 224-225).

CHAPTER FOUR

Preparing a Bed for Brigid

Not only was there a belief in Brigid's return on the holy night, but in certain areas, it was understood that she may want to spend the night in a particular house, and so, a bed should be prepared for her – *Leaba Bhríde*, Brigid's Bed.

The following account shows the nature of the belief and practice:

'Another old lady still makes a St Brigid's Bed but it is made of the ends cut off the rush crosses. All the ends are put in a corner in the form of a bed and covered by a white linen sheet. After the bed is made, this old lady when night falls, goes to the door and says in a loud voice: "Come Saint Brigid" and returns to the rush bed leading imaginatively St Brigid by the hand' (IFC 904; 310; Imelda O'Loan, Krook-na-hai, Glenravel, Co Antrim, Narrator; T. Marrion, Creeve, Randalstown, Co Antrim; Scribe).

In another neighbouring district, *Leaba Bhríde* used to be made also, but in this case it was made of the crosses themselves, holy water was sprinkled on it and the people of the house said the rosary around it:

'This (*Leaba Bhríde*) was left all night in the kitchen and the door left open for St Brigid. In the morning if the bed of crosses remained undisturbed, a cross was hung outside every door of the building (IFC 904; 310; Imelda O'Loan, Krook-na-hai, Glenravel, Co Antrim, Narrator; T. Marrion, Creeve, Randalstown, Co Antrim; Scribe).

It is clear from this account that the bed was examined in the morning to find out if Brigid had slept in it. There is another reference to this practice from Ballymena, Co Antrim, and in this case the writer put a direct question to the Narrator: 'Had the old people any beliefs about St Brigid's Bed?'

'St Brigid herself came and lay in it. The old people would swear to that. They said that they always found traces of where she had lay (lain) in it' (IFC 904; 279; William John Campbell, Craigsdunloof, Ballymena, Co Antrim, Narrator; Pádraig Mac Giolla Bhuí, 12 Larne St, Ballymena, Scribe).

It will be noticed, however, from the earlier account that it was not always certain that Brigid occupied the bed, and in a case such as that, in which no signs of Brigid's occupancy could be found in the morning, the St Brigid's crosses were hung up outside each door of the house. In this case, the crosses had already been made and, indeed, they formed the material for the bed. They were waiting for Brigid to touch them and so bless them. The blessing which the crosses received from contact with Brigid would bring protection and healing to those people and animals who were touched by them.

It will be noticed from a former account that when the bed was examined in the morning it was seen that Brigid had not come to occupy it during the night. The crosses of which the bed was made had not been touched by Brigid and so were not blessed. Hence they would be ineffective in bringing a blessing to people and animals who were touched by them. In this case, the crosses were hung outside the doors of the houses in the morning. Perhaps it was believed that Brigid had been delayed in her journey throughout the country and that she would pass by hurriedly later in the morning and bless the crosses.

We will now see that a similar form of *Leaba Bhríde* was in vogue in Gaelic Scotland. Since Antrim and Scotland are so close it is reasonable to suppose that they had some cultural links. Alexander Carmichael gives a comprehensive description of the ritual in *Carmina Gadelica* (Edinburgh 1972), 1, 167-168:

The older women are also busy on the Eve of Bride, and great preparations are made to celebrate her Day, which is the first day of spring. They make an oblong basket in the shape of a

cradle, which they call 'leaba Bride', the bed of Bride. It is em-
bellished with much care. Then they take a choice sheaf of
corn, generally oats, and fashion it into the form of a woman.
They deck this ikon with gay ribbons from the loom,
sparkling shells from the sea, and bright stones from the hill.
All the sunny sheltered valleys around are searched for
primroses, daisies, and other flowers that open their eyes in
the morning of the year. This lay figure is called Bride. When
it is dressed and decorated with all the tenderness and loving
care the women can lavish upon it, one woman goes to the
door of the house, and standing on the step with her hands
on the jambs, calls softly into the darkness, *Tha leaba Bride
deiseal*, Bride's bed is ready. To this a ready woman behind
replies, *Thigeadh Bride steach, is e bealha Bride*, Let Bride come
in, Bride is welcome.

The woman at the door again addresses Bride, *A Bhride,
Bhride, thig a steach, tha do leaba deanta. Gleidh an teach dh'an
Triana*, Bride, Bride, come thou in, thy bed is made. Preserve
the house for the Trinity. The women then place the ikon of
Bride with great ceremony in the bed they have so carefully
prepared for it. They place a small straight white wand (the
bark being peeled off) beside the figure. The wand is variously
called *slatag Bride*, the little rod of Bride, *slachdan Bride*, the
little wand of Bride, and *barrag Bride*, the birch of Bride. The
wand is generally of birch, broom, bramble, white willow, or
other sacred wood, "crossed" or banned wood being carefully
avoided. A similar rod was given to the kings of Ireland at
their coronation, and to the Lords of the Isles at their instate-
ment. It was straight to typify justice, and white to signify
peace and purity – bloodshed was not to be needlessly
caused.

The women then level the ashes on the hearth, smoothing
and dusting them over carefully. Occasionally the ashes, surrounded by a roll of cloth, are placed on a board to safeguard
them against disturbance from draughts or other contingen-
cies. In the early morning the family closely scan the ashes. If

they find the marks of the wand of Bride they rejoice, but if they find *lorg Bride*, the footprint of Bride, their joy is very great, for this is a sign that Bride was present with them during the night, and is favourable to them, and that there is increase in family, in flock, and in field during the coming year.

Should there be no marks on the ashes, and no traces of Bride's presence, the family are dejected. It is to them a sign that she is offended, and will not hear their call.

The account of the 'Leaba Bhríde' tradition in Co Antrim, corresponding as it does to the more elaborate Scottish presentation, illustrates the riches of the cult of Brigid in the centre of the county, especially in the area northeast of Ballymena. Not only was there a profound understanding of the return of Brigid on the holy night, but this was presented dramatically in the *Gnás na Tairsí* or threshold rite to be discussed later, and the rite of the *Leaba Bhríde*.

This area might well be designated as the *Leaba Bhríde* District as it conserved a unique feature of the cult either unknown or not emphasised in other parts of the country.

Professor Séamas Ó Catháin comments on the domestic features of the cult of Brigid: 'Much of the indoor activity associated with the celebration of the feast took place in the vicinity of the hearth or, as with the preparation of the modest ceremonial repast, was actually centred upon it. A symbolic extra place might be set for the visiting saint and similarly, sometimes a 'shakedown' bed of straw was laid out for her by the fire-side' (1995, 53).

CHAPTER FIVE

The Cult of Brigid among the Clerics

Despite the difference between the general attitude of the official church to the saints and the belief of the people in the annual return of Brigid on the holy night, her cult seems to have flourished among the clerics as it did among the ordinary faithful.

Evidence for this is to be found in the Liturgical Calendars of various churches and in the number of churches dedicated to her.

As regards dedications previous to the Reformation, the research carried out by E. G. Bowen illustrates the very considerable extent of her *cultus*. The map produced by him shows a number of chapels dedicated to St Brigid in East Scotland; then turning to the west, a continuous line of dedications goes from the south-west of Scotland down the coast of England spreading throughout Wales. A small number are found in Devon and in East Cornwall, and then they branch off to the northern and western coast of Brittany.

'It is estimated that there are (or were) as many as forty dedications to St Brigit in the three departments of Cotes-du-Nord, Finistere, and Morbihan. In attempting to assess the significance of St Brigid in Brittany, we have to remember not only the early Irish pirates and settlers who may have carried her name thither, but also the fact that in later times Irish missionaries and scholars spread the name of Ireland and Irish Christianity far and wide throughout western Europe and the cult of St Brigid almost certainly followed in its wake. It is said, for example, that the great abbey of Landevennec, on the coast of Finistere, had the closest contacts with Ireland, especially before the Northmen occupied Brittany in 919. In its neighbourhood we find several churches and chapels dedicated to St Brigit. Furthermore, we must not think of these Irish contacts solely in piratical or even in ecclesiastical terms – there would appear to be much legitimate commerce as well' (Bowen, 1973-1974, 46).

A strange inconsistancy appears in the dedications to St Brigid in Ireland. The majority are, of course, in Leinster, but there is a notable shortage of dedications in the northern portion of the country – north of a line going from Dundalk across to southern Co Mayo. The same phenomenon is noticeable in Munster (Bowen, 1973-1974, 36).

It is possible that this has some connection with the large monasteries of the medieval period. On the other hand, John O'Hanlon asserts that when Colgan was editing the *Life of Brigid* he was limited by the fact that he had in his possession only a partial list of dedications – those pertaining to the dioceses of Dublin, Tuam, Kildare, Elphin, and Lismore (O'Hanlon, 1875, 2, 193). When it is taken into account that some of those areas deficient in dedications are, nevertheless, rich in folkloric accounts and customs, it may be assumed that there were two levels to the cult of Brigid – one of the official ecclesiastical type and the other of a more primitive popular type containing echoes of archaic thought and sensibility.

The Calendar of Glastonbury (10th century), the great medieval Benedictine Monastery in Somerset so often associated with King Arthur and the Knights of the Round Table, has the heading: '*KL Februarii. Sanctae Brigidae virginis*' for the first day of February (Wormald, 1934, 45). Evidence for the cult of Brigid is found in the area. Glastonbury is called *Glostimber na nGoedel* (Glastonbury of the Irish) in *Félire Oengusso* (Stokes, 1905, 188), and the place is connected with *SeanPhádraig* (Old Patrick). Some Irish used to live in nearby Beckery. The name is thought to be derived from *Becc Ériu* (small Ireland). According to tradition, Brigid lived near the small shrine of St Mary Magdalen, and her bell and spindle used to be shown to pilgrims. A plaque on the tower on top of the 'Tor' shows Brigid milking her cow

(Michell, 1990, 10-11). A similar plaque is to be found in St
Mary's Chapel in the old Abbey and it is thought that this goes
back to the 12th century (Mann, 1986, 15).

In Ireland itself, the *Martyrology of Tallaght* (8th-9th century)
announces for the 1st of February: *Dormitatio sancti Brigitae lxx
aetatis suae* (Best and Lawlor, 1931, 14) (The falling asleep/death
of Brigid in the seventieth year of her life). Similarly *Félire
Oengusso Céli Dé* (8th-9th century) announces:

> 'Mórait calaind Febrai fross martir már glédenn, Brigit bán
> balc núalann, cenn cáid caillech n-Érenn' (They magnify
> February's calends, a shower of great, pure-coloured mar-
> tyrs; Brigit the fair, strong, praiseworthy, chaste head of
> Erin's nuns) (Stokes, 1905, 58).

Strangely enough, the official liturgical book of the Roman Rite,
the *Martyrologium Romanum*, when announcing her feastday, referred to one of the miracles mentioned in the *Lives*:

> 'In Scotia sanctae Brigidae Virginis, quae cum lignum altaris
> tetigisset in testimonium virginitatis suae, statim viride fac-
> tum est' (Martyrologium Romanum; 1913, 35). (In Ireland,
> (the Feast of) St Brigid, the virgin; when she touched the
> wood of the altar in witness to her virginity, immediately the
> wood turned green.)

The cult of Brigid was also located in certain areas of continental
Europe: 'The saint of Kildare enjoys a remarkable popularity
through all western Europe. There is no doubt, moreover, that
this popularity is due to the very intense propaganda carried on
in favour of their national saints by Irish monks, missionaries,
and peregrini wherever they penetrated' (Gougaud, 1923, 104).
Among the notable places are: Reichenau, Echternach, Nevelles,
Sankt Gallen, Liege, Mainz, Strasbourg, Schotten, Liestal,
Genova.

In certain cases, the cult is not as ecclesiastical as one would
expect and sometimes there are accounts of farmers performing
rites for the protection of their cattle, as so often happened in
Ireland.

This feature of devotion to Brigid was associated with the areas of Saint-Omer, Fosses, Koln, Amay. In Fosses, in Belgium, little sticks were blessed in honour of St Brigid and the farmers touched the cows with them to transfer the blessing from the wands to the cows. In Amay, in Belgium, the priest blessed clay; the clay was then spread on the ground on which the cows walked and in this way Brigid's protection was obtained for the herd (Gougaud, 1923, 103-112).

This widespread cult of Brigid abroad is a testimony to its vitality in the country of its origin. While certain clerics of strict orthodoxy might have some misgivings about certain features, such as the annual return of Brigid and her close connection with fertility, nevertheless, the official Church of Rome cast a benign eye on the great Brigid, the 'Mary of the Gael'.

CHAPTER SIX

Brigid, the Goddess and the Saint

As previously stated, a certain aura of archaic religion surrounds Brigid and differentiates her from the vast majority of the saints of the Roman Martyrology. Several scholars have commented on this and have endeavoured to make a distinction between Brigid the Christian saint, Patron of Kildare, Patroness of Ireland, on the one hand, and Brigid the Celtic goddess of pre-Christian times on the other:

'Another goddess attested by inscriptions both in Gaul and Britain is the goddess Brigid … She appears to have been Christianised as St Brigid, whose shrine is at Kildare, where her sacred fire was kept burning' (Dillon and Chadwick, 1967, 144).

'Brigid est, a la difference de Minerve, dans le panthéon classique, l'unique divinite feminine celtique. Elle n'est guere attestée sous ce nom a cause de l'assimilation ulterieure a la sainte chretienne' (Le Roux et Guyonvarc'h, 1982, 369).

(Brigid, unlike Minerva in the classical Pantheon, is the unique feminine Celtic divinity. She is hardly encountered under this name because of its later assimilation to the Christian saint.)

'But paradoxically, it is in the person of her Christian namesake St Brighid that the pagan goddess survives best. For if the historical element in the legend of St Brighid is slight, the mythological element is correspondingly extensive, and it is clear beyond question that the saint has usurped the role of the goddess and much of her mythological tradition' (McCana, 1970, 34)

'De toutes les deesses du panthéon irlandais, la plus vénérée

a du etre san aucun doute Brighid, la fille du Daghdha, si l'on
en juge par l'importnce du culte adressé, non seulement en
Irlande mais a travers toutes les terres celtiques, a celle
qu'une habile politique de l'Eglise catholique lui a substitu-
tée; sainte Brigide de Kildare' (Sterckx, 1974-1975, 229-233).

(Of all the goddesses in the Irish Pantheon, there is no doubt
but that the most venerated of all was Brighid the daughter
of the Daghdha. If one is to judge by the importance of the
cult addressed to her not only in Ireland but throughout all
the Celtic territories by the subtle politics of the Catholic
Church which substituted for her St Brigid of Kildare.)

In this assessment, Professor Sterckx goes from the cult of Brigid
the saint to Brigid the Celtic goddess and argues for an even balance between the two. Brigid the saint was venerated more than
any other female saint in Ireland; therefore, the goddess Brigid
must have been venerated more than any other goddess.

If it be true that Brigid of Kildare – the saint – took the place,
to some extent, of the Celtic goddess Brigid, then it is likely that
there were certain resemblances between the two from the beginning, or that certain likenesses were composed so that the
two characters could blend more easily with each other and
allow an easy transition from pagan goddess to Christian saint.
This type of policy is in harmony with the directive given by
Pope St Gregory (6th century) to St Augustine, Bishop of
Canterbury, on his mission to the English:

'… fana idolorum destrui in eadem gente minime debeant,
sed ipsa quae in eis sunt idola destruantur. Aqua benedicta
fiat, in eisdem fanis aspergatur, altaria construantur,
reliquiae ponantur, quia si fana eadem bene constructa sunt,
necesse est ut a cultu daemonum in obsequium veri Dei debeant commutari, ut dum gens ipsa eadem fana non videt destrui, de corde errorem deponat, et, Deum verum cognoscens
ac adorans, ad loca consuevit familiarius concurrat' (Migne,
1849, 1, 1176).

(… the pagan sanctuaries should not be destroyed but as little as possible, but the idols in them should be destroyed.

Water should be blessed and sprinkled on these temples.
Altars should be installed and Relics should be put into
them. If these sanctuaries are well built they must be turned
away from the cult of idols to the worship of the true God.
The people will see that their temples are not destroyed and
they will gather together in the places to which they are accustomed. In this way they will be led to give up their errors
from their hearts and acknowledge and adore the true God.)

With this sensible provision, St Gregory laid down the directives
for this question which must have been of importance to
Christian missionaries of the period. The principle could easily
be extended to cover other elements besides pagan sanctuaries.
If the church could accept these, with a certain amount of reser-
vations and accomodations, it could, no doubt, shelter under its
voluminous cloak some other features of the Old Religion dear
to the hearts of the people since pre-Christian times. In the rural,
non-urbanised civilisation of the Celtic areas, the fertility of the
land, of animals and humans would have been of prime concern
and this would be a challenge for Christianity with its urban
roots and echoes of imperial organisation and structure.

A strange little note in the *Annals of the Four Masters* under
the year 1176 recording the death of Strongbow in Dublin, connects him with the destruction of churches and the vengeance of
Brigid. He died from an infection of the foot and it was thought
that this was caused by the curse of St Colm Cille, St Brigid, and
other saints as he had destroyed many of their churches. 'At con-
nairc siumh féisin Brighit andarlais ag a mharbhaidh'
(O'Donovan, 1856, 3, 24). (He himself thought that he saw Brigid
killing him.)

Brigid shows herself again in a military context in 'Cath
Almhaine' (The Batle of Allen). The story which is found in
Leabhar Buí Leacáin and *The Book of Fermoy* concerns the battle be-
tween 'Leath Choinn' and 'Leath Mhogha' in the year 718 or 722.
Feargal Mac Maoldúin was defeated and killed along with Donn
Bó the renowned musician of Ulster, though he was later
brought back to life through the power of St Colm Cille. Colm

Cille gave no help to his own Ulster people during the progress of the battle as Brigid was to be seen hovering over the army of Leinster. This appearance of Brigid encouraged the Leinstermen immensely:

'Níor fhan meanma Cholm Cille le Uí Néill chun fóirthint orthu sa chath sin ar bhfeiscint díibh Bríd, ag foluain os cionn sluaite Laighean ag cur sceoin i muintir Leath Choinn, agus ba le hamharc Bhríde amhlaidh sin a briseadh an cath ar Fheargal agus ar Leath Choinn le Murchadh mac Bhrain, rí Laighean, agus le Aodh, rí dheisceart Laighean' (Ó Floinn agus Mac Cana, 1956, 214).

(Colm Cille's favour was not bestowed on the Ui Neill in order to help them in that battle. Brigid was seen flying above the army of Leinster and this terrified the army of Leath Choinn. It was the sight of Brigid in this guise that led to the defeat of Feargal and Leath Choinn by Murchadh mac Brain, king of Leinster and Aodh, king of southern Leinster.)

In The Battle of Allen it is clear that Colm Cille is a Christian saint, but one who in normal circumstances would favour his own Northern people in battle. But in this case, the northern group has invaded Leinster, and moreover, Brigid, on the side of Leinster, is seen floating above the Leinstermen. Here we have the ancient Celtic goddess of war – the *Badhbh Chatha* the scald-crow who flies above the warring armies. Professor Pádraig Ó Riain remarks that the same position is adopted by Brigid elsewhere (1978, note 81).

In the poem *A Choicid Choin Chairpri Cruaid* by Orthanach, Bishop of Kildare, who died in the year 839, it is the Battle of Luachra which is in question:

'Cath lond Luachra, huasa tuas
at chess Brigit, nib firt fas'
(The fierce battle of Luachra, up above it was seen Brigid, it was no vain miracle) (*Éigse*, Vol 10, 177, 187)

In *Cath Maighe Tuireadh* it is the *Badhbh* who brings the news of the great victory of Lugh and the Tuatha Dé Danann over Balar

of the Evil Eye and the Fomhoraigh to the royal heights of
Ireland, to the *Aos Sí*, to its chief waters and to its rivermouths
(Gray,1982, 71).

Cormac Mac Cuileannáin, 9th century scholar and king-bishop
of Cashel in his glossary, *Sanas Cormaic*, discusses Brigid the
goddess:

'Brigit.i. banfile ingen in Dagdae. Isí insin Brigit bé n-éxe .i.
bandéa no adratis filid. Ar ba romor ocus ba roán a frith-
gnam. Ideo eam deam vocant poetarum. Cuius sorores erant
Brigit bé legis ocus Brigit bé goibne ingena in Dagda, de
cuius nominibus paene omnes Hibernenses dea Brigit voca-
batur' (Meyer, 1912, 150)

(Brigid, that is to say, the goddess, daughter of the Daghdha,
she is , then, the Lady of Poetry, the goddess that the poets
used to worship, for very great and very noble was her care.
Because of this they call her goddess of the poets. For sisters
she had Brigid Lady of Medicine and Brigid Lady of
Metalwork, daughters of the Daghdha. From these names,
the name Brigid used to be given to almost every Irish goddess.)

This means that 'Brigid' was more of a title than a personal
name, and this is in accordance with the fundamental meaning
of the word – 'the high one', 'the exalted one':

'As regards function, therefore, Brighid was patroness of poetry and learning, of healing and of craftsmanship, and, as regards status, such was her prestige that her name could be
used as a synonym for 'goddess' (Mac Cana, 1970, 34).

Ó hÓgáin accepts this conclusion:

'It is apparent that a goddess with whatever name could in
archaic times be called 'brigit', this being an epithet for 'exalted' goddesses' (1990, 60).

In certain cases, some elements of the surrounding landscape
may be of import in distinguishing a pre-Christian sanctuary.
Professor Pamela Berger discusses this phenomenon:

'A study of ancient sites suggests that to our prehistoric ancestors, twin hills symbolised breasts, which in turn were envisioned as belonging to a reclining mother goddess of the earth. Such twin mountains, in different parts of the world, are oftern given appellations equivalent to "paps" or "breasts". Archeology has shown that prehistoric temples were frequently placed in alignment with such breastlike land formations' (1988, 124-125).

In Ireland, we seem to have a very clear example of this in the two hills in Kerry called 'The Paps', 'Dhá Chíoch Anann ', the two breasts of the goddess Anu. There in all her magnificence, the great mother – Anu /'Ana' – in her nourishing aspect is outlined on the landscape. She is, according to *Sanas Chormaic* the mother of the gods of Ireland – the *Tuatha Dé (D)Anann*.

Now, apart from these two natural breastlike hills there is, some distance away, the sacred stone fort of Cathair Chrobh Dearg enclosing a holy well (the City Well) much frequented into fairly recent times at *Bealtaine* (May Eve). Rounds were made at the well and cattle were brought from considerable distances to drink the water. Formerly there was was much merrymaking and a large attendance of hucksters. The awesome character of the landscape enhances the religious atmosphere of the place (MacNeill, 1982, 272).

What is most remarkable, however, is what appears to be the alignment of Cathair Chrobh Dearg with Dhá Chíoch Anann so that two straight lines drawn from the Cathair to the two breasts form an isoceles triangle. It is unknown if this happened by accident of if it were deliberately planned.

At any rate, perhaps the same phenomenon occurred at Kildare. On a map, at least, the two great hills, Knockaulin (Dún Ailinne) and the Hill of Allen (Cnoc Almhaine) are of almost the same height, and almost of equal distance from St Brigid's Cathedral, so that they, too, with Cill Dara, form an isosceles triangle. The great hill fortress of Dún Ailinne is associated with the kings of Leinster, while Cnoc Almhaine features strongly in the literature of Fionn Mac Cumhaill and the Fianna.

The question arises, however of the visibility of these two

hills from the actual Cathedral and this is a matter which may be
of interest to local inhabitants familiar with the landscape.

CHAPTER SEVEN

Brigid and the Ever-Living Fire at Kildare

In the year 1185 King Henry the Second sent the cleric Giraldus Cambrensis to Ireland on a visit. Having spent some time in the country, Giraldus returned home and proceeded to write his famous book *Topographia Hiberniae*. In this work he described the many wonders which were to be seen in Ireland. Among these was the perpetual fire in St Brigid's Monastery in Kildare and this was for him an object of great interest:

'At Kildare, in Leinster, celebrated for the glorious Brigit, many miracles have been wrought worthy of memory. Among these, the first that occurs is the fire of St Brigit, which is reported never to go out. Not that it cannot be extinguished, but the nuns and holy women tend and feed it, adding fuel with such watchful and diligent care, that from the time of the Virgin, it has continued burning through a long course of years; and although such heaps of wood have been consumed during this long period, there has been no accumulation of ashes.

As in the time of St Brigit, twenty nuns were here engaged in the Lord's warfare, she herself being the twentieth; after her glorious departure, nineteen have always formed the society, the number having never been increased. Each of them has the care of the fire for a single night, the last nun, having heaped wood upon the fire, says: 'Brigit take charge of your own fire; for this night belongs to you.' She then leaves the fire, and in the morning it is found that the fire has not gone out, and that the usual quantity of fuel has been used.

This fire is surrounded by a hedge, made of stakes and brushwood, and forming a circle, within which no male can enter; and if any one would presume to enter, which has been sometimes attempted by rash men, he will not escape the divine vengeance. Moreover, it is only lawful for women to blow the fire, fanning it or using bellows only, and not with their breath' (Wright, 1887, 96-97).

The perpetual fire remained lighting until the Reformation apart from a short interval as explained by Archdall:

'1220. In this year Henry de Loundres, archbishop of Dublin, put out the fire called unextinguishable, which had been preserved from a very early time by the nuns of St Brigid; this fire was however relighted, and continued to burn till the total suppression of monasteries. The ruins of the Fire-house, or rather of the Nunnery, may yet be seen' (Archdall, 1886, 329).

It is difficult to know if Giraldus Cambrensis was influenced by the Classics when describing St Brigid's perpetual fire, but it is strange that he mentions the number 20 as the number of nuns – the same number from which the Vestal Virgins of ancient Rome were chosen. In Ireland, one would expect the number 9 to predominate. A. and B. Rees give examples of the widespread use of 9: 9 hazels of wisdom; Morgan La Fee and her 8 women; Ruadh Mac Rigdoinn and the 9 damsels of the sea; the druid Cathbhadh and his 8 disciples; Fionn Mac Cumhaill and his 8 Caoiltes, and so on (Rees, 1976, 192-193).

It is clear that the taboo forbidding blowing on the fire with the breath to kindle its flame was of some importance, as Giraldus mentions it again at a later stage. According to his story, a soldier once crossed over the wall and breathed on the fire. He immediately jumped back out of the sacred place severely disturbed. From that time onwards he used to go around breathing on people's faces, saying: 'That is how I breathed on Brigid's fire' (O'Meara, 1951,71).

Contrary to this, Rees refers to an ancient Welsh poem in which nine damsels blow with their breath on the fire under the cauldron of Pen Annwn (1976, 193). Here we have a divergent custom within a Celtic context. Perhaps a tentative approach to a solution may be arrived at by referring to the goddess Minerva to whom Brigid is sometimes compared. On the evidence of Caesar, Minerva was the founder of the Arts (Tierney, 1960, 272) and as such would resemble Brigid as Lady of Ironwork, Lady of Medicine and Lady of Poetry.

According to a legend, Minerva was once seated by a stream playing a flute. She happened to look into the water and saw her face distorted and her cheeks puffed out by the effort of blowing into the instrument. In disgust at her appearance she threw the flute into the stream, never to play again (Guerber, 1986, 55).

Perhaps this incident influenced the account, or, indeed, it may well be that the nuns of Kildare found it more dignified to wave their fans gracefully than to indulge in strenuous puffing.

De Vries, in discussing Minerva, refers to her likeness to Brigid in the context of *Aquae Sulis* the great Celto-Roman sanctuary of Sulis-Minerva at Bath in Britain, where the steaming thermal baths of the goddess are still to be seen with the tradition of a perpetual fire:

'Il faut rappeler a ce sujet la déesse "Sul" adorée a Bath; Solin l'assimile a Minerve et dit qu'elle est une déesse des sources, entendons des sources thermales. Dans son temple brulait une flamme perpetuelle. Cela rapelle la déesse latine du foyer, Vesta, mais aussi la déesse irlandaise Brigit. Le nom "Sul" doit signifier "soleil" (1977, 86-87).

(In this regard, it must be remembered that the goddess 'Sul' worshiped at Bath is assimilated to Minerva by Solinus who says that she is a goddess of springs, that is of thermal wells. In her temple a perpetual fire burned. This brings to mind Vesta the Roman goddess of the hearth, but also the Irish goddess Brigit. The name 'Sul' must mean 'sun'.)

Again, Professor McCone speaks of this theory concerning Minerva and the boiling medicinal well at Bath (*Aquae Sulis*):

'It thus seems quite likely that the Bath cult and its Christianised Kildare counterpart related ultimately to the same goddess, variously known as "Briganti", "exalted one", or

"Sul" "sun" cognate with Latin "sol", Welsh "haul",
semantically shifted Irish "súil" "eye" and so on. At all
events, the pagan Brigit's association with sun and fire seems
to be beyond reasonable doubt' (1990, 164-165).

In this context it may be recalled that several holy wells in
Ireland are known as *Tobar na Súl* (Ó Muirgheasa, 1936, 155, 158)
and these are connected with the cure of ailments of the eyes.
Tobar na Sool near Ballymena, Co Antrim, is one of these as is
Tobar na Súl on Slieve Sneacht, Co Donegal (Logan, 1980, 77).
One might well wonder if these are not connected with the god-
dess 'Sul' of Bath.

An ancient poem attributed to St Colm Cille describes Brigid
as: 'Fax aurea, praefulgida' and 'Sol fortis et irradians' (Kelly,
1857, 188) (a golden gleamhing torch; a strong and radiating
sun). This reference to sun and fire recalls the fire-element *aoibheall*, (*aibhleog* – ember, spark) in the names of the of the well-
known goddesses of Munster, Aoibheall na Carraige Léithe,
Ébliu (Eibhleann) , Aoife, Áine, Grian (Ó Corráin and Maguire,
1981, 15; 82; 16; 19; 115).

Six Vestal Virgins took care of the perpetual fire in the
Temple of Vesta in Rome, but in the case of a shortage of voca-
tions to the sisterhood, a choice was made from 20 virgins. No
men were allowed enter the temple and it was a major calamity
if the fire were extinguished as the ever-living fire of Vesta was a
symbol of the Roman Republic. The virgin responsable for let-
ting the fire go out was punished severely and the fire was relighted by means of a ray of sunshine passing through a glass
(Lempriere, 1866, 714).

On the first day of March the Vestal Virgins rekindled the fire
by rubbing two pieces of wood together until the emerging
sparks ignited some very dry combustable material from which
the fire of Vesta was lighted according to the ancient custom.
The lighting of the fire after it had been deliberatly extinguished
at the end of the year marked the beginning of the new year
which began in March according to the old Roman calendar
(James, 1961, 161).

The type of wood used by the Vestal Virgins is discussed by Frazer:

'In pointof fact, it appears that the perpetual fire of Vesta at Rome was fed with oak-wood, and that oak-wood was the fuel consumed in the perpetual fire which burned under the sacred oak at the great Lithuanian sanctuary of Romove' (1923, 665).

In these considerations a distinct pattern emerges linking Kildare and Rome:

KILDARE (Brigid)	ROME (Vesta)
1 A Perpetual Fire	A Perpetual Fire
2 Cared for by Virgins	Cared for by Virgins
3 Men Excluded	Men Excluded
4 A Circular Hedge Enclosure	A Circular Temple
5 The Use of Oak	The Use of Oak
6 The Number Twenty	The Number Twenty

According to tradition, there was a perpetual fire in Cloyne, Co Cork (Killanin, and Duignan, 1976, 175); in Inishmurray, off the-coast of Sligo (idem 311) and in Saighir Chiaráin, Co Offaly (idem 120) as well as at Cill Dara.

A perpetual fire legend records that there was in the monastery of Ciarán Óg (the Younger) at Clonmacnoise on the Shannon a foolish malevolent child. Crithid was his name. He came on a visit to Old Ciarán at Saighir and remained there for some time. Ciarán (the Older) asked him not to extinguish the fire he had blessed at Easter until the year was over but to tend it and keep it blazing. Tempted by the devil, however, the child quenched the fire. Ciarán told his community of monks that vengeance would overtake the child for this and that he would die tomorrow. This proved to be true as next day a wolf killed him. When Ciarán of Clonmacnoise heard of the death of the child he came with some of his followers to Saighir and they were given a great welcome. However, there was no fire in the monastery as it was from the perpetual fire that the ordinary fire for cooking was lighted each evening. Ciarán had said that there would be no fire until next Easter unless God himself sent fire from heaven. There was snow on the ground and Ciarán went out and stretched out his arms in fervent prayer to God. Then, a great glowing ember fell from heaven and with that Ciarán lighted the fire of the monastery (O'Grady, 1892, 1, 14-15).

In this case, the perpetual fire of Saighir Chiaráin was quenched just before Easter so that its relighting at the Easter Vigil would mark the beginning of a new era. Neither at Saighir or at the Temple of Vesta was the fire entirely perpetual in the sense that it was never extinguished. It was extinguished at the end of a fixed period and then relighted to show that a new period was beginning. Saighir Chiaráin was obviously christianised as it followed the Christian Liturgical Cycle as we have it today with the quenching of all lamps and candles in the church on Holy Saturday and their relighting from the New Fire at the Easter Vigil at around 11.00 p.m. on Holy Saturday night. The usual Insular Celtic practice was to extinguish all fires and re-light them from a central bonfire at *Samhain* and *Bealtaine* to mark the beginning of the dark and bright halves of the year. As a great Christian Centre, Easter was in all probablity, as in Saighir close at hand, the point at which Brigid's Fire was quenched and relighted.

The gravity of the offence of quenching the fire at the wrong time is highlighted in the Saighir story by the intervention of providence in the killing of the child even though he was later brought back to life by St Ciarán of Clonmacnoise. For a similar offence a Vestal Virgin would be whipped (Schilling, 1987, 15; 251).

In the account of Mide in the Dinnseanchas the importance of the hill of Uisneach (Co Westmeath) as the great Centre and Navel of the country is set forth and this is natural enough considering the geographical position of the hill and the extraordinarily extensive view from the summit. Mide lighted the first fire here for Clann Neimhidh and it was from that fire that every other principal fire was ignited. On that account, it is lawful for Mide's successor to receive a bag of corn and a pig from every chief household in Ireland (RC. 15, 297).

Aodh Mac Bric (Bishop Aodh) had a monastery in Cill Áir

near Uisneach and in it was a building dedicated to Brigid (Gwynn and Haddock, 1970, 392). Bishop Aodh, as well as being a renowned physician, was a great friend of Brigid and 'Aodh' means 'fire' (McCone, 1990, 165). This suggests a link between Brigid, and Aodh and Uisneach – 'symbolic centre of Ireland and site of an erstwhile fire ritual according to the Metrical Dindsenchus 2, 42,' (Gwynn, 1906).

As regards Saighir Chiaráin, Killlanin and Duignan say: 'The place may previously have been a pagan sanctuary; a perpetual fire is said to have burned there' (1967, 120).

In a similar vein, McCone says of Kildare: 'the twelfth century visiting cleric, Giraldus Cambrensis, describes a fire cult at her main church of Kildare that can hardly be other than a pre-Christian survival and is quite reminiscent of the Vestal fire tended by a college of virgins in ancient Rome' (1990,164).

In a remarkable insight Professor McCone builds up an argument for a connection between fire and Brigid as *'Bé Fhilíochta, Bé Leighis agus Bé Ghaibhneachta'* (Lady of Poetry, Medicine and Ironwork), as well a pointing out her connection with three men who are associated with these three functions.

It is by the use of fire that cooking is done, that is to say the transformation of food from the rough form in which it is eaten by animals into the softer more delicate form in which it is consumed by humans. Symbolically, this is the transition from wild nature to culture. In the same way, it is through the use of fire that the blacksmith transforms rough formless masses of metal into implements for agriculture, horseshoes, brooches, works of art. Similarly, through fire, the physician prepares his herbal brews for medical purposes. Thus, Brigid, fire, culture, ironwork and medicine are related.

The practice of these functions is not always pronounced in the *Lives* of Brigid but it may be there in a hidden way through her connection with three men who are typical of these particular professions. They belong to the *Aos Dána* or learned class in early Irish society so that Brigid was their patroness. However, in the actual cult of Brigid as it has come down to us, she is very largely associated with cows and sheep and corn, with agriculture in general.

This area of life belonged to the *Bó Airí* – the farmers. And so it would appear that while Brigid was at a very early stage associated with the *Aos Dána*, the farmers at some point appear to have hijacked her and made her their own.

As regards the three men associated with both Brigid and the three functions – culture, medicine, ironwork – there is firstly the renowned poet Dubthach maccu Lugair, then Aodh Mac Bric the famous physician, and finally Conlaed, Bishop of Kildare, a distinguished metal worker, *primcherd Brigte* (Brigid's chief artisan) as *Félire Oengusso* describes him (Stokes, 1905, 128).

Dubthach wanted to marry Brigid but she refused. She directed him, however, to a beautiful woman whom he married without delay (*Bethu Brigte*, par.2 6) When Brigid had a headache she went to Aodh Mac Bric to be cured (*Bethu Brigte*, par. 26)

It appears then that the characteristics of Brigid which link her to the *Aos Dána* are spread out among three men who are closely associated with her life.

According to Caesar, the Celts worshipped Mercury above all the other gods and they considered that it was he who was the inventor of all the arts: *Deum maxime Mercurium colunt … hunc omnium inventorum artium ferunt* (Tierney, 1960, 244). In Caesar's mind, apparently, Mercury (Greek *Hermes*) was the equivalent of the Celtic god Lugh. Before the Battle of Moytirra (*Cath Maighe Tuireadh*) Lugh portrays himself as the *ildánach* – skilled in all the arts. It is remarkable that both Caesar and the Gaelic text use practically the same phraseology (Gray, 1982, 40).

In the same text, Caesar describes Minerva (Athena of the Greeks): *Minervam operum atque artificiorum initia tradere*, that is to say that Minerva is the founder of the arts and sciences – an echo of what he has already said regarding Mercury.

From the Irish point of view, however, there is a distinct similarity between Caesar's statement about Minerva and Cormac Mac Cuilleannáin's description of Brigid as goddess of poetry, medicine and ironwork (Stokes, 1862, 8).

Something of an equivalence then, can be distinguished between Minerva and Brigid and, as Professor Mac Cana has remarked, it demonstrates the high status of technological expertise among the Celts at an early period (1970, 34).

Brigid as pagan goddess was *ildánach* – possessing all the arts in herself. Brigid, as Christian saint, however, has her talents divided up among three men-friends.

In the *Lives* of the saint, much attention is given to her hospitality; she provides food for the poor; she is engrossed in household affairs; she turns water into beer (*Bethu Brigte*, par.8); she provides meat to make up for what she has given to the dog (Idem par.13); she multiplies the quantity of ale to supply the clergy of 18 churches for Easter Week (Idem par.21), and so forth.

While all of this conforms to the great Christian virtue of hospitality it also has echoes of the Celtic *Bruíon* (*bruidhean*) or Official Hostel open to all comers and presided over by a wealthy *Brughaidh*, provided with extensive lands and cattle by the *tuath* or local political unit. McCone surmises that there may be some influences on the life of Brigid from *Brig briugu* (Brigid the Hospitaller/Hotelier) mentioned in the legal tract *Cethirslicht Athgabhala*: 'The Christian St Brigit's cult or attributes may then be partly based upon those of the mythical female hospitaller whose name is preserved in a legal context as Brig the '*briugu*' (1990,162).

In the story *Scela Mucce Meic Datho* it is said that there were five 'bruidhean's in Ireland: Mac Da Tho's in Leinster; Bruidhean Da Derga in Co Wicklow, probably; Bruidhean Fhorgaill Mhanaich in Lusk; Bruidhean Mhic Da Reo in Breifne (Cavan/Leitrim area) and Bruidhean Da Choca in Co Westmeath (Thurneysen, 1935, 11, 7-10).

In a remarkable article 'Religious Beliefs of the Pagan Irish', J. O'Beirne Crowe surmises that a link may be noticed between the Irish word *Brudin* (*bruidhean/bruíon*) and the Greek *Prytaneion* – that there is a resemblance between both the words and the reality they express. The Prytaneion was connected to a political unit. It had *Hestia/Vesta*, the goddess of the hearth, as its patron and a perpetual fire burned there. In the case of a new colony being established, the fire in the Prytaneion of the new political unit was lighted from the old Prytaneion to show its continuity with the mother territory. Like the bruidhean's of Ireland, it was a hostel where both the aristocracy and travellers in general could receive hospitality (*JRSAI*, 1869, 326-327). As the hearth was the heart of the household, so the Prytaneion was the heart of the political unit (Smyth, 1853, 313).

Could it be that a Bruidhean, with a female Hospitaller called Brigh or Brighid in charge, once existed in Kildare and that the warm hospitality and ale-parties of this benign hotelier filtered down to the later St Brigid and her Convent of Nuns? Something of this spirit is to be found in the poem of the ale-feast, attributed to St Brigid, in which she expresses her desire to entertain Christ and the people of heaven:

I should like a great lake of ale
For the King of Kings;
I should like the family of heaven
To be drinking it through time eternal.

I should like cheerfulness
To be in their drinking;
I should like Jesus
Too, to be there (among them)

I should like the three
Marys of illustrious renown;
I should like the people
Of heaven there from all parts (O'Curry, 1878,616).

I was reminded of this tradition quite by chance just a few days before writing this. In the beautiful church of St Bride (Brigid) in Fleet St., London, with its ancient Crypt revealing the remains of the previous seven churches, and a well, now dry, (Bride Well) the water of which was used for sprinkling the royal route at coronations, the guide showed us the elegant, lifesize statue of St Bride, 'and', he remarked, 'she kept a fine ale-house.'

The existence of the perpetual fire probably indicates the religious element in the presence of a fire-goddess or goddess of the hearth, whether we call her Vesta, Hestia, Sulis, Minerva, or Brigid. It is remarkable that the word 'Da' occurs in four out of the five named 'Bruidheans' and may indicate divinity or cultic associations. The strange, otherworldly atmosphere pervading 'Bruidhean Da Derga' hints at a ritual site, and the violence described in some of the classical Bruidheans would induce the ordinary peaceful traveller to seek alternative accomodation such as was, according to tradition, provided by Brigid. O'Beirne Crowe suggests that with the introduction of the Christian monasteries with their tradition of hospitality, the Bruidheans are less in evidence and this may indicate that they may have been pre-Christian cult centres (*JRSAI*, 1869, 325) This would mean that a 'Christian Cultic and Hospitality Centre' was replacing a 'Pagan Cultic and Hospitality Centre' with the gradual establishment of the new religion. The characteristics of the Bruidhean and the Christian monastery may be compared as follows:

AN BHRUIDHEAN	CILL DARA
1 A centre of hospitality	A centre of hospitality
2 Extensive lands	Extensive lands
3 An easily accessible site	An easily accessible site
4 Connected to a 'Tuath'	Connected to a 'Tuath'
5 Hosteller and Staff	Hosteller and Staff
6 A Perpetual Fire	A Perpetual Fire

As already seen, this square area of Co Kildare having as its corners Kildare (Cill Dara), Hill of Allen (Cnoc Almhaine), Naas (Nás na Rí), and Knockaulin (Cnoc Áilinne) and Maigh Life (the Plain of the Liffey) and the Curragh of Kildare (Cuirreach Life), contained within it was an area of immense political and religious importance.

It seems probable, or at least alternating with an alternative site near Carlow as suggested by Smyth (1982, 34-35), that the great Aonach Carman was held here for a week every three years at Lughnasa (around 1st August). The *Book of Leinster* and

the *Book of Ballymote* (cf. O'Curry, 1873, 3, 522ff) describe the
horse-racing, the music, poetry, storytelling, the artistry, the
lament for dead ancestors, the markets, the proclamation of
laws:

> Seven mounds without touching each other,
> where the dead have often been lamented;
> seven plains, sacred without a house,
> for the funeral games of Carman.

> Three markets in that auspicious country;
> a market of food, a market of live stock,
> and the great market of the foreign Greeks,
> where gold and noble clothes were wont to be.
> (*Margaid mor na n-gall n-Gregach,*
> *i m-bid or, is ard etach*) (O'Curry, 1873, 3, 546-547).

Patrick, Brigid, Kevin and Colm Cille are said to be dominant
over every group and the fair of the saints is celebrated with
pomp, for it is meet, at first, to pay homage to God (Idem 539).

The fertility of the land came as a result of holding the
Aonach:

> *Ith ocus blicht doib ar a denam* (Corn and milk to them for its
> holding).

> *meth, ocus suba la cach saintreib, ocus cach mess mara thaidbsin,*
> *ocus lina lan o uiscib, ocus almuire co tir lagen* (prosperity and
> comfort for every household, and fruits of every kind in
> abundance, and abundant supplies from their waters,and
> imports to the land of Leinster) (Idem, 531).

While some authors favour the Carlow, Burren/Barrow area as
the site of Aonach Carman, which in any case is of no great distance from the Knockaulin, Curragh area, Orpen after much research favours the latter and remarks that Aonach Carman has
been compared, not inaptly, to the Olympic Games of Greece
('Aenach Carman: its Site'; *JRSAI*, 1906, 11ff). The presence of
Greek merchants at Carman is to be remarked and we can tabul-
ate some items of resemblance between the two events and sites
(cf Swaddling, 2004).

AONACH CARMAN	OLYMPIA
1 Cnoc Almhaine – Sacred Hill of god Fionn	Sacred Hill of god Kronos
2 Cuirrech Life – The Curragh	Stadium and Gymnasium
3 Sacred Oak at Cill Dara	Sacred Olive Tree
4 Temple of goddess Brigid	Temple of goddess Hera
5 Perpetual Fire	Perpetual Fire
6 Bruidhean	Leonaidon
7 Ancestral Burials in Curragh	Pelopion (Burial Mound)
8 Games and Horse Racing	Games and Horse Racing
9 Artistic Work	Artistic Work
10 Large Gathering	Large Gathering
11 Trumpeters	Trumpeters
12 Archaic Religious Background	Archaic Religious Background
13 Every Three Years	Every Four Years
14 Fertility association (Brigid)	Fertility association (Ge)
15 Lasted one Week	Lasted Five Days
16 Held at Lughnasa (August)	Held at Autumn (Aug/Sept)

(Swaddling, J., *The Ancient Olympic Games*, The British Museum Press, 2004)

Many features of the life of Brigid are more easily explainable if she is seen within a milieu alive with activity involving agriculture, economics, sports, local kingship, archaic religion, a newly-introduced religion, ecclesiastical organisation, herbal medicine, international trading, artistic work. Into this complex and pulsing area, the saint sought to introduce the unifying spirit of Christianity.

CHAPTER EIGHT

The Place of the Sun in Ancient Religion

While many references to the cult of the Sun may be found in ancient Irish Literature and to the mark it left on certain Irish saints, Brigid among them, that is not to say that the ancient Irish practised an exclusive worship of the sun such as is frequently attributed to the Egyptian Pharaoh Akhenaten.

Traditionally, the supernatural race – the Tuatha Dé Danann or Aos Sí – are connected in a special way to the fertility of the land. They have power over milk-production and plant growth and the human population who live on the surface of the land are dependant on the Aos Sí who live underground in the Sacred Hollow Hills and Megalithic Sites. The human population has to have the good will of the Tuatha Dé Danann for the prosperity of their farms.

The tenacity of this type of religion, lasting on to some extent to our own days, is shown in the research carried on by Kate Muller-Lisowski on the cult of Donn Fírinne in Co Limerick. People used to climb the slope to Cnoc Fírinne, (Knockfierna, near Croom) and gifts of eggs, pieces of dead animals and cocks, as well as bunches of wild flowers were laid in the grass or in the corn fields in honour of Donn. Blood was sprinkled to protect the house and land at Bealtaine (May Eve), at Samhain (Halloween) and on the 10th of November the eve of the Feast of St Martin of Tours (Martinmas) – this latter was really an alternative for Samhain as the calendar had gone out of line with the sun (*Béal.* 1948, 160).

The god Donn had power over the crops:

'Blight on crops, potatoes, was caused by Donn and his "sluagh" (company) who fought battles for the crops. These

76

battles took place in autumn between the fairies of Cnoc
Áine, (Knockainey in east Limerick) led by Áine and those of
Knockfierna led by Donn Fírinne. The struggle took the form
of a cross-country hurling match. The victors carried the best
of the potato-crop to their side of the country' (Béal.
1948,160).

In this case, the quality of the potato-crop for the year depended
on a supernatural hurling match between the goddess Áine
Chliach of east Limerick and her team and the god Donn Fírinne
of west Limerick and his team. There were no goalposts as in
modern hurling. The idea was to get the ball back to one's own
territory. Cnoc Áine and Cnoc Fírinne are about 20 miles apart
so that the ball would have been thrown in about half way between the two areas. Then the hurlers would have to play over
fields and bogs, over streams and ditches in an endeavour to get
the ball back to their home ground. If Áine succeeded in bringing the ball back to Cnoc Áine, then the potato-crop in east
Limerick would be excellent that year while that in west
Limerick would only be fair, and vice versa. Here, the game of
hurley is seen as a divine activity, a ritual performed by the
gods, having repercussions on the food-supply of the humans
under their control.

This modern example, however, corresponds to the ancient
account, *De Gabhail in tSida*. Just as in the case of Donn and Áine,
the great god, An Daghdha, has control over the fertility of the
land and the human population have to recognise this.

The humour can be seen in the situation in which Clann
Mhíle defeat the Tuatha Dé Danann at the Battle of Tailteann
and they (TDD) go underground into the Síthe, the sacred
Hollow Hills. Hardly have they disappeared from view, however,
than they show their power by causing the crops to fail. The
human population have to go, hat in hand as it were, and
humbly ask the Daghdha to restore the crops. The Daghdha
grants their request graciously.

The Tuatha Dé Danann/Aos Sí, however, expect recognition
of their power by little gifts, observance of seasonal rites, respect

for their sacred sites and so forth. If this is done all will be well
and the land will prosper. We might see this arrangement in
terms of a circle of reciprocity: the Tuatha Dé Danann give a
good harvest and a plentiful supply of milk *(Ith agus Blicht)*. The
human population show their gratitude by making offerings
such as laying cakes outside a Sí or sacred hill and by giving a
generous present to the masked children, representing the *Aos
Sí*, who go around from house to house requesting gifts at
Samhain. If the humans are grateful and keep acknowledging
their dependence in these small ways, the circle will remain unbroken and the Tuatha Dé Danann will give prosperity to the
land. If, however, the humans become neglectful and ungener-
ous and begin to treat the sacred sites with disrespect, then the
circle is broken and bad weather, blight and disease will result.
It is unnecessary to point out the parallels with contemporary
exploitation of the land, rain forests, sacred sites and natural re-
sources. This reciprocal attitude towards creation must indeed
be one of the glories of the ancient religion and one which we
disregard to our cost.

Another facet of the Creideamh Sí was the peculiar arrangement of Celtic kingship in which the human, mortal king, the
representative of his people, was symbolically married to the
goddess of the land, a supernatural woman of the Tuatha Dé
Danann, in the rite of the *Bainis Rí*, 'the wedding of the king'. If
the king were good and just his divine consort guaranteed the
prosperity of his reign and his kingdom.

In Ms 3.18.565 in Trinity College, Dublin, it is said that
Munster is more fertile than any other Province as Ana, the god-
dess of fertility, is worshipped there and the two breasts of Ana
(*Dhá Chíoch Anann*, near Killarney) derive their name from her:
'*Muma: mó a hana nás ana cach coigid, ar is inti noadrad ban-dia int
shonusa .i. Ana a hainm sein; ocus is uaithi side is berar dá chig
Anann*' (*JRSAI*, 1869, 317)

According the story *Tochmarc Treblainne*, the Clann Míle
aristocracy used to take the sons and daughters of the Tuatha Dé
Danann in fosterage from the Sí (sacred hill) nearest them so that

they (TDD) would not destroy the corn, milk and fruit of the humans during their lifetimes (*PRIA*, 1879, 169).

This was a clever move on the part of the Celtic aristocracy as the system of fosterage created very strong bonds between the fosterers and the fostered. Of course, it seems to imply that the Tuatha Dé Danann, normally invisible to human eyes, made themselves visible throughout the period of their fosterage.

Many of the well-known practices such as pouring a little milk on the floor at milking time, avoiding building a house on a path between two Síthe used by the Tuatha Dé Danann on their frequent round of parties, carrying the Scian Coise Duibhe (a black-handled knife) as protection when passing a Sí, and so forth, are readily explainable in terms of the double population assumed by the Creideamh Sí.

A human and a divine population were living close at hand and had to accomodate themselves to that situation. As one would expect in a rural civilisation, very dependent on the land, the Creideamh Sí was largely a fertility religion concerned with life and growth and prosperity.

In the epic *Táin Bó Chuailnge*, Cú Chulainn is hard-pressed by his enemies and calls on the elements – the sky and the earth and the local river 'Crón' to come to his aid. And with that, the river-rises up in a flood as high as a tree to prevent his enemies advancing further (LU, 5512-5520).

In the story *Comthoth Loegairi*, in *Leabhar na hUidhre*, King Laoghaire comes to Leinster to collect the Boramha – the much opposed tribute. The Leinstermen defeat him at the Battle of Áth Dara and he swears by the elements – sun and moon, water and air, day and night, sea and land – that he will never come again to collect the tribute. The Leinstermen accepted his oath sworn on the elements. But next year, he was back again, and this time the offended elements killed him (LU, 9794 -9815).

Even the God of the Christians is referred to as 'Dia na nDúl' – the God of the Elements, of earth, air, fire and water. The Lorica (protection prayer) *Ateoch friut an dechmad*, invokes God through the elements:

Atteoch friut an usci,
Ocus inn aer nangaid;
Atteoch friut an tenid,
Atteoch friut in talmain (Plummer, 1925,102-107).
(I beseech you through water and through the stormy air; I
beseech you through fire, I beseech you through earth.)

Although the sun is of overwhelming importance, at the same
time, it is only one of the elements. Earth, air and water are also
involved in the growth of crops, and the fertility of the land op-
erates within a complex system of interrelationships in which
each of the elements plays its part.

It appears that balance and harmony between the different
parts of creation was what was sought for in the ancient religious philosophy. In an episode in *Cath Maighe Tuireadh*, the
Tuatha Dé Danann refuse to grant their enemy Breas his life on
the promise that he would enable them to produce four crops
per year from the same field. They said that they were quite sat-
isfied with the normal system – the spring for ploughing and
sowing the corn, the summer for the growth and strengthening of
the grain, the autumn for ripening and saving the harvest and the
winter for consuming (Gray, 1982, 68). Obviously, the Aos Sí must
have been aware, that four crops per year would have given enormous profit. Nevertheless it was rejected in favour of the ordinary
annual round which conformed to the laws of nature.

It appears that to a certain extent the deities were personific-
ations of the forces of nature. Certain characteristics of the sea
may be discerned in Manannán Mac Lir, the god of the sea, and
those of the sun with Lugh. The goddesses Bóinn, Eithne, Sionna
and Brighid have given their names to rivers, and Éire, Banbha
and Fodhla to the country itself.

A number of early Irish adventurers' stories give descriptions of the Celtic Otherworld known by many names such as
Eamhain Abhlach, Tír na nÓg, Maigh Dá Cheo, Maigh Mel, Tír
na mBeo, Tír na mBan, Ynys Afallon, etc.. While the Druids proclaimed the immortality of the soul and the continuity of life
after death, it is difficult to know if everybody went to this pleas-

ant paradise automatically after death. At any rate the Celtic Otherworld is often portrayed as a place of wonderful music, beautiful women, fine food (the pigs eaten today will be alive again tomorrow) and delicious drink. It was a place of sport and feasting, and perhaps St Brigid's Ale-Feast was not uninfluenced by such a strong tradition. It appears that the Celtic heaven was a place of great merriment, totally unlike the grim Hades of Greek and Roman literature (MacKillop, 1998, 317-318).

When it comes to descriptions of the Otherworld and life after death, Christianity is obviously at a disadvantage as its vision of heaven is of a state so transcendent and beyond all human experience that an adequate vocabulary to describe it is unavailable.

It is within this vast complex of ancient philosopical thought, and a lore of connections between a myriad of phenomena that seem so distinct, that the life of Brigid is to be situated. Since the power of the sun is so marked in the processes of the natural world, it is a feature of her cult and her Feast of Imbolc on the first of February marks the public return of the sun, with its hot fertilising power, into the world of nature having finally escaped from its period of imprisonment by the dark forces of winter in a dark underground cave, according to ancient traditional ideas. Not without reason did the great King-Bishop of Cashel, Cormac Mac Cuilleannáin explain the name 'Brigit' as derived from *Breoshaigit* – a fiery torch arrow (Stokes, 1862, 8).

As well as Áine and Grian, well-known goddesses of Co Limerick whose names link them to the sun, there is also Ébliu (Eibhle) from whom Sliabh Éibhlinne (Slieve Felim) is derived, on the borders of Limerick and Tipperary (*JRSAI*, 1, 96)

Aoibheall na Carraige Léith is the renowned goddess of Co Clare linked to the kingly family of the O'Briens, who as their Bean Sí, cries on the death of a member of the group. As well as that, Aoibheall is judge in the women's court in *Cúirt an Mheáin Oíche*, and it is near Loch Gréine (Lake of the Sun) that Brian Merriman fell asleep and was led by the damsel to the palace of Maigh Ghréine for the sitting of the Court (Ó hUaithne, 1968, 9).

In this way, the link between Grian and Aoibheall is marked. Similarly Grian and Áine are connected by Aogán Ó Rathaille:

'do ghuil Áine i n-Árus Gréine' (ITS, 3, 2nd ed., 224) (Áine wept in the palace of Grian.)

The two names Éibhle and Aoibheall are connected to *aibhleog*, 'ember', embracing the idea of 'fire, spark, radiance. All come together in 'Aoibhgréine' (radiance of the sun, ray of sunshine), daughter of the ill-fated Naoise and Deirdre of the Sorrows (Ó Corráin and Maguire, 1981, 15).

The fire element in Brigid is shown in her connection with the Feast of Candlemas (Purification of the Blessed Virgin Mary/Presentation in the Temple) which takes place on the second of February, the day after that of Brigid. According to tradition, St Brigid, put a ring of lighted candles on her head and led the Virgin Mary into the temple in Jerusalem (IFC 903; 26, 28). For this reason, St Brigid's Feast precedes that of Mary. The Blessing and Procession of Lighted Candles at Candlemas with their ideas of light, protection and fertility are parallel to some extent to the cult of Brigid.

While the origins of the Candlemas Blessing and Procession are somewhat obscure, the actual blessing of the candles developed enormously in the West as may be seen in the *Missale Romanum* of the Tridentine Rite: '... there is the increasing preoccupation with the blessing of the candles to the point of blessing the source of light, before the candles in some places' (Stevenson, 1988, 340).

In some places such as Braga and Narbonne a new fire was kindled and the candles were lighted from this to signify a new beginning, parallel to that of Easter.

In parts of Scotland, bonfires blazed on the Feast of the Presentation. The practice was known as the 'Candlemas Bleeze' (McNeill, 1959, 34).

In certain areas in Ireland, the custom of the burnt firebrand was to be found. The end of a little wooden branch was burned in the domestic fire on St Brigid's Eve and when quenched, a cross was marked with it on the arms of members of the family

(IFC 900, 99). This resembles the widespread practice of throwing burning branches from the bonfire on St John's Eve (23rd June) into the fields and orchards to keep away disease and promote fertility. In this case, the domestic fire may have taken the place of the bonfire.

E. O. James describes the ritual use of the domestic fire in Scotland also: 'In Scotland, for example, the sacred fire of St Bride, or Bridget, was carefully guarded and on the Eve of Candlemas a bed made of corn and hay was surrounded with candles as a fertility rite, the fire symbolising the victorious emergence of the sun from the darkness of winter' (1961, 233).

CHAPTER NINE

The Brídeog

One of the more remarkabe features of the cult of Brigid is undoubtedly what is known as the Brídeog. This is a procession
which takes place on the Eve of the Feast. A large doll or image,
often made of straw and clothed in white or in various colours
according to the customs of the particular area, is carried from
house to house by a group of people known as 'Lucht na
Brídeoige'. The group may be of men, of women, or of children,
or a mixture of all. They are usually dressed in quaint attire and
are often masked. In some places, especially in Kerry, very elab-
orately woven hats of straw are worn. They often carry musical
instruments and play when they enter a house. They sometimes
announce their arrival at a house by blowing a horn.

The image is called the 'Brídeog' but the name is also given to
the actual rite of visitation.

The rite varies somewhat from place to place but generally
speaking when the group enters a house the person carrying the
Brídeog (doll) props it in the corner of the room so that the
Brídeog 'presides' as it were over the proceedings. The Brídeog
members usually do a little dancing, collect some money from
the household, and then, carrying the image, depart for the next
house.

While the Brideog was once very widespread, especially in
the southern half of the country, it is rare nowadays except in
some areas of Kerry and notably Kilgobnet near Killarney.

This is the basic outline of the rite but we will see that the details varied considerably inside the general structure. To obtain
a general idea of the procedure we begin with an account of the
Brídeog from Co Waterford:

'Long ago, a group of girls from the district used to get some
long article, generally a broom. They used to dress it up in
the form of St Brigid and go around from house to house collecting money. The head was made from a little round bag

stuffed with straw and rags and had eyes, nose, mouth and ears painted on it. The arms were made from two old stockings stuffed likewise and tied on the handle of the broom. All this was covered with a long white frock and a cloak which was made from a shawl' (IFC 900; 209-210; Na cailíní scoile, Cruach agus Cill Aodha, Contae Phort Láirge).

This account from East Co Waterford makes it clear that in 1942 or thereabouts the Rite of the Brideog was no longer practised in that part of the country. Nevertheless, it describes certain features of the Brídeog quite clearly so that it may be presumed that the demise of the Brídeog had taken place comparatively recently.

It describes the image itself and how it was made. In this area it was girls who formed 'Lucht na Brídeoige' and as usual they went from house to house collecting money.

In the parish of Baile Bhóirne in West Cork, it was children who went around in the Brídeog:

'Trathnona oíche 'le Briíde, d'imíodh aos óga ó thigh go tigh le Brídeog socair suas acu i bhfuirm babáin. Bhídis ag brath ar airgead d'fháil díreach fé mar a bhíodh lucht dreoilín lá 'le Stiofáin' (IFC 900; 87; Amhlaoibh Ó Loingsigh, (69), Cúil Aodha, Maigh Chromtha, Contae Chorcaí, Narrator; Cáit Bean Uí Liatháin, Cúil Aodha, Scribe).

(On the evening of St Brigid's Night, the young people used to go from house to house with a Brídeog arranged in the form of a baby. They expected to be given money just like the Wren Boys on St Stephen's Day.)

From Killorglin, the place of Puck Fair at Lughnasa, comes a description which gives certain details of the rite enabling us to build up a comprehensive picture of the proceedings:

'A figure was carried in procession from house to house, boys and girls dressed up and wore masks. The men usually wore women's clothes and tall hats made of straw. They carried a horn which they blew on approaching every house. They danced in every house and before they left, the woman

of the house stuck a pin in the Brídeog and left it there. The
brídeog was made from a churn-staff and the body stuffed
with straw. People who were not 'dressed up' usually followed the Biddy. It was customary to 'break up' at the house
where the Biddy was made and to dance the remainder of the
night. There were no songs and no hymns used on the occasion. There is no logical explanation of the origin of the custom' (IFC 899; 26-28; E. Foley, Killorglin, Scribe)

Another wonderful description of the Brídeog comes from Dún
Caoin in Kerry. This places great emphasis on the welcome
given to the image-bearers on their arrival at the house:

'Lá 'le Bríde, téitear amach sa Bhrídeog fós anseo timpeall.
Fadó is iad na cailíní óga suas go ceithre bliana déag nó mar
sin a ghabhadh timpeall leis an mBriídeog ach anois téann
garsúin bheaga chomh maith leis na gearrchailí beaga amach
… Nuair a thagadh an lá ghabhadh na cailíní beaga timpeall
leis. D'iompraídis í ina mbaclainn go hoscailte go dtagaidis
go béal an dorais. Stadaidis ansan agus chuireadh muintir an
tí fáilte roimh 'Bríd' no 'Naomh Bríde'. 'Móire is daichead ar
maidin duit, is a Chríostaí Óig tá an bhliain seo caite, is tánn
tú tagaithe arís 'nár dtreo' (bean a' tí a chuir fáilte roimh
Bhrídeog), nó 'Dé bheathasa, a Bhríd.' Sin é a ndeirtí agus
ansan thogadh bean a' tí ina baclainn an bhrídeog agus phóg-
adh sí í.

Uibhe cearc, ceann nó dó, nó trí a gheobhadh lucht na
brídeoige ins gach tigh. Ní chuirfí amach 'Bríd' gan rud éigin'
(IFC 899; 153-155; Muiris Ó Dálaigh, Baile Bhiocaire, Dún
Caoin, Scribe).

(On St Brigid's Day, people still go out in the Brídeog in this
area. Long ago it was the young girls up to fourteen years of
age or thereabouts who used to go around but nowadays
young boys go around as well. When the day would come
the young girls would go around with it. They used to carry
the Brídeog (image) in their arms until they came outside the
door. They would stand then and the people of the house
used to welcome Brigid or St Brigid saying: 'Moire is daich-

ead ar maidin duit - Luck and forty welcomes of the morning to you, and O Young Christian, another year is past and you have come again to us'. (It was the woman of the house who welcomed the Brídeog procession). Or, she would say: 'Welcome Brigid.' That was what they used to say, and then the woman of the house would take the Brídeog (image) in her lap and kiss it. The Image-Bearers would get one or two or three hen-eggs in every house. Brigid would not be allowed to go out of the house without receiving something.)

A remarkable and saddening account of how the custom of the Brídeog came to an end in one area through the influence of a 'town woman' is the following:

'Strange as it may seem, I havent heard much about St Brigid in the parish. I know this, however, that when we first came to live there in 1889, that the Brídeog was still carried around by the little girls on the eve of the Feast Day, but alas, my mother was a townie intolerant of the 'superstitious' practices of the country people, and I know that the little girls that came round with the Brídeog to Fallduff Lodge did not get a cordial welcome but rather a lecture on the insult to the saint by carrying around a thing like that in honour of the saint. I was too young to quite agree with my mother's attitude, though I did not venture to express such an opinion. I had a sympathy with the novelty of the whole thing which I did not come into contact (with) before and was disappointed when our visitors were not welcomed, instead having their feelings hurt. I wonder if that was one of the first reactions against the town mind that I felt.

The sad part of the whole thing was that my mother's lecture damned the old custom ever after, in that part of the parish anyhow, and I never heard of the little girls carrying around the Brideog after that' (IFC 903; 82-83; John O'Dowd, 'The Laurels', Westport).

An amusing and enlightening account of a local form of the rite comes from Gort some miles north of Castlebar, Co Mayo:

'On the vigil of St Brigid's Day, a quaint custom is observed
in this district. Two girls who call themselves "brídeogs"
dress themselves in old ragged clothes, and carrying a blackthorn stick in their hands, they go from house to house.
When they come to the door they knock and say: "Brigid is
coming." The door is then opened to them and they are invited in. They walk into the kitchen carrying a doll and a big
"brídeog cross". If anybody attempts to tear the false face off,
they strike them with the blackthorn stick. One of them sits
on a chair and plays a flute or a fiddle while her companion
dances a reel or a jig. When the dance is finished, the bean a'
tí gives them money and they say, 'If ever you be short Brigid
will give you some.' They are given a drink of milk and after
partaking of it they say, 'May none of your cows die during
the year' (IFC 903; 133-134; Bríd bean Uí Rabhlaigh, Gort,
Caisleán an Bharraigh, Narrator; Mairéad Bean Uí Ríagáin,
OS, Scribe).

Apart from the humour contained in this account, it will be noticed that an archaic ritual style prevails. At the doorstep there is
the ritual acclamation 'Brigid is coming' with the invitation to
enter the dwelling. This type of threshold dialogue is known
from other areas. What is surprising is the smallness of the number, but these two girls are masked and carry the doll and cross
as well as a musical instrument and a blackthorn stick for protection and perhaps also to help them over rough ground as in
other examples. The stepdancing may represent the movement
of the seasons – the transition from winter to spring which occurs with the feast of Imbolc, St Brigid's Day, the Dance of the
Seasons. Then they are given money and they reply ritually with
a formula corresponding to the money offering: 'If ever you be
short Brigid will give you some.' Here they speak in the person
of Brigid. Then they are given a drink of milk, and again, the ritual response corresponds to the nature of the gift: 'May none of
your cows die during the year.' This response recalls the fact
that the Rite of the Brídeog begins a cycle of a year which will
last until the next eve of Imbolc. This particular form of the

Brideog is remarkable for its robust character and clearly proclaims the rite as concerned with the fertility and luck of the
coming year.

In the area of Kilcorban near Portumna, Co Galway, St
Brigid's Day used to be a holiday, with Mass and a sermon on
the life of the saint. It was on the day itself (1st February) and not
on the Eve (31st January) that the Brídeog took place:

'Tar éis an Aifrinn téann na buachaillí fásta mórthimpeall ag-
bailiú airgid. Bíonn siad deisithe in éadaí bána agus tugtar
Brídeoga ortha. Ní bhíonn aon Bhrídeog a hiompar acu ná ní
chanann siad amhráin ar bith. Ní fios cad a dhéantar leis an
airgead a bhailítear' (IFC 902; 215; Lorcán Ó Cillín, Cill
Chorbáin, Port Omna, Narrator; Seosamh Ó Dunaí, An
Cillín, Port Omna, Scribe).

(After Mass, the grown-up boys go around collecting money.
They are dressed in white clothes and are called Brídeoga.
They do not carry a Brídeog (image) nor do they sing any
songs. It is unknown what they do with the money.)

Here, in Portumna, the role of the church, with Mass and sermon and the change to the day rather than the eve, is oviously
stronger than in other more rural areas. The narrator must have
known other forms of the Brídeog as he remarks on the absence
of the doll and the singing of songs in this local version. A casual
observer could easily have missed these features but it appears
from his remarks that Lorcán Ó Cillín had a detailed knowledge
of the rite in other forms.

Later, we will see that this area provides a remarkable example of the connection of St Brigid's cross with the sowing of the
corn.

The Brídeog in Co Donegal

Donegal is not generally regarded as an area in which the
Brídeog was practised. There are several accounts of the
'Threshold Rite' and it is true that this is more characteristic of
the county. Despite this, however, we have a description from
the Ross Goill area in the north of the county of a Brídeog pro-

cession of quite a remarkable form – perhaps a mixture of the
northern 'Threshold Rite' and the southern Brídeog. The
Narrator speaks first of the Threshold Rite and then of the
Brídeog:

'Roimhe seo, théadh daoine ó theach go teach leis an
Bhrídeog. Ba é an sort ruda a bhí ins an Bhrídeog ná samhailt
de éadach a bheadh cosúil le Naomh Bríd, agus chuirtí clóca
gorm uirthi i gcuimhne an chlóca ghoirm a bhíodh ar Naomh
Bríde nuair a bhí sí beo. Ba ins an teach a bheadh ag ceann na
comharsanachta a dhéantaí an Bhrídeog. Nuair a bhíodh sí
déanta théadh cupla duine den líon tí sin go dtí an chéad
teach eile. Nuair a thagadh siad go leac an dorais scairteadh
siad amach in ard a gceann trí huaire: 'Gabhaigí ar bhur
nglúine, osclaigí bhur súile agus ligigí isteach Bríd
Bheannaithe', agus thugtaí mar fhreagra istigh orthu: 'Sé
beatha, 'Sé beatha, na mná uaisle.' Théadh cupla duine as an
líon tí sin go dtí an chéad teach eile agus mar sin de a rachadh
siad. Cupla duine as líon tí amháin ag gabhail go dtí an chéad
teach eile nó go mbeidis ag ceann na comharsanachta. Ba é an
fáth a bhí leis an Bhrídeog ná deirtear go samhluigheann
(sabhálann) Naomh Bríd gach teach a bheirtear an Bhrídeog
go dtí é, ó gach contúirt i rith na bliana agus go gcuireann sí
an droch-uair thar an líon tí gan chaill ar feadh na bliana
fósta de reir bharúill na seandaoine' (IFC 904; 188-190; Seán
Ó Siadhail, Cnoc Dumaigh, Narrator; Tomás Mac
Fhionghaile, Carraig Áirt, Leifear, Co Dhún na nGall, Scribe)
(Formerly, people used to go from house to house with the
Brídeog. The Brídeog was an image – kind of statue – wearing the type of clothing that would have been worn by St
Brigid with the blue cloak she wore when alive. It was in the
house at the head of neighbourhood that the Brídeog used to
be made. When it was made, a couple of people from this
household would go to the next house. When they would arrive at the threshold they would shout out loudly three
times: 'Go on your knees (kneel down), open your eyes and
let Blessed Brigid enter,' and those inside the house answered

'She is welcome, the Noble Lady is welcome'. Then, a couple of people from that house would proceed to the next house and this is how it was done – a couple of people from one household going to the next house until the original house at the head of the neighbourhood was reached.

The purpose of the Brídeog procession was this: it is said that St Brigid protects every house visited by the Brídeog from every danger throughout the year and that she drives misfortune away from that house throughout the course of the year. The is the opinion of the old people.)

This description of the Brídeog from Co Donegal introduces a different type of observance from what is normal. Instead of the same group of people carrying the Brídeog from house to house and covering the whole locality as is the usual procedure, in this case two people carry the Brídeog to the house nearest to them, leave it there, and return home. They travel far less than in Munster.

Suppose that there are five houses in the area – houses A, B. C, D, and E. House A is at the head of the settlement – perhaps the biggest house or the house nearest the public road, at any rate the most prominent house in the area. It is in this house that the Brídeog, the doll, is constructed from straw, wood, and so forth, and the clothes put on. When the Image is made, two people or more, carry it to the next house (house B) and perform the threshold rite as described, standing outside the door and shouting out the ritual summons: 'Go on your knees, open your eyes and let Blessed Brigid enter.' They shout this three times through the closed door. Those inside answer: 'She is welcome, the Noble Lady is welcome' to each acclamation. Then the people inside the house open the door and the Brídeog enters. The Image-Bearers can now return home to House A, their part of the relay system having been completed, leaving the Image/ Brídeog behind them

In this account, masks and special dress for the performers is not mentioned, so presumeably they wore their ordinary dress. If the houses were very close to each other and each group had

to travel only a very short distance, perhaps it was considered
not worth while assuming the highly ritualised dress of the
south where the Brídeog was time-consuming and a very considerable walking-tour was involved. It is not stated that there
was dancing, singing, dining, or collecting in any house, and
perhaps these did not take place, as the ritual only involved
next-door neighbours. One could have wished, however, that
the narrator were more lavish with the details of the case.

What is impressive in the rite is the elaborate, three-fold
'Threshold Dialogue' in which, in front of a closed door, Brigid
seeks entry into the family home and from inside is given an as-
surance of welcome. Then the door is opened and Brigid comes
in. The Brídeog (Image), then, having been faithfully deposited
in house B, it is now the turn of a group from this house to carry
it to the nearest house – house C. Here the same ritual is performed – Threshold Rite, and Entry. A group from house C take
the Brídeog to house D. A group from house D takes it to house
E, and finally a group from house E takes the Brídeog back to
house A – the house in which it was made. The Threshold Rite
and Entry probably also take place here, as the construction of
the Image is distinct from the ritual tour. In this way, the whole
area is visited and a kind of relay system is used the avoid travelling long distances on a dark night. On the other hand, it lacks
the flamboyance of some of the southern performances.

The Brídeog in Co Wicklow

A fine description of the Brídeog comes from Co Wicklow, from
the artist Benedict Tutty as he looked back on the days of his
youth in the village of Hollywood (Cillín Chaoimhín). As the
name implies, the place has connections with St Kevin
(Caoimhín) of Glendalough, and it is thought that the pilgrims
to the monastery used to pass that way. It is here that the
'Hollywood Stone' was found. On the stone a labyrinth is sculptured, indicating to the pilgrims that they were now entering
into a sacred and mysterious realm of many turnings and secret
recesses where the Minotaur wandered. They must confront

him bravely, relying on divine help before arriving at the peace of the City of God. The 'Hollywood Stone' is now in the National Museum in Dublin.

According to the narrator, the Brídeog group did not belong to Hollywood itself but to the area of Cryhelp, about five miles away. But they came to Hollywood with the Brídeog and it was there in the public house belonging to the narrator's father that they actually ended the season of visits to houses around the third week of February – quite late in February at any event.

The Brideog began in the Cryhelp area at the usual time, the 31st January. It was a large area with many houses to be visited and this explains the late arrival in Hollywood. The narrator was unsure if they had any break within the 3-week period.

At any rate, the Brídeog arrived in the village of Hollywood at about seven o'clock in the evening towards the end of the month of February and proceeded to visit each house in turn. The account covers the years 1935-1948, and some time after that the Brídeog seems to have ceased.

The Brideog group consisted of from 15 to 20 members, all male, married and single alike. Certain families, such as the O'Kearneys and the O'Kellys, were well represented and for many years one of these families acted as leader. The leader had a well-recognised status. When he gave the signal to begin the Rite or to move to another house, or any other directive, he was obeyed instantly. He was masked and he alone was garbed in straw. All members of the group wore masks and were dressed in quaint clothes – whatever was at hand. However, the members of this particular Brídeog did not wear white.

Around the end of February, the sun sets at around 5.30 and the narrator remembered the group marching into the village in the darkness with the white Brídeog leading the way. The scene filled him with a sense of the primeval.

The Brídeog was made from a churn-dash; the circular top was used to form the head with a veil around it and the rest was covered with a long white dress. The Brídeog was always carried in front of the procession and while the rite was being performed in a house the Brídeog-Carrier always kept the Brídeog standing. He did not join in the ritual dancing, his function was to attend to the Brídeog.

When all was over, and the last performance of the year had ended in the public house in Hollywood, a party took place, a kind of 'Biddy Ball' as it was called in Kerry.

No 'Rann' or ritual verses were recited or 'Threshold Dialogue' as in Co Donegal. The ritual consisted of dancing – sets – with the music supplied by melodions. Music was also played by the Brídeog as they entered the village in the dark.

An atmosphere of mystery prevailed during the performance of the rite. There was no conversation, no joking. Looking back over the years, the narrator felt that the performers themselves were immersed in the ritual and were drawn into a world of mystery, another dimension. No collection of money took place and the narrator was unsure if it took place in other houses of the area.

For the party, or 'Biddy Ball', the group retired to another room and some of the formality disappeared but not all. The members of the Brídeog drank and sang and danced with the local women. The leader never took off his disguise. While the masks were simple they were effective and the local people, who might know some of the performers, were unable to recognise them until they took off the masks after the last performance. It was clear to all that the Brídeog marked a turning-point in the year. The narrator felt that the Brideog was a religious rite generating an atmosphere of mystery and operating outside the boundaries of ordinary life (Benedict Tutty, Glenstal, Murroe, Co Limerick, Narrator; Seán Ó Duinn, Scribe).

CHAPTER 10

The Threshold Rite

While the Brídeog procession from house to house was very popular in the southern part of the country, as we have seen, the 'Threshold Rite' held sway in certain areas in the northern part of the country. Accounts from different places, beginning with Co Donegal, will illustrate the situation.

The Threshold Rite in Co. Donegal.
A clear comprehensive description of the Threshold Rite comes to us from the Ros Coill area – from the same place as the account of the unusual 'relay-type' of Brídeog procession and from the same narrator – Seán Ó Siadhail. Firstly, he looks back on how things were a short time before:

'Le tamall anuas tá an sean-nós a bhíodh acu ag comóradh an Fhéile Bríde ag gabhail i bhfuaradh ach b'fhéidir le cúnamh an Rí go n-éireodh sé beo arís níos láidre agus níos bláthmhaire ná mar a bhí sé riamh. Níl acu anois ach nós ag déanamh crosanna agus brúitín oíche Fhéile Bríde, ach seal tamaill ó shin nach acu a bhíodh na sean-nósanna breátha. Seo an dóigh a chomórtaí an Fhéile Bríde seal tamaill o shin.
Le clapsholas go díreach ní bheadh le feiceáil ag leac dorais achan (gach) tí ach ualach feaga. Nuair a thagadh an oíche dhéanfaí réidh pota breá brúitín (prataí beirithe brúite) agus go díreach sula mbrúití iad théadh fear an tí amach go leac an dorais agus de ghuth ard scairteodh sé amach:
'Gabhaigí ar bhur nglúine,
Osclaigí bhur súile,
Agus ligigí isteach Bríd Bheannaithe'
Déarfadh an líon tí, ag tabhairt freagra air:
'Se beatha, 'Se Beatha na mná uaisle.'

95

Deireadh siad an rann céanna athuair agus thugtaí an freagra
céanna orthu. I ndiaidh é a rá an triú uair agus an líon tí freagra a thabhairt air, bheireadh sé isteach na feaga (feagacha)
agus chuireadh sé faoi phota an bhrúitín (prátaí) iad nó go
mbíodh siad brúite. Ansin, d'itheadh siad a suipéar. I ndiaidh am suipéara thosódh an sport agus an siamsa sa dóigh
cheart. Shuíodh an líon tí síos, siar ar fud an tí ag déanamh
crosanna. Bhíodh na seandaoine i gclúdaigh chomh
gnóthach le cách ag déanamh crosanna ach san am céanna
bhíodh siad ag scéalaíocht nó ag tairngreacht nó ag fian-
naíocht. Lá 'le Bríde choisrictí na crosanna a dhéantaí an oíche
roimh ré agus chrochtaí suas iad' (IFC 904; 187-188; Seán Ó
Siadhail,   Cnoc   Dumhaigh,   Narrator;   Tomás   Mac
Fhionghaile, Carraig Áirt, Leifear, Scribe).

(For some time now, the old custom of celebrating the Feast
of St Brigid has been declining, but perhaps with the help of
the King (Christ) it may arise again stronger and more fruit-
ful than it ever was before. Nowadays, there is only the making of the crosses and *brúitín* (mashed potatoes) on St Brigid's
Eve, but a short while ago there were fine old customs to be
seen. This is how St Brigid's Feast was observed a short time
ago:

At twilight at the doorstep of each house, a bundle of rushes
was to be seen. When night came, a fine pot of mashed potatoes was prepared and immediately before they were
mashed the man of the house used to go outside to the
doorstep and with a loud voice say: 'Go on your knees; open
your eyes; and let Blessed Brigid enter.' The family inside
would answer: 'She is welcome; Welcome to the Noble
Lady.' They used to say this verse again and with the same
answer and after saying it the third time with the same answer he would bring in the rushes and put them under the
pot of potatoes until they were mashed. Then they used to
eat their supper. After suppertime the sport and entertainment began properly. The household would sit around the
house making crosses. The old people tucked away as busy

as everybody else making crosses, but at the same time they used to tell stories or make predictions or tell stories of the Fianna. On St Brigid's Day the crosses made on the previous night used to be blessed and hung up in the house).

In another account from Donegal it is shown again that the bundle of rushes was put under the pot of mashed potatoes and an interesting detail is added – the woman of the house covered her head with a veil when welcoming Brigid into her house (IFC 904; 199-201). Here, the close connection between the food and the bundle of rushes is emphasised and this phenomenon occurs over and over again. In both of these accounts, it is clear that the bundle of rushes was prepared beforehand and placed in a convenient spot outside the house. The person who was to carry the bundle of rushes (the equivalent of the Brídeog/doll in other areas) into the house could take up the bundle, recite the threshold dialogue with those inside and then carry the bundle of rushes inside the house and place it under the pot. As potatoes are a late introduction to Ireland it is conceiveable that they replaced a cauldron of meat as in the old stories of the Bruíon.

In a report from Cill Mhic Réanáin, Co Donegal, some of the regulations for the Threshold Rite are given:

'Crosses are made on the Eve of the Feast. They are made from green rushes, and the rule is that you must have them cut and left on the doorstep before the sun sets' (IFC 904; 179).

The setting of the sun takes place about 4.30 on St. Brigid's Eve. Another important rule is mentioned in the same report:

'It was an old custom to make "poundies" (mashed potatoes) on the Eve of the Feast, and the rushes had always to be brought in before the "poundies" were eaten' (IFC 904; 180).

At this stage, we can discern the order of events governing the Threshold Rite:

1. Before sunset on 31st January, rushes are cut and placed in a bundle outside the door.
2. While this is taking place outdoors, potatoes are being prepared, boiled and mashed in a pot indoors.

3. When this is ready, the man of the house or somebody else goes outside, closes the door after him, takes the bundle of rushes in his arms and recites the threshold dialogue with those within the house.

4. When the dailogue is completed, the door is opened by the woman of the house wearing a veil.

5. The man/woman enters carrying the bundle.

6. He/she deposits the bundle of rushes under the pot – presumeably the bundle was laid on the floor and the the pot was placed on top of it.

7. The supper then takes place, the mashed potatoes being taken from the pot resting on the bundle of rushes.

8. When supper is over the pot is removed.

9. The members of the family divide the rushes among them and proceed to make St Brigid's crosses.

A report from Co Longford recognises the link between the rushes and the meal:

'It (the Feast) used to be kept in the following way: On the evening of the Eve the man of the house cut some rushes which he hid in an outhouse. When the great supper given on the Eve was ready, he brought the rushes into the house. Immediately all in the home fell on their knees while he recited some prayer in Irish. He remained standing for the prayer; the rushes were put under the table where they remained until the tea was over. Then they were put in the middle of the floor and the people of the house gathered round and began making St Brigid's crosses' (IFC 906; 181-182; Thomas Gill, Bóthar Mór, Co Longfoirt, Narrator; Lughaidh Ó Maolamhlaidh, Scribe).

A somewhat different method was used in some areas but still the link between the food and the rushes was maintained: 'In some districts, the making of the crosses preceded the Brigid's Supper or Tea, and the plate or plates containing the pancakes rested upon the table on a cross or crosses. It was more usual, however, to make the crosses following the meal' (IFC 905; 39-

40; 41; T.S. F. Paterson, Armagh, Scribe) In this case the rush-es / crosses were used as plates on which the food rested – a different version of the pot of potatoes resting on the bundle of rushes, as in the example from Co Donegal.

A short but very interesting report comes from Collon in which a new feature is introduced, that is, the circumambulation of the house as part of the Threshold Rite, and this is not the sole example of the procession around the exterior of the dwelling:

> 'The rushes are carried around the house outside three times until someone inside says 'Céad fáilte romhat, a Bhríd.' Then the rushes are brought in, placed on the kitchen floor and all lend a hand to make the crosses' (IFC 906; 26-27; Mairéad Bean Uí Dhonnagáin, Woodlawn, Collon, Co Louth, Scribe).

From the pointof view of ritualism one of the most interesting reports at hand comes from Co Wexford and here is seen a fuller account of the circumambulation of the the house spoken of in the report from Collon:

> 'I have heard from the oldest man in this district, William Graham, who is 86 years (in 1942) of age, and who has stories about the Eve of St Brigid's Day which were told to him by his father, who died 50 years ago at the age of 93, that on the Eve of St Brigid's Day, a feast used to be given in the house. After sunset, the man of the house used to cut a bundle of rushes with a reaping hook unawares of the people inside, and hides it outside the house until the time for the feast arrrives. He again leaves the house, and walking round it in the direction of the sun, picks up the bundle and completes one circuit. When he reaches the open door, all inside kneel down and listen attentively to his petition:

> 'Go down on your knees;
> Open your eyes;
> And let St Brigid in.'

They all answer: 'She is welcome, she is welcome'

> He makes a second circuit, and a third circuit of the house, always with the same petition at the door, and the same an-

swer is given. At the end of the third petition, the man of the
house enters, lays the bundle of rushes under the table, says
grace, and invites all to partake of the meal. After the feast,
the rushes used to be placed in the middle of the room, and
the family used to weave the crosses of St Brigid. Next day,
the crosses used to be blessed and hung up in each room and
every outhouse' (IFC 907; 174-177; Cáit Ní Bholguibhir, Rath
an Iúir, Inis Córthaidh, Contae Loch Garman, Scribe).

In this magnificent report, the description of the man's threefold
circumambulation of the house in a sunwise direction carrying
the bundle of rushes corroborates the report from Collon. This is
the well-known ritual of the Celts – the *Cor Deiseal*, the
righthanded (sunwise) procession around a sacred object such
as a holy well or standing stone. This ritual can be seen at pilgrimage sites such as Croagh Patrick, Gleann Cholm Cille, Baile
Bhóirne and many other places. The pilgrims march around the
sacred object three or nine times in single file, always keeping
the well or sacred tree or other object at the right hand side
(*deiseal – lámh dheis*). The early Greek writer Athanaeus, in describing the drinking habits of the Celts, remarked that a common container was used for the beer and each one took a mouth-
ful but they did it rather often. The server carrying the vessel
moved towards the right not towards the left. 'That is the
method of service. In the same way they do reverence to the
gods, turning towards the right' (Tierney, 1960, 247). In following the course of the sun one put oneself into harmony with the
rhythyms of the cosmos.

In this area of Rath an Iúir (Rathnure), Co Wexford, the archaic ritual of the *Cor Deiseal* or sunwise turn is gloriously present. The man goes out to collect the bundle of rushes (representing the Brídeog/Brigid). He takes the bundle in his arms
and carries it around the house proceding sunwise, keeping the
house to his right. Having completed the round he stands outside, before the open door, and recites the formula: 'Go down on
your knees; Open your eyes; and let St Brigid in.' The people inside the house answer: 'She is welcome, she is welcome'. The

Image-Bearer, however, does not go in, but procedes around the house for the second time until he arrives again in front of the open door and recites the formula. The people inside again say 'She is welcome, she is welcome' but the man does not enter. He makes a third circumambulation of the house and this time when he arrives in front of the door and says the formula and those inside say 'She is welcome, she is welcome', he enters the house carrying the bundle of rushes. He lays the bundle of rushes under the table on which the meal is eaten, in this way showing a connection between the food and the image. When the meal is over, the rushes are taken from underneath the table and the-members of the household begin the making of the crosses from them.

It is likely that the sunwise circumambulation of the house was a normal feature of the Threshold Rite in many places but only survived in Collon and Rathnure and some other areas into a late period. In this circumambulation using the sacred number three, Brigid must have been seen as forming a triple ring of protection around the house to save it and its inhabitants from all evil during the course of the coming year.

The 'Cor Deiseal' or ritual sunwise movement is the lucky movement of luck and prosperity well-known to the Hindus under the name 'Pradaksina'. One goes sunwise around a sacred tree, well, shrine, house or fire (Hastings, 1909, Art. Circumambulation).

It is said that St. Patrick consecrated the Cathedral of Armagh by going around it sunwise, and St Senan consecrated a church in the same manner. It was the custom for people to walk sunwise three times around a house, a field, or a boat on the last night of December (Hastings, op.cit.).

Even in areas where the actual circumambulation had ceased to be performed, the triple threshold dialogue may indicate that it once existed.

An elaborate ecclesiastical form of the Threshold Rite is to be-found in the Liturgy of Braga, in Portugal. In the Rite of Braga, on Palm Sunday the priest, accompanied by deacon and subdea-

con and other ministers, goes to the door of the church. The door
is closed. The celebrant raps the door with the processional
cross, singing the formula: *'Attolite portas, Principes, vestras; et elevamini, portae aeternales, et introibit, Rex Gloriae'* (Lift up your
heads, O gates; and be lifted up, O ancient doors; that the King
of Glory may come in). Those inside the church answer: *'Quis est
iste Rex Gloriae?'* (Who is the King of Glory?) The priest answers
from outside: *'Dominus potens in proelio'* (The Lord mighty in battle) (Psalm 24:7-8). This dialogue is repeated three times, then
the door is opened from inside and the celebrant and his assistants enter the church (*Missale Bracarense*, Roma 1924; 152-154)

A similar type of threshold ritual is found in a Missal of the
Mozarabic Rite of Spain (Martene, 1706, 212) and in many of the
great cathedrals of Europe (Martene, 1706, 196).

There is no circumambulation of the church involved in these
examples but in the Consecration (Dedication) of a Church in
the Roman (Tridentine) Rite, the consecrating bishop went
around the church three times – antisunwise twice and sunwise
once, and at the end of each circumambulation there took place
the knocking on the closed door with the crozier. On the third
occasion, the word *'Aperite'* (Open) was sung three times and
then the door was opened to allow the bishop to enter the
church (*Pontificale Romanum*, 1868, 140-142). While going around
the church the bishop sprinkled the walls with holy water. The
prayers recited by the bishop ask God to protect the building
from attack by the devil and demons and to make of this church
a place of peace and harmony.

Although there is some similarity between the Brigidine
Threshold Rite and these Official Liturgical Rituals of the
Catholic Church, it is difficult to say if one is derived from the
other or if they all have a common origin in some archaic source.
Obviously, the circumambulation of the house with the image of
St Brigid resembles in a simple form the magnificent ritual of the
Dedication of a Church as laid down by the Pontificale
Romanum. In this ritual, the relics of the saints (a small amount
of bone) are interred in a little cavity called the 'Sepulchre'

carved out for them in the High Altar. When the bishop has placed the relics in this sepulchre they are cemented in. They receive a new burial-place in the altar of the newly-consecrated-church. A consecrated church may be distinguished from a non-consecrated church by the presence of 12 candleholders on the interior of the walls, each one above a painted cross on the wall. These 12 crosses were anointed with chrism and incensed during the consecration ceremony. Before their interring in the altar, the relics were taken from another nearby church or oratory where they had been kept overnight and carried in solemn procession from there to the new church. Clerics carrying torches and incense preceeded the small container of relics which rested on a bier carried on the shoulders of four priests clothed in red vestments. Instead of the four priests, the bishop himself might carry the vessel of relics in his arms. The bier with the relics was carried in procession around the church once, in an antisunwise direction, before being taken into the church where the relics were buried in the altar. At the entrance of the relics into the church there is no threshhold dialogue so that the Brigidine Threshold Rite resembles rather the earlier threefold circumambulation of the church during which the bishop sprinkles holy water on the walls. Here, the threshold dialogue between the bishop outside the door and a deacon within took place after each round and the bishop entered the church on the third occasion.

However, at a later stage in the Rite of Dedication, the vessel containing the relics of the saints was carried around the church and the carrying of the bundle of rushes (Brídeog) around the house bears a marked likeness to this – a sacred object being taken around a building before being taken inside. An Antiphon sung during the procession gives a basic understanding of the rite: 'Surgite Sancti Dei, de mansionibus vestris, loca sanctificate, plebem benedicite, et nos homines peccatores in pace custodite.' (Rise up, O Saints of God from your resting places, sanctify the area, bless the people and preserve us, sinful men as we are, in peace). These sentiments are not far distant from the basic intention of the Threshold Rite. Brigid's circumambulation of the house will preserve it from harm such as storms and floods and her entrance to the house will bring the blessings of peace and prosperity to the family. It does seem that what we have here is a miniature, domestic form of the consecration of a church on an annual basis, with the house taking the place of the church building and the family taking the place of the church congregation.

The righthanded turn comes to the fore again in an account by Domhnall Ua Murchadha in the context of the Threshold Rite. It is difficult to determine the area to which the usage belongs but it displays some unusual features:

'Nuair a bhíonn crosa ag daoine dá chur fé sna fraightheachaibh oídhche Fhéile Bríde, níor chead d'éinne focal a labhairt go mbeadh ádhbhar na croise tabharta abhaile; agus tar éis teacht go dtí an tigh, b'é an nós gabháil timpeall an tí trí huaire; agus tar éis an tríomhadh huair timpeall, do sáidhthighe na broibh fén ndoras iadhta' (1939, 96).

(When people are putting crosses under the rafters on St Brigid's Eve, it is not permitted to anyone to speak a word until the material for the making of the crosses is brought home. And, having arrived at the house, it was the custom to circumambulate it three times, and after the third circuit, the rushes were pushed in [into the house] under the closed door).

Judging from the type of Irish used in this report it is evident that it comes from Munster. This part of the country, however, is not usually associated with the Threshold Rite and we may wonder if the author were speaking of some northern area. At any rate, the carrying of the material for the crosses around the house three times is made perfectly clear, and then, when the third round has been completed, the rushes are pushed in under the closed door. One wonders why the man himself doesn't bring them in in the usual manner.

As regards the silence observed while procuring the material for the crosses as described here, a similar rule prevailed in other places.

The narrator describes the man of the house going outside to procure a bundle of rushes in Paróiste an Chnoic, Co Galway: 'I ngan fhios a théadh sé amach' (IFC 902; 71). (He used to go out secretly.)

The same phenomenon is found in Co Longford: 'On the evening of the Eve the man of the house cut some rushes which he hid in an outhouse' (IFC 906; 181).

From Co Kerry comes a still clearer account of the holy silence to be observed while cutting the dry grass-stalks for St. Brigid's crosses:

'Théimis ar na portaithe a mbaint Oíche 'le Bríde – gan aon fhocal a labhairt lena chéile chun go dtagaimís abhaile leo ach ag paidreoireacht' (IFC 903; 239; 264). (We used to go to the bogs cutting them without saying a single word to each other until we arrived home with them, but only praying.)

The same tradition is found in a report from Co Mayo:

'… the man of the house goes out without telling anyone and pulls the thraneens (dry grass-stalks) for the cross and when the house is quiet sits down and makes it' (IFC 903; 155).

It appears that a very archaic practice lies behind this observance of sacred silence. Other examples of this are found in traditional treatment of diseases such as disease of the hips and mumps. It will be noticed that here, also, the silence is connected to the actual preparation of the materials:

'Take three green stones, gathered from a running brook, between midnight and morning, while no word is said. In silence it must be done. Then uncover the limb and rub each stone several times closely downwards from the hip to the toe, saying in Irish:

'Wear away, wear away,

There you shall not stay,

Cruel pain – away, away' (Wilde,1888, 199).

The sacred silence was acknowledged in ancient Greek rites also. 'Observe silence; observe silence' Didaiopolis cries to begin the Country Dionysia in the Acharnians (Sommerstein, 1980, 59) and the word 'euphem-ew' was used to proclaim the ritual quiet (Liddel, Scott, Jones,1958, 736).

At the beginning of Mass in the Gallican Rite, it was the function of the deacon to proclaim '*Silentium facite*' (Make silence) (Lietzmann, 1935,22).

It appears then, that the silence feature of the Threshold Rite is to be situated within a complex of sacred rites embracing Europe and the classical world.

The Threshold Rite in Co Mayo

A survival of the sunwise turn may be discerned also in a wonderfully comprehensive account of the Threshold Rite from the parish of Kilcommon, Iorras, Co Mayo. Here, the bundle of straw (not rushes) was wrapped around with clothing so that it took on the form of the Brídeog/doll/image representing Brigid so familiar in the Brídeog procession of the southern part of the country. As well as this, the image and the 'Brat Bhríde' (a piece of cloth representing St Brigid's cloak, used for cures and protection) are connected for the Brat is part of the clothes in which the image is wrapped:

> 'Before nightfall, usually the man of the house procured a garment for a 'Brat Bríde'. The article of clothing selected was one which would be in greatest use by the member of the house whose occupation was the most dangerous. As the head of the family was generally a fisherman and exposed to the dangers of the deep for the current year, and the one most in need of the saint's protection, a coat or waist-coat of his was used for the 'Brat'. Frequently the man's muffler – one of the large home-made mufflers which covered nearly the whole head and was worn on night fishing – became the 'Brat'.
>
> The man took out this article of clothing into the haggard, drew a good long sheaf of straw out of the stack and wrapped the garment around the sheaf in a manner giving it as far as possible the rough outline in appearance of a human body. He then reverently carried the object between his arms,

in the manner one carries a child, and deposits it outside the back door. He leaves it there and comes into the house.

The preparation for the supper is proceeded with, the fire on the hearth is kept well stoked and burning brightly, and radiating cheer and happiness. Then when supper is laid on the table and the inmates are ready to sit in, the man of the house announces that he is now going out to bring in Bríd, as she too must be present at the festive board. The man goes out and around to the back door, where he kneels, and then in a loud voice says to the people inside who are expectant and waiting for the coming request:

'Téigí ar bhur nglúine, agus osclaigí bhur súile agus ligigí isteach Bríd.'

Response: 'Sé beatha, 'sé beatha, 'sé beatha'

The people within continue repeating the third response 'Sé beatha. On the third response, 'Sé beatha, from the people within, he takes up the bundle, gets up off his knees and comes around to the open door, while the people within continue repeating the 'Sé beatha as he is coming round (to the front door), and when he enters the door they finish the response with 'Muise, 'sé beatha agus sláinte.'

Then the object (the sheaf of straw and brat) is laid carefully and respectfully leaning against the leg or rail of the table and under the table. The family then sit down to the supper preceded by a short prayer or invocation such as:

'A Bhríd Bheannaithe, go gcuire tú an teach seo thar anachain na bliana.' (O blessed Brigid, may you deliver this house from the troubles of the year.)

When supper is finished there was the ejaculatory prayer – the usual one of: 'Dia graisias le Dia, agus cumhdach Dé ar lucht shaothrú na beatha.' (Deo gratias / thanks to God and the protection of God on those going through life.)

Then the supper vessels are removed and the table cleared, and things put in order, the 'brat' is stowed away in a secure place. In addition to the article or garment used for the 'brat' previously referred to, frequently a piece of new cloth was used to supplement the garment. Strips of this cloth were subsequently used for cures in cases of headache, or as they used to say 'bad heads', such as dizziness, etc.

The next operation was the making of St Brigid's cross from this particular sheaf of straw. Some people went to great pains in making the cross and I have seen some very large and artistic ones made, and it certainly looked a nice emblem when it was stuck or secured to the ceiling or rather to the scraw (thatch), usually above the kitchen window, in line with the kitchen bed. The cross was supposed to be a safeguard against storm or the blowing away of the roof of the house during the coming twelve months. It was supposed this danger of the winter's storm or its crisis had passed on St Brigid's Eve when provision was made for protection against the next winter by the exhibiting of Brigid's cross in the manner described' (IFC 903; 50-54; Michael Corduff, The Lodge, Ros Dumhach, Ballina, Co Mayo).

This is a wonderfully detailed and careful account of what happened and it will be noticed that frequently a piece of cloth is added to the muffler wrapped around the sheaf of corn to give it the appearance of a child – Brigid in her youthful form to symbolise the infancy of the year at the beginning of Spring. This extra piece of cloth must be seen in the same terms as the muffler as the clothes of Brigid in close contact with her body. It is this extra piece of cloth which is torn up into strips and a piece given to each member of the family as part of the 'Brat Bhríde', St Brigid's cloak, to be used by them for the cure of headaches, etc.. Obviously, the knitted muffler, itself, was too valuable to be destroyed. The important point was that the strip of cloth given to each person was a piece of Brigid's clothes – a kind of relic – through which Brigid's power of curing and protecting was communicated to the owner of the Brat or piece of the Brat.

We have seen examples of a bundle of rushes with no clothing used as a Brídeog. These are cases, perhaps, in which the rite has degenerated. Undoubtedly, the body of the image would have been formed from the bundle of rushes. Originally it would have been clothed to resemble a child as in the case of the

Brídeog of the south. Then, over the years, people would have grown careless. Dressing up the bundle of rushes was a troublesome affair and the bundle of rushes would suffice. The wonderful collection of folklore made in the 1930s and 1940s came just in time to save a massive amount of information on ancient rites, customs, songs, stories, riddles and calendar lore. The country and indeed the world owes a great debt of gratitude to the Irish Folklore Commission, for the collection and preservation of so much of the past. When the reports were submitted the rituals were in decline or had already vanished in many cases. But parts of a rite which had disappeared or degenerated in one area remained on in another area and so, by using a comparative method, we can reconstruct with a fair amount of validity, the original form of the usage.

In this particular report from Co Mayo, great emphasis is laid on the presence of Brigid, a focus on her return from the Otherworld on the Holy Night. When the meal is ready the man of the house announces that he is going out to bring in Brigid. The presumption here is that she was to share the meal with the family. This would be a case of someone from the Otherworld with a spiritual body partaking of a supper meant for living people of this world. One thinks, of course, of the appearance of the Risen Christ to his disciples and his eating with them, as for instance in John 24:41-43: "Their joy was so great that they still could not believe it, and they stood there dumbfounded; so he said to them. "Have you anything here to eat?" And they offered him a piece of grilled fish, which he took and ate before their eyes.'

It is uncertain if eating, even of a spiritual non-physical form is involved here, however, for the figure representing Brigid is placed 'leaning against the leg or rail of the table or under the table'. We have seen that in other instances the figure (in the form of a bundle of rushes) was under the pot containing the food (IFC 904;199-201); (IFC 904; 187-188); 'under the table where they remained until the tea was over' (IFC 906; 181-182); 'the plate or plates containing the pancakes rested upon the table on a cross or crosses' (IFC 905; 39-40; 41). In this latter case the plate with the pancake on it may be compared to the pot with the potatoes in it – both the plate and the pot are containers of food – in one case the container of food lies directly on the image; in the other case the container of food lies directly on the cross made from the image. In both cases the food is brought into contact with Brigid.

It seems uncertain then, if the idea of Brigid actually eating a meal with the family was envisaged. It seems, rather, that she was vitally present and the food was brought into contact with her so that her power entered into it and, by means of this food which the people ate, her health-giving power was communicated to them.

The image or Brídeog, whether in the form of an undressed bundle of rushes or straw or a dressed image, represents Brigid in the Otherworld and is used in the rites as a bridge connecting the two worlds. It is by the ritual use of the Brídeog that the healing and protecting power of Brigid in heaven reaches us, as in the case of the use of the relics of the saints in the Catholic and Eastern Orthodox Churches. In the Hymn for Lauds for the Feast of St John the Baptist (24th June) we have an exposition of the Otherworldly power of the saint:

Nunc potens nostri meritis opimis
Pectoris duros lapides repelle;
Asperum planans iter, et reflexos
Dirige calles.
(Now rendered powerful by thy rich merits, pluck out the stony hardness of our hearts, make plain the rough way, and make straight the crooked paths.)

This is what John had been doing strenuously while on earth (Luke 3; 4-5) but now that he is dead he is more powerful and better able to get things done than he was while he was alive in this world. This is the realm of the saints – our spiritual ancestors.

When the supper is over the clothing is taken off the image. The muffler is given to the father as a protective talisman against the violence of the sea. The other pieces of clothing are cut up

and a strip given to each person to use for protection and healing and the pains of childbirth. The bundle of straw which forms
the body of the image is divided up and from it St Brigid's crosses
are made for the protection of the house against storms and fire.
In some cases *buaracha* or straw ties are made and put around
the cows' necks so the the blessing of Brigid might be communicated to them. In other cases, the rushes from the image were
brought into contact with the corn seed so that Brigid's blessing
might accompany the seed into the ground and produce an
abundant harvest. The Brídeog then was a means of bringing
Brigid's supernatural power to bear on a variety of aspects of
social and agricultural life.

Another fine report comes from Thomas Mason from
Inishere:

> On the first day of February old women get some straw, also
> some clothing and dress up the image of St Brigid. They then
> go from house to house, saying a prayer as they enter the
> house. From this straw each person takes some of it and
> makes a cross the same as enclosed. This cross is nailed to the
> rafter inside the roof in remembrance of St Brigid. This is the
> ceremony of the 'Brídeog' (1943, 164).

It is unfortunate that Mason did not give a more detailed account and include the prayer – said in Irish no doubt in Inis Oírr.

However, it is clear that what amounts to a dismemberment
of Brigid takes place as in the example from Ballina, Co Mayo.
Brigid was dismembered and pieces of her body were used as
instruments of protection, abundance and healing. If this interpretation is correct we are entering an area of archaic thought
with cosmic implications.

An Indo-European and perhaps even a more widespread tradition speaks of the 'Dismemberment of Purusa' as a well-
known Creation Myth. Purusa, in this tradition, is the
Primordial Man who is sacrificed by the gods and dismembered. Bruce Lincoln mentions a Middle-Persian text of the 9th
century which gives a particular version of the Myth:

> This also is said (by the Manicheans): the bodily, material

creation is of the Evil Spirit – all the bodily creation is of the
Evil Spirit. More precisely, the sky is from the skin, the earth
is from the flesh, the mountains are from the bone, and the
plants are from the hair of the demoness Kuni (Lincoln, 1991,
180).

The same type of cosmological thinking occurs in the
Scandinavian 'Edda':

From Emir's flesh the earth was made and mountains from
his bones; Heaven from the skull of the rime-cold giant and
from his blood, the sea' (Lincoln, 1991, 180).

It is, basically, the theme of the connection between the world
and the body of the deity, between the macrcosmos (world) and
micro-cosmos (body).

Moreover, there is a certain likeness between members of the
body and parts of the universe – a certain correspondance between flesh and clay; between bone and stone; between breath
and air; between blood and water; between hair and vegetation,
and so forth.

Following the ancient view, however, there is more than a
likeness between them. The microcosmos and macrocosmos
inter-relate with with each other. In Indian thought, the elements of the cosmos – sun, moon, sky, earth, air, etc. – derive
from the sacrificed and dismembered body of Purusa. Likewise
with Ymir and with the female demon Kuni – it is from the
separated parts of her body that the various parts of the universe
are formed. This movement from the microcosmos to the macrocosmos is called a 'cosmogany'.

But in the Indo-European context it was thought that sacrifice and dismemberment of a victim on earth was a re-enact-
ment, a ritual copying of the initial, primordial sacrifice and dismemberment of Purusa. This initial sacrifice and dismemberment was the cause of the creation of the universe: 'When they
(gods) divided the Man, (Purusa) into how many parts did they
apportion him? … The moon was born from his mind; from his
eye the sun was born … and from his vital breath the wind was

born ... from his head the sky evolved.' Thus speaks the 'Purusa-Sukta' or 'The Hymn of Man' in the *Rig Veda*, 10.90. (O'Flaherty, Penguin 1981, 29-31).

These examples belong to the primal, archypal event of the creation of the universe from the body of the god in the 'time of the gods', 'in the time outside time', 'in illo tempore', 'en arche', 'fadó, fadó'.

But it was perceived by people as an obvious phenomenon, that at certain periods, the world, nature, got tired, as it were and needed renewal, re-invigoration, re-creation.

At the end of the year when winter comes, the earth appears to be exhausted. The leaves fall from the trees, grass and vegetation decay, the land becomes barren. In the depths of winter death prevails.

People feel that this exausted world of nature, of which they themselves are a part, needs a new awakening, a new injection of life and vigour – in short, a new creation. How is this to be done, how can the world be re-created?

The answer, in the mind of ancient peoples was, that the world and nature could be renewed, re-created, as it were, by employing a ritual which imitated or copied the method by which the world was first created – in other words, by taking a man, who represented Purusa, sacrificing him and dismembering him, repeating the primordial act by which the world had been made in the original creation. The head of this human (or animal) sacrifice would strengthen and renew the sky; his blood would renew the rivers and seas; his flesh would renew the soil (poultices of clay were used by women to renew ageing flesh); his hair would re-invigorate vegetation (notice the tradition of burying the hair after a hair-cut; vegetation springs up which might become a herbal tonic to improve the condition of the hair); his bones strengthen the rocks and mountains. In this way the Purusa Creation Myth gives something of the mythic background for the idea of sacrifice. By ritual sacrifice and dismemberment of the victim, the various parts of the universe were renewed, giving to sacrifice something of cosmic significance.

According to this theory it was not an act of savagery or barbarism but something which kept the universe in motion and prevented its falling into decay. The victim, in some cases at any rate, may have gone to his death willingly and proudly, believing that he was chosen to undertake a great work of renewing the land in the interests of his people.

According to the account given by Herodotus of the rites of the Persians, the Magi sang a Creation Hymn while an animal was being sacrificed and dismembered. This was done for the benefit of the various elements of the universe, that is to say for the sun, the moon, the fire, the water, the wind (Lincoln, 1991, 168-169).

According to Herodotus, the ritual poem sung by the Magus gave an account of the origin of the gods; and among the early Persians the elements and the gods were the same. For that reason, they had no images of the gods nor had they a temple. Their custom was to go up to the top of a mountain in the sight of the heavens and there to sacrifice and cut up the victim into several pieces (Herodotus, *Persian Wars*, 1, 131-132; Edit: Rawlinson, C., New York, 1942)

Like the Persians, the Celts did not sacrifice without a druid, according to Diodorus Siculus: 'Their custom is that no one should offer sacrifice without a philosopher; for they say that thanks should be offered to the gods by those skilled in the divine nature, as though they were people who can speak their language' (Tierney, 1960, 251).

The author Pomponius Mela, writing around 41 AD, refers to the Celtic practice of dismemberment:

'(The Gauls/Celts) are arrogant and superstitious, and at one time they were so savage that they believed a man to be the best and most pleasing sacrificial victim for the gods. Vestiges of their past ferocity remain, so that while they refrain from the final dismemberments (*ultimis caedibis*), nonetheless they take off a little portion (from the victims) when leading the consecrated ones to the altars' (*De Situ Orbis* 3.2 18-19).

Professor Lincoln (op. cit., 169) mentions the regulations governing the directing of the severed parts of the sacrificed animal towards the different parts of the universe:

'Cause its eye to go to the sun; send forth its breath to the wind; its life-force to the atmosphere; its ear to the cardinal points; its flesh to the earth' Thus (i.e. with this sacred formula and the accompanying gestures) the priest places this victim into the parts of the universe' (*Aitareya Brahmana* 2.6).

In this way, the concept of sacrifice and dismemberment of the victim was bound up with the creation of the world. They were considered to be ritual enactments of the primordial sacrifice and dismemberment of Purusa by which the universe came into being. The ritual enactment, the liturgical rite, had the effect of re-creating the universe in the sense of re-invigorating a world grown old and tired and restoring it to the vigour and freshness it had when it was first created.

In the Indo-Europian context, it is easy to understand the classical authors' assertion that the Celts sacrificed prisoners of war (Tierney, 1960, 196, 206, 251, 252). Behind the barbarism, there was a profound understanding of the relationship between microcosmos and macrocosmos. Possibly, behind the small wars and cattle-raids of the Celts there was the idea of providing material for sacrifice. For, in the light of the Purusa Myth, providing regular sacrifices kept the world in motion. We might wonder, for instance, if the cult of the severed head, in which a great hero such as Cú Chulainn cut off the heads of his brave enemies and nailed them on to the door of his house with great respect for a vanquished but brave and distinguished warrior, had not something to do with the kingship. The head was the guiding force and organisational centre of the human body. The king was the guiding force and organisational centre of his people. May not the severing of the head of a great and generous hero lead to the strengthening of the monarchy according to the norms of the Purusa philosophy?

When the Greek writer Strabo says (iv, 4, 4) that the Celts believed that the crops would be good in a year in which there were a large number of murders, we are faced with what is at first sight a very puzzling thing, as the connection between murders and good crops is not obvious. However, when it is taken into consideration that the Celtic Druids ,who were considered to be the most just of men, acted as judges, a large number of murders gave them the excuse of condemning the perpetrators to death – that is to be sacrificed and dismembered. In the light of the Purusa Myth this would result in good crops and the fertility of the land (cf MacCulloch, 1911/1991, 235).

Professor Lincoln remarks: 'I would note briefly, for instance, the analysis of birth and death which formed an important part of this awesome inclusive system, for death was regarded as nothing less than a cosmogonic action – a final sacrifice, in which the material substance of the body was transformed into its macrocosmic alloforms, while birth was the anthropogonic reversal of death, in which cosmic matter was reassembled in bodily form' (op. cit., 172).

The Irish story of Miach directs the Purusa Myth into the realm of medicine. The Tuatha Dé Danann god Nuadha lost an arm in the first battle of Maigh Tuireadh (Cunga). Dian Cecht, the great physician, made a silver arm for him instead. However, Dian Cecht's son, Miach, was a much better physician than his father and he made an arm for Nuadha which was as good as his former natural arm. Dian Cecht went wild with jealousy and in a rage murdered his son. From Miach's grave 365 herbs sprang up. Miach's sister, Airmedh, herself a brilliant physician who could diagnose a patient's complaint from looking at the smoke coming out of the chimney of his house, arrived at Miach's grave, spread her cloak on the side of the grave and proceeded to pluck the herbs and place them on the cloak in the exact order in which they grew from the body. They point was, of course, that the herb which grew from Miach's forehead would cure headache, the herb coming from his heart would cure heart disease, and so on. However, before Airmedh had time to memorise the exact position of each herb, Dian Cecht arrived, caught up the cloak and scattered the herbs all over the place. From that day to this we do not know which herb will cure which disease and this explains the inadequacies of our Health Service (*Cath Maige Tuired*, 33-35).

The 365 herbs – one for every day of the year and one for every joint and sinew of the body – are a symbol of completeness. It is from the various joints and sinews of Miach that the various herbs spring (from the microcosmos to the macrocosmos) and now healing is coming back from the herbs to the various parts of the human body (from the macrocosmos to the microcosmos). The fact that the medical knowledge is lost is due to the jealousy of the human agent Dian Cecht – not to the inherent validity of the Purusa system.

This question of the dismemberment of Brigid arose from an analysis of the Threshold Rite as practised in Kilcommon, Co Mayo (IFC 903; 50-54), as in that particular account it is clear that the dressed sheaf represents Brigid. In the case of Inis Oírr it is equally clear, and in the instances where the bundle of rushes or straw is not dressed, it seems most likely that the lack of clothing is due to decadence in the performance of the rite and that the bundle still represents Brigid, and the crosses are made from her dismembered body for the purpose of protection, prosperity and healing.

The use of figures made of rushes in the Lemuralia of Italy is mentioned by Smith: 'The symbolic sacrifice of human figures made of rushes at the Lemuralia also shows that in the early history of Italy human sacrifices were not uncommon' (1853, 324).

If this interpretation is correct and if the Purusa Myth is the myth underlying the ritual, then the idea of an annual sacrifice and dismemberment of Brigid in a highly ritualised form lies at the heart of the Threshold Rite.

This may not be such a highly dramatised idea when one considers the ordinary Roman Catholic doctrine of the Eucharist where the priest gives the host to the faithful with the words: 'The body of Christ' and the chalice with the words: 'The blood of Christ' and the recipient must believe that this is so. Perhaps the primitive character of the Euchrist in the Catholic and Eastern Orthodox tradition is not always appreciated.

What is also worthy of consideration is the procession in which the Brídeog is carried around the house before being brought in. There is evidence for a procession of this type around the altar in some ancient rites of sacrifice. The *Rig Veda* of India, speaking of the horse sacrifice, says: 'When, as the ritual law ordains, the men circle three times, leading the horse that is to be the oblation on the path to the gods, the goat who is the share for Pusan goes first, announcing the sacrifice to the gods' (O'Flaherty, 1981, 90).

At Holy Wells a circumambulation of the well takes place and a token offering such as a comb, a medal, a pen and so forth is made and deposited on a ledge of the surrounding wall. Similarly in the Mass of the Roman Rite a circumambulation of the altar with incensation accompanies the offering of the bread and wine. In the impressive 'Procession of the Lamb' in the Coptic Rite, the priest and deacon carry the bread and wine wrapped in veils in a procession around the altar. At the consecration of a church, the relics of the saints were carried around the exterior of the building in the elaborate form in the *Pontificale Romanum*. The circumbulation delineated a sacred boundary which protected and honoured a temple. The Threshold Rite appears to have had something of the character of the consecration of a church, but in this case the church was the family home and the consecration was on an annual basis. This yearly consecration of the dwelling was meant to bring protection, peace and prosperity to the family through the supernatural intervention of Brigid.

The English song 'John Barleycorn' gives a truly remarkable exposition of the agricultural cycle linked to the Purusa Myth and helps to illustrate the mind-set behind Brigid's rituals.

A group of people from Haxey in Lincolnshire come together on 'Plough Monday', close to the Feast of the Epiphany (6th January), at the beginning of the ploughing season for an ale-drinking session in honour of 'John Barleycorn'. The song sung during the session describes the various adventures of John and the vissicitudes he endured at the hands of his tormentors, before rising triumphantly, overcoming them all and proving himself 'to be the stronger man'. The song is a wonderful exposition of the seasonal cycle of the corn, and again, one can see its affinities to the rites of Brigid:

> Three men came from the west and made a solemn vow that John Barleycorn (personification of the barley and consort of the goddess) must die:
>
> 'They ploughed, they sowed, they harrowed him in
> Throwed clods upon his head'
>
> They left him for dead but when the rains came John amazed them all by appearing above ground. The growth of the barley is then described, its harvesting, threshing , milling and conversion into beer, and in this form, in the glass, he proves to be the stronger man at last for he makes them all drunk and, at least for a while, takes away all their anxieties and cares:
>
> 'Twill make a man forget his woe;
> Twill heighten all his joy;
> Twill make a widow's heart to sing,
> Tho' the tear were in her eye'
> (Dames, 1977, 16-17; Pennick, 1989, 250).

A report from Corra Cluana and Coillte Clochair in Co Leitrim shows that the threshold dialogue had fallen into abeyance but that the bundle of rushes was kept under the table during the meal, thus ensuring the connection between the image and the food. An impressive circumambulation of the house is described, probably of the outside of the house, with the openings of the house (through which bad luck could enter) used as 'Stations' at which the cross-bearer stopped to utter a prayer for protection:

> 'On the evening of the feast, a bunch of rushes is cut, and placed under the table. After the supper, the cross is made. The cross I always make is the rush cross, and to make this properly you require 49 rushes. One of these is unbroken and

the other 48 bent and form the 4 sides of the cross. The unbroken rush represents Jesus Christ and the twelve on each side represent the 12 Apostles. St Brigid always had great devotion to Jesus Christ and the 12 Apostles and hence the number of rushes …

When the cross was made, the head of the house went round the house with it and placed it in every window and door round the house and said at each entrance or window: 'St Brigid, save us from all fever, famine and fire' (IFC 902; 283-286).

CHAPTER ELEVEN

St Brigid's Cross

A familiar aspect of the cult of Brigid is St Brigid's Cross which in many houses and shops hangs on the wall over the door. It is usually woven from straw or rushes and is renewed every year with the arrival of the feast.

St Brigid's Cross takes different forms which may be classed as follows:

1. The four-armed or 'Swastika' type.
2. The three-armed type.
3. The diamond or 'lozenge' type.
4. The interwoven type.
5. St Brigid's Bow.
6. St Brigid's bare cross.
7. The Sheaf Cross.

1. The four-armed type

This is a very famliar type of St Brigid's Cross, sometimes called the 'Swastika' form from its particular shape. The arms are not in an exact line across from each other so that it gives the impression of being a wheel in motion rather than a cross.

This type of cross is usually made of rushes, although straw is sometimes used. No wooden support is needed and a very simple cross might have only a few rushes, while a large specimen might have up to twenty. The four arms are bound together at the ends with a piece of string. This type of cross is widely distributed, especially in Ulster and Leinster (Danaher, 1972, 17).

The idea of motion comes to mind again if this type of cross is compared with a design on the High Cross in Kilcullen, Co Kildare, where four dancers, holding each other's long hair, perform a circular dance.

2. The Three-Armed Cross

In areas of Ulster a three-armed cross is found. It is made of straw or rushes and looks like a simplified form of the four-armed cross. Again, no wooden frame is required in making this type of cross.

This does not resemble the conventional kind of Christian cross to any extent, but like the four-armed type suggests a wheel in motion. This idea is appropriate for the Feast of St Brigid, the ancient Feast of Imbolc, which marks the movement from winter to spring. In this way it may be a sun-symbol – the great wheel of the sky. Jane Harrison, in discussing the sun-chariot discovered in Trundholm in which a horse is shown pulling a chariot containing a great sun-disc, remarks: 'It is of course the wheel in motion that has power magically to compel the sun to rise. The wheels in sanctuaries were turned by ropes with the like intent' (1989, 524).

3. The Diamond or Lozenge-shaped Cross.

This is the most widely distributed cross of all and is found in all provinces, especially Connaught. In Ulster it was found in Cos Donegal, Armagh, Monaghan and Cavan. In Leinster it was found in Cos Meath, Kildare, Offaly and Wexford. It was found in every county in Munster also (O'Sullivan, 1973, 72). John O'Sullivan omits Co Cork probably because it was not mentioned in the folklore manuscripts but, as a child, I remember an old house near Fermoy in which a large number of diamond-shaped Brigid's Crosses were attached to the thatch – a new one being added each year and the old ones allowed to remain.

For the diamond cross a framework of wood – two sticks crossed – was required, and it was usually made of straw though rushes were sometimes used, or indeed, a mixture of straw and rushes which gave the cross a beautifully artistic appearance. The four ends of the wooden frame were sometimes allowed to extend so that four more diamond crosses could be formed to make a very elaborate production, but the single diamond remained as the basic form.

Not only is the diamond cross the most widespread but its design goes back over the ages. The same design is found on statues of the goddess of fertility in Old Europe. The same design is found on the belly of a goddess from Gladnice near Pristina in southern Jugoslavia. The statue goes back to 6000 BC. (Gimbutas, 1989, Plate 203).

Similarly, the same design was found, again on the belly of a goddess, in north Moldavia and on this occasion the diamond is divided into four parts with a little mark at the centre of each square (Gimbutas 1989, Plate 204).

Again, from Bordjos in northern Jugoslavia comes the figure of a naked woman holding a large vessel and and on the stool on which she is sitting the diamond design is clearly carved. Professor Gimbutas suggests that this may be an invocation for rain – that the rain may come and fill the vessel she is holding (1989, Plate 94).

A statue of the goddess from Bulgaria called 'The Lady of Pazardsik', and dating from about 4500 BC, again carries the diamond design on each buttock (Gimbutas, 1989, Plate 209). Professor Gimbutas comments:

'The dot representing seed, and the lozenge symbolising the sown field, appear on sculptures of an enthroned pregnant goddess and are also incised or painted on totally schematised figurines. A lozenge with a dot or dash in its centre or in the corners must have been the symbolic invocation to secure fertility. Less abstract are the Early Cucuteni figurines from western Ukraine where the entire body, particularly the abdomen and buttocks, were impressed with real grain ... A lozenge is often the most pronounced feature, the rest of the female body serving only as a background to the ideographic concept' (Gimbutas, 1989, 205).

Later, we will see in a custom from Co Wexford, an illustration of this phenomenon.

Marija Gimbuta stresses the importance of the diamond figure as a symbol of the goddess of fertility and her connection with the field in which the corn is sown: 'The seed must have

been recognised as a cause of germination and growth, and
the pregnant belly of a woman must have been assimilated to
field fertility in the infancy of agriculture. As a result, there
arose an image of a pregnant goddess endowed with the pre-
rogative of being able to influence and distribute fertility.
The belief that woman's fertility or sterility influences farming persists almost universally in European folklore. Barren
women are regarded as dangerous; a pregnant woman has
magical influence on grain because like her, the grain 'becomes pregnant'; it germinates and grows.

The Pregnant Goddess can be deciphered either by means of
her quasi ideogram – a dot or a lozenge within a lozenge – incised or painted on her belly, thighs, neck or arms, or by the
naturalistic portrayal of a pregnant female with hands above
the belly. She is related to the square, the perennial symbol of
earthbound matter' (Gimbutas, 1989, 201).

The diamond design is found again in Brú na Bóinne,
Fourknocks and in Knowth (Eogan, 1986, 153).

P. Ó Síocháin makes the interesting observation that the
lozenge/diamond design is found in the Aran sweater. So it
would appear that a megalithic design is still to be seen in common use in St Brigid's Cross and in the pullover from the Aran
Islands (1967, 179, 181).

This diamond design is also to be found in ecclesiastical sites
in Ireland: on the High Cross of Donaghmore, Co Tyrone; in the
Round Tower, Kildare Cathedral; Killaloe Cathedral, Co Clare;
Killeshin Church, Co Laoise; St Saviours's Church, Glendalough,
Co Wicklow; the Nuns' Church, Clonmacnoise, Co Offaly;
Tuamgraney, Co Clare; Clonfert Cathedral, Co Galway and on
the High Cross of Moone, Co Kildare (JRSAI, XL11, part 1, 1912,
Fig 6).

The same design is found on the Tara Brooch and the on the
brooch found in Roscrea.

This diamond design is found, then, in a variety of places and
in a variety of situations and goes back to the megalithic age –
Newgrange is usually dated at around 3200 BC. From the exten-

sive research carried out by Marija Gimbutas in Old Europe, it is clear that the design is connected with the goddess of fertility who is associated with growth and reproduction. The huge lozenge-shaped stones of the West Kennet Avenue in Avebury, Wiltshire, are considered to represent the broad-hipped body of the goddess (Dames, 1977, 84).

It can be seen, then, how appropriate this design is for the Feast of Brigid who returns from the Otherworld to end the dark season, to stretch the brightness of the days, to re-start the growth of vegetation, to introduce the lambing season and the fishing season, to initiate the ploughing season and the sowing of crops.

4. The Interwoven Cross
This type of St. Brigid's Cross is made from rushes, or straw or a type of strong grass/sedge (cib). The strands are interwoven in the form of a cross. Unlike the types described already, this type is clearly recognisable as a form of Christian cross.

This type is found in Kerry, Cork and Clare in Munster; in Sligo and Leitrim in Connaught; in Donegal, Derry, Armagh and Monaghan in Ulster (O'Sullivan, 1973, 78).

This design is to be found in a sculptured stone in St Saviour's Church, Glendalough.

5. St Brigid's Bow
This is a cross within a circle. According to the samples preserved in the National Museum they were made from stiff grass, from straw or from sally. This type was found only in counties Cork, Limerick and Tipperary (O'Sullivan, 1973, 76). While the distribution is small, this is a very handsome, artistic type of St Brigid's Cross.

6. St. Brigid's Bare Cross
In this type of cross, ornamentation is absent and it is readily recognisable as a Christian Cross. It is often made of two plaits of straw or rushes bound together at the centre. Distribution was

not widespread but they are found in some counties of Connaught, Leinster and Ulster (O'Sullivan, 1973, 78).

An even simpler form of this is found, consisting of two pieces of wood bound together or nailed at the centre (O'Sullivan, 1973,78). In some cases, the two pieces of wood were bound together at the centre with straw. This may indicate that the diamond-shaped cross once prevailed here, but that in the process of time, decay had set in. Less attention was being paid to the making of the crosses and a hasty tying of two pieces of stick together with a piece of staw was all that remained of the great artistic and symbolic diamond cross. If this is correct, it would indicate that the diamond cross was even more wide-spread than hitherto suspected.

7. The Sheaf-Cross

This type bears no resemblance to the conventional cross. It consists of two small sheaves of corn – unthreshed so that the grain is still attached to them – bound together with a *scolb* – a split piece of branch used in thatching. The *scolb* binds the combined sheaves to the thatch on the inside of the house. Sometimes, a potato was included as well, the *scolb* pinning both the potato and the sheaves to the thatch.

The Sheaf-Cross is associated with East Galway and Co Roscommon and it is likely that these were once areas of extensive corn growing.

In the fine report given by Anne Tuohy, Ballygreaney, Ballymacward, Co Galway (IFC 902; 182) she explained how a sheaf of oats and a potato used to be placed on the doorstep on St Brigid's Night. Then, they were hung up in the house at bedtime. A little later in the spring, when the corn was being sown in the fields, the grains were taken off the sheaf and mixed with the seed-corn to be sown. The same was done with the potato – it was mixed with the rest of the seed-potatoes and went into the ground with them.

James Delaney reports on the extensive amount of folklore hecollected in the area around Tobar Bhríde, Camach, Curnalee,

Grange, in south Roscommon. He describes how Tom Dolan made the Sheaf-Cross from two sheaves of oats, a potato and a *scolb*. When the time for sowing the oats came, the Sheaf-Cross used to be taken down from the rafters, the grain removed and the cross put up on the rafters again.

Perhaps this same type of fertility ritual to ensure good crops is indicated in the famous painting of the Wedding Feast by Pieter Brueghel. On the wall behind the table on which the bride is seated, two small sheaves hang which closely resemble the description of the Sheaf-Cross in Co Roscommon (Cammaerts, 1945, Plate 32).

It does appear that ancient customs survived for a long time in the area surrounding Tobar Bhríde. The well itself attracted a large number of pilgrims on the Pattern Day, 'Domhnach Chrom Dubh' in this case, that is to say the last Sunday in July, but it is likely that people went to the well on St Brigid's Feast also. To this well came Raghnall Ó Dónaill, who later became Earl of Antrim, along with his wife in 1604 to ask Brigid to give them a child. A child was born to them and the Earl returned to give thanks and donated the ornamental gate at the entrance to the well (Mac Neill, 1982, 11, 633).

On the western side of the Shannon, from Portumna to Lough Ree, there was a fairly extensive area in which the connection of the cross with the sowing of corn was clearly celebrated. This same phenomenon occurs – mixing grain from the sheaf-cross with the grain being sown in the field – in a remarkable account from Co Wexford:

'Crosses were made by some at home – if crosses you could call them. It was made of straw and were (was) started by rolling the straw round a grain of corn – by the ends. When finished it took the shape of a diamond and was fixed to the rafter by a small nail.

When the first grain was being sown, this grain was taken out and put into the first bucketful. The straw was left in position and the age of a house might be determined by counting the 'crosses'. I cannot say if the custom still exists' (IFC

907; 164-165; F. Mac Nioclàis, Bun Clóidí, Fearna, Loch
Garmáin, Scribe).

Here, in Bunclody, in Co Wexford, in the twentieth century, we
have what appears to be the ritual expression of what is contained in a Figurine with a dotted lozenge on the belly, in
Gladnice near Pristina, southern Yugoslavia. c. 6000 BC (Gimbutas,
1989, Plate 203).

Gimbutas gives several illustrations of the 'dot and lozenge'
from remote antiquity – Plates 204; 206; Figs 158; 159; 160; 162,
163 – and states: 'The dot, representing seed, and the lozenge,
symbolising the sown field, appear on sculptures of an enthroned pregnant goddess and are also incised or painted on totally schematised figurines. A lozenge with a dot or dash in its
centre or in the corners must have been the symbolic invocation
to secure fertility' (1989, 205).

From Yugoslavia to Ireland, for 8000 years, the 'dot and
lozenge' motif illustrated the corn sown in a field, a woman's
pregnant womb. It expressed the human need for the continuation of life through the fertility of the earth and the fertility of
woman.

In other places the link between the cross and the fertility of
the earth was expressed in another way, that is to say by burying
the old cross:

> 'In County Armagh when Brigid's Crosses are made they
> must not be lightly thrown aside when they can no longer be
> preserved. They must then be burned or buried. No reason
> was given to me for the burning but I have been told that the
> burial conveyed Brigid's blessing to crops' (IFC 905; 40; T. S.
> F. Paterson).

In different places in Co Donegal the burning of the old crosses
is mentioned (IFC 904;33;161) but generally they were left where
they were, and in an account from Co Galway it was said that up
to 50 could be seen in certain houses (IFC 902; 181). It seems that
people were reluctant to take them down when the new one for
the current year was hung up as these old crosses, in a sense,

were bound up with the history of the household as a moving
account from Co Kerry indicates:

> 'As each generation passed out, the old crosses were taken
> down and the series began anew. In this way, the number of
> crosses on the rafters denoted the number of years spent in
> married life by the couple then living'(IFC 899; 192; Annraoi
> Ó Conchúir, Ceann an Tóchair, Trá Lí, Narrator; Annraoi Ó
> Conchúir, OS, Rath Uí Mhuirthille, An Tóchar, Trá Lí,
> Scribe).

A report from Co Cavan describes a unique type of cross used in
Corrloch. It was closely connected with milk. The cross was like
the four-armed cross but was made of wood. When a person
was pouring milk into a vessel he would lay the cross on the
mouth of the vessel. The foot of the strainer would be placed
within the cross. In this way, the milk, while being poured into
the vessel would actually pass through St Brigid's Cross and so
receive her blessing (IFC 905; 177). This was certainly an extraordinarily clever method of using a strong, wooden, robust type
of St Brigid's Cross in the ordinary course of domestic life.
Taking into consideration St Brigid's traditional connection with
cows, it is rather surprising that this type of use was not more
widespread.

When the cross was made of straw it is reasonable to presume that it was connected to the rites pertaining to the end of
harvest and to the *Cailleach* or 'Last Sheaf".

The account given by T. G. F. Paterson on the *Cailleach* or
'Last Sheaf' corresponds more or less with the usage in vogue in
Scotland and England. Firstly, a sheaf was made of the very last
remaining section of the cornfield but the corn was left uncut.
Then the reapers stood back and each one in turn cast his reaping hook at the standing sheaf of corn in an effort to cut it. When,
finally, one of the reapers succeeded in cutting the last sheaf –
the *Cailleach* or old woman representing the corn crop just harvested – the sheaf was taken home and placed around the neck
of the farmer's wife during the harvest supper. Later it was hung
up in the kitchen. In some cases, it was left there until the next

harvest, but otherwise the grain was rubbed off and mixed with the seed being sown in the springtime (Evans, 1975, 198). In this way, the continuous cycle of the death and resurrection of the corn was shown and the Corn Lady accompanied the process in all its aspects.

In his book *Mythic Ireland*, Michael Dames gives some wonderful photographs of a harvesting scene from Toome, Co Antrim, taken before 1914. In one of them (p. 56) he shows a line of corn stooks from the reaped field. Beside one of them the grandmother of the family sits eating her lunch. She, more than the younger members, comes closest to the experience of the life-cycle of the corn – birth, death, rebirth. Another photograph shows the reapers throwing their reaping hooks at the *Cailleach*. In this picture they are not blindfolded, as was sometimes the case, as a reaper might feel reluctant to be the one to kill the goddess. But it had to be done, for, ' unless a wheat grain falls on the ground and dies, it remains only a single grain; but if it dies it yields a rich harvest' (John 12:24).

Another picture (p. 246) shows the same family at the 'Harvest Home' supper while the Last Sheaf hangs from the ceiling presiding over the feast. When sowing time comes the grain from the Last Sheaf or Corn Dolly will be mixed with the seed-corn to descend into the earth from which a next year's harvest will spring. And so it will go on, for ever and ever – 'The Myth of the Eternal Return'.

In Scotland, the Last Sheaf was known by different names:
'The name Bride is given to the last sheaf in districts as far apart as Midlothian and the mearns. In later times the distinction between the Cailleach and Bride was not everywhere maintained. In some districts, if cut before Hallowmas, it was called the Cailleach or Carlin. In the West Highlands, it is commonly called the Cailleach, whenever cut, and in the Central and East Highlands, it is always the Maighdean-Bhuana, the Reaping Maiden. It has other names' (McNeill, 1959, 2, 120).

The 'Bride' is connected to the motherly aspect of the goddess in her role as mother of the harvest, the Corn-Mother. When the harvest is over and Samhain comes, she is the Cailleach. But these titles only represent different aspects of the same goddess.

Michael Dames looks at the great megalithic monuments of Avebury in Wiltshire as basically a sanctuary consisting of four stations representing the four seasons in the yearly life-cycle of the goddess. The four-armed Brigid's Cross, with its suggestion of a wheel in motion, may represent the four stages through which the gooddess travels in the course of a year. For a cycle of one year is basic.

The same phenomenon may be seen in the Christian Liturgical Calendar. It is widely held that historically Our Lord lived for 33 years. However, in the Liturgical Calendar, we begin in Advent with a period of preparation for his birth which we celebrate on the 25th December (c. the winter solstice). Then follows the period of Lent in preparation for his death and resurrection and transition from the conditions of this world to the glory of eternity. A period of celebration of Easter follows, in which we rejoice in the fact that the Risen Christ has broken through the barriers and opened up the gates of heaven to us. This long period of rejoicing for 50 days brings us up to the Feast of Pentecost. The remaining part of the year is spent celebrating the action of the Holy Spirit in the church and we are back to the First Sunday of Advent when the cycle begins again.

At *Samhain* (1 November) the goddess is in her winter form as *Cailleach*.

At *Imbolc* (1 February) she assumes her infant form as Brídeog.

At *Bealtaine* (1 May) she is the young woman ripe for marriage – the Bábóg.

At *Lughnasa* (1 August) she is the Mother, the Lady of the Harvest.

The different stages through which the goddesses goes in a single year represent the natural seasonal changes of vegetation, animal life and the earth. As Michael Dames expresses it:

'... the overall picture of the entire ensemble was to celebrate

the annual life cycle of the Great Goddess, at temples which
were her seasonal portraits. The worshippers moved around
this extended gallery of symbolic architecture in time with
the changing seasons and the farming year, synchronised
with the comparable events in the lives of the human community, namely birth, puberty, marriage and death' (1977,
122-123).

The theory is that there were fundamentally four significant
sites in Avebury to represent the four stages of the life of the
goddess. The people would have made a pilgrimage to each of
those sites in turn at the appropriate dates and in this way, as it
were, identify themselves with the life-cycle of the goddess and
become one with her.

Perhaps a remnant of this same annual cycle may be inferred
from the feastdays of three saints associated with the Barony of
Dúiche Ealla (Duhallow) in West Cork, on the borders of Kerry.
These are three female saints well known in that locality. The
first is St Lasair who has her holy well at Cill Lasrach and a pilgrimage to this took place at Imbolc. This pilgrimage has fallen
into decay but the well may still be visited by a few at this date.
The next saint is St Iníon Bhuí and her holy well is at Drom
Tairbh, a few miles to the south of St Lasair. A pilgrimage takes
place here at Bealtaine. Another few miles to the west brings us
to the holy well of St Laitiaran and a pilgrimage takes place here
at Cullen, at Lughnasa. Another few miles to the north is
Kishkeam (Coiscéim na Caillí – the footstep of the Cailleach/
hag/old woman) and a legend of this small square area has it
that at some part of the year the saints – who are sisters – 'go underground'. This probably refers to the winter period when all
nature dies – the period of the Cailleach.

It is surely significant, that in this small area three female
saints have holy wells more or less equidisant from each other
and have their feastdays on three of the insular Celtic
Calendrical Quarter Days, Imbolc, Bealtaine, Lughnasa with a
site referring to the Cailleach, thus pointing to Samhain, as a
completion of the annual cycle.

This area appears to be a Christianised version of a great out-door sanctuary of the goddess, in the form of a square with a cult area at each corner. By going on a short pilgrimage to each of those four sites at the appropriate dates, the people could identify themselves and unite themselves mystically with the different phases of the life-cycle of the goddess. This small square area of Dúiche Ealla, hemmed in by rivers and hills, may possibly have been a *Neimheadh*, a hidden sanctuary with a ritual calendar laid out on the landscape (cf *Seanchas Duthalla*, 1991, 50-54).

For the most part, it is probable that ploughing began earlier in Britain than in Ireland – immediately after 'Plough Monday' – that is to say, shortly after the Epiphany (6th January).

In the Irish examples, the grain used to be taken from the small sheaves or from the cross, to be put into the earth along with the seed, but the body of the sheaf, or cross, was left hanging on the rafters throughout the year. In this fashion Brigid was operating on two levels: she was with the grain in the field in the process of growth and, at the same time, she was acting as guardian of the house and helper in domestic affairs.

The reason, then, for placing a sheaf outside the door, on the Holy Night (31 January) can be understood. It could be said that the goddess was already present in the sheaf – she was there in her winter form as 'Cailleach'. But with the arrival of spring this form was no longer suitable. With the return of Brigid from the Otherworld at Imbolc, she assumed a new form – that of Brídeog – the infant goddess, to mark the infancy of the year in spring-time. The Last Sheaf of the old harvest was dismembered to be-come a cross and assume different modes of operation as fertiliser of the new harvest, as protector and domestic helper. It was as Brídeog (in her springtime form) that she was carried from house to house to give her people new hope and new courage for the coming year, just as in the previous procession from har-vest field to harvest feast (Harvest Home) she had been in the form of 'Cailleach', the Last Sheaf, the Old Lady of the corn just harvested.

While the emphasis on corn-growing may have been greater

in England than in Ireland, nevertheless, it is clear that the Brídeog Procession from house to house was in the same tradition of fertility as the rites of Plough Monday in Britain.

Sometimes, Plough Monday occurred in early February, quite close to St Brigid's Day. Boys, known as 'Plough Bullocks', or unmarried women, would drag a plough through the village. The plough was gaily ornamented and the onlookers would contribute some money. Among the characters involved in the play was the 'Fool', dressed in an animal hide, and the 'Bessey'/'The Betsy' – a woman or a man dressed in a woman's clothes. At the end, a dance was held in the barn. The Betsy would sit on the plough and the young men would perform a sword dance. The Betsy represented the goddess (Berger, 1988, 80).

An account from the year 1938 describes the ritual form of Plough Monday: 'The Fool, representing the spirit of the year, after providing amusement for the onlookers, is killed by the sword-dancers, who perform a mock funeral procession around him as he lies dead on the ground. The ceremonial plough now moves around the dancers in a circle and penetrates their ranks where, at its fertilising touch and the cry of "Speed the Plough", the Fool springs to life and the dancers finally move off, dragging the plough behind them' (Whitlock, 1978, 24). In this case the spirit of the year is in male form.

In some areas in England, the Kern Baby, or Corn Dolly (Last Sheaf), which had been kept in a place of honour by the hearth throughout the autumn, was taken out on Plough Monday and reverently laid on the first furrow. 'It held, so it was thought, the spirit of the Corn Goddess, who gave life to the sown seed. The plough turned over the soil in a brown, curving wave to bury her, and there she was, safe in the womb of the earth, ready to accomplish her annual miracle. From death came life; from darkness, light; it was always so in the cycle of the country year' (Whitlock, 1978, 24-25).

Pamela Berger discusses the importance of the month of February as the great period of fertility rituals with ideas of the productivity of the land underlying certain Christian saints whose feastdays occur throughout the month aints such as St Brigid (1 February); St Blaise (3 February); St Valentine (14 February); St Milburga (23 February), St Walpurga (25 February). The shadow of the goddes lies behind their life-stories (1988, 62, 71, 81, 85, 69).

CHAPTER TWELVE

Brat Bhríde/St Brigid's Cloak

A piece of cloth, popularly known as *Brat Bhríde* and used for various purposes such as protection and healing, is a well-known feature of the cult of Brigid. A personal account comes from Baile na nGall in Kerry:

'An Cochall Bhríde (Brat Bhríde): Brat do (de) línéadach ar nós haincisiuir póca a leataí amach faoin drúcht an oíche roimh Lá 'le Bríde – Oíche 'le Bríde – tar éis dul faoi den ghréin. Tógtaí ansin ar maidin é roimh éirí gréine is d'fhilltí suas é, is bhíodh sé ag mná cabhartha ... Bhíos ana-olc i luí seoil ar an gcéad leanbh is chuir Neillí Ní Chiabháin (an bhean ghlúine) an Cochall Bhríde ar mo cheann is fuaireas faoiseamh' (IFC 899; 108; Mein Mháire an Ghabha (Bean Uí Mhaoileoin), An Clochán, Baile na nGall, a d'aithris; Seán Ó Dubha, OS, a scríobh).

(St Brigid's Cloak: a piece of linen like a pocket hankerchief that is laid out under the dew on the night before St Brigid's Day – that is St Brigid's Night – after the sun has set. It is lifted up again next morning before the sun has risen and it is folded up and it is used by midwives ... I was very ill while having my first child and Neillí Ní Chiabháin (the midwife) put St Brigid's Cloak on my head and I found relief).

Similarly, in a report from Co Mayo, it is said that a red cloth is put out in the same place as the bundle of rushes outside the door immediately before bringing in the rushes in the Threshold Rite at supper time. This piece of cloth is not brought in with the bundle of rushes, however. It is left outside all night but brought in, in the morning before the sun rises and stored away (IFC 903; 12-13).

This practice of putting out the brat after sunset and bringing it in again before sunrise is described very clearly in a report from Co Tipperary:

'This ribbon, generally black, is put out on a tree or bush after sunset on Saint Brigid's Eve and is taken in in the morning before sunrise ... This ribbon is a cure for certain ailments, especially headaches' (IFC 901; 153-154; Micheál Ó Dubhshláinge, Ard Fhionáin, Cathair Dhún Iascaigh).

The same practice is found in Ros Muc, Co Galway (IFC 902; 36).

There was no formal regulation regarding the colour of the brat. Some people held that it should be one of the colours of the Mass vestments – that is white, green, red, violet or black.

In certain areas in Co Cork, it was forbidden to wash the brat (IFC 900; 21;53; 175). The same tradition was found in Clais Mhór, Co Waterford:

'Fanann an bheannacht ar na rudaí sin go ceann bliana, mura ndéantar iad a ní. Mar sin, ní ceart na hearraí seo (a leagtar taobh amuigh den doras) a ní ar chor ar bith; má dhéantar, imíonn an bheannacht díobh agus ní bhíonn aon leigheas iontu' (IFC 900; 225; Mrs Ellen Kiely and Mrs Bridget Foley, Clashmore, a d'aithris; Íde Bean Uí Chofaigh, Bun Machan, a scríobh).

(The blessing remains on these things (Brait) for a year unless they are washed. Therefore, it is not right to wash these goods left outside the door at all. If they are washed, the blessing leaves them and they have no healing power.)

In Cúil Aodha, in West Cork, it was the women and girls who put out the Brat and men had no part in it (IFC 900; 88).

In Kilbehenny in Co Limerick the brat was about 30 inches long and 3 to 4 inches wide, rather like a bandage (IFC 899;217). It was almost of the same dimensions in Newcastle, Co Tipperary (IFC 901; 164). This was a convenient length as it enabled a person suffering from headache to wrap it around his head and tie it at the back.

In an account from Anglesborough, Co Limerick, the reporter

said that he himself had seen men wearing the brat at Mass. These were men who were subject to headache (IFC 899; 263-264).

The piece of cloth known as Brat Bhríde was not, of course, a part of St Brigid's personal clothes. It was not a relic in the ordinary sense of being part of a saint's body or clothing. Moreover, it was not permanent – it had to be renewed each year. Its power of healing and protection was on an annual basis. This being so, one might well ask from whence did it receive its power.

It appears that it received its supernatural power from Brigid's visit on the Holy Night. We have seen that a basic concept in the cult of Brigid is her return from the Otherworld and her visitation of the homes of her devotees. She puts her blessing on whatever is left outside the door as she passes and so she blesses the brat hanging on a bush or hanging from the latch of the door itself. The Brídeog procession from house to house is probably a ritualisation of Brigid's invisible return – a dramatic presentation of the myth or sacred story.

Although the brat was very popular as a cure for headache, it is also mentioned in connection with toothache in Co Leitrim (IFC 902; 285-286) and with sore eyes in Co Clare (IFC 901;46).

While St Brigid's Cross was essentially stable, belonging essentially to the interior of the house to safeguard its inhabitants from 'fire, famine and fever', the brat was mobile and could be taken to any place or situation where it was required. It could be brought to a sick cow; it could be carried by the fisherman going to sea, in his pocket or sown on to his coat; the midwife could take it with her when going to assist a woman in childbirth, and it could be hung up on a tree near the house when a storm was raging. Its mobility gave it prime importance.

W. Danaher, recalls conversations he had with old people from the parish of Athea, Co Limerick, at the beginning of the twentieth century: 'Prayer to St Brigid cured ringworm and allied skin trouble' (Mrs. John Ahearne). 'Her influence kept the Evil One (Satan) far from the sick bed' (Dan Carroll); 'The brat blessed in St Brigid's name was supposed to drive out the demon from a girl possessed by the devil' (Richard E. Woulfe,

Cratloe, 1904) and was so used by Father Ahearn, PP, about 1800).

Go gcuire Dia a neart,

Muire a Mac,

Bríd a Brat,

Colm a Leabhar

Idir sinn agus poll a' bháite,

saol cráite,

bás obann,

náire saolta,

deamhan Fírinne,

diabhal coimhdeachta (IFC 899; 206).

(May God send his strength; (May) Mary (send) her Son; Brigid her Brat; Colm(cille) his Book (of the Psalms) to stand between us and the pond that could drown us; (between us and) a life of misery; sudden death; public scandal; the demon of (Cnoc) Fírinne; our acompanying devil.)

This is a wonderful example of a popular simplified type of protection prayer or *Lúireach*, of which the best-known one is *Lúireach Phádraig*, St Patrick's Breatplate. The name *Lúireach* is a Gaelicised form of the Latin *Lorica* – the metal breastplate worn by Roman soldiers which stood between them and sword thrusts. The Christian Celts, being very conscious of the fact that the Christian is a soldier of Christ who is subject to attack by the forces of evil, as Christ himself was attacked by the Evil One in the desert, on the roof of the temple and on a mountain (cf Mt 4:1-11), developed this type of 'shielding prayer' to a degree unusual in the rest of Christendom. Sometimes the various members of the body are mentioned as needing protection, as in the early Lúireach of Maol Íosa Ó Brolcháin (Ó Duinn, 1990, 73-74). God, the angels and saints, the elements, form protecting circles around the person so that the evil forces surrounding him to attack him will be unable to penetrate the defences and reach him. A remnant of this type of spiritual warfare or 'psychomachia', as it was called in early Christianity, is preserved in the triple renunciation of Satan at the Easter Vigil.

St Brigid's Brat finds a place as a protective device within the context of the 'spiritual warfare' which formed such a basic part in the thinking of early Christianity. The anointing with oil of the child's chest at baptism – like a Roman athlete about to enter the contest – is another reminder of the military character of the Christian religion as it confronts its demonic enemies.

The 'deamhan Fírinne' mentioned in the Lúireach is obviously Donn Fírinne, the god of the dead in Gaelic tradition. He is also connected with the fertility of the land, and with storms. He has a sanctuary on Cnoc Fírinne (Knockfierna) near Ballingarry in Co Limerick quite near Athea. In the minds of the people of the surrounding area, Donn could be both benevolent and dangerous, and so he is mentioned in the Lúireach to be on the safe side (cf *Béaloideas* 18 (1948),144ff).

The 'diabhal coimhdeachta', the 'accompanying demon', is also mentioned. This probably lies in opposition to the 'aingeal coimhdeachta', the 'accompanying angel' or 'guardian angel'. The people apparently believed that each of us carries around with him an 'accompanying demon', and how right they were.

In some places, the person putting out the brat said an accompanying prayer. A fine example of this comes from the parish of Macroom in West Cork:

Bríde agus a brat,
An Mhaighdean Mhuire agus a Mac,
Mícheál agus a sciath,
Éist amháin le Dia'
(on hanging it)
'Cas orainn aniar anocht
Agus bliain ó anocht,
Agus anocht amháin le Dia' (IFC 900; 82-83; Neans Ní Shúill-eabháin, Cill na Martra, a d'aithris; Pádraig Ó Deas-mhumhan, Maigh Chromtha, a scríobh).
(Brigid and her cloak, Virgin Mary and her Son, Micheal and his shield, listen to God alone. Return to us from the west tonight, and a year from tonight and tonight only with God.)

The prayer expresses clearly the idea of Brigid arriving from the Otherworld on her annual visit.

With regard to Brat Bhríde, a question arises as to its connection with another feast, that of Bealtaine. Seán Ó Súilleabháin, in discuusing Oíche Bhealtaine (May Eve), asks: 'Was a garment (e.g., the wedding-tie of the man of the house) exposed on a bush that night for some purpose?' (1942, 333).

Here he is speaking of May Eve – not St Brigid's Eve, but the ritual is the same – exposing a piece of cloth outdoors on this other Holy Night, that of Bealtaine. It is the dew of Bealtaine that is important here and the piece of cloth kept outdoors all night is the instrument by which the dew is collected and applied to the body for cosmetic purposes. May dew was extremely popular among women both in England and Ireland until comparatively recent centuries, for it was believed that it contained remarkable powers for conferring beauty on women who washed themselves in it prior to the rising of the sun on May Morning. A popular English poem expresses the idea clearly:

The fair maid who,
the first of May,
Goes to the fields
at break of day,
And washes in dew
from the hawthorn tree,
Will ever after
Handsome be (Opie and Tatem, 1992, 246).

The folklorist Christina Hole speaks of the custom, as it was practised in Derbyshire, of laying a sheet on the ground to collect the dew of May: '… delicate children used to be anointed with it. A sheet was spread out on the grass overnight, and the dew thus collected was rubbed next day into the child's loins' (1978, 193).

In the report from Kerry (IFC 899; 108) which we have seen already, there is a reference to putting the brat out under the dew after sunset and bringing it in again in the morning before sunrise. (Brat … a leataí amach faoin drúcht an oíche roimh Lá

'le Bríde – Oíche 'le Bríde – tar éis dul faoi den ghréin. Tógtaí
ansin ar maidin é roimh éirí gréine is d'fhilltí suas é.) Here we
have the equivalent of the Derbyshire use but occuring at Imbolc
rather than at Bealtaine. In both cases, dew is involved and the
cloth spread on the ground, or hanging from a bush, is there to
collect the dew.

A report from Co Cork gives a similar description of the
usage:

'A clean piece of cloth is put out on a whitethorn bush on St
Brigid's Eve. This cloth must be the best material in the house
– if possible linen. The rag (cloth) is soaked with dew in the
morning. It is dried and preserved carefully during the year
and is used as a cure' (IFC 900;31; Séamas Mac Coitir,
Beantraí, Narrator; Mary A. Crowley, Beantraí, Scribe).

We have seen, also, that it was forbidden to wash the Brat in certain areas in Co Cork (IFC 900;21; 53; 175) and in Clashmore (IFC
900; 225). Perhaps the reason for this prohibition was to preserve
the dew, for if the curative and cosmetic power were in the dew
as in the case of Bealtaine, then the washing, in destroying the
dew would also the destroy the power. This is probably also the
reason why the brat had to be brought in to the house before the
rising of the sun. If left outside, the risen sun would soon dry up
the dew and render the brat useless. It is unfortunate that
Séamas Mac Coitir did not give a more detailed account explaining what he meant by 'It is dried'. If it were dried before a fire,
this would be the equivalent of leaving it out under the risen sun
and would dissipate the dew in the same way. At any rate, if the
power were in the dew, then it was vital to preserve the cloth
unwashed and undried.

This, of course, puts a different complexion on the question
of Brigid's visit and her blessing of the brat as being the source
of the brat's healing and protective power. In this latter theory,
the power comes from the dew on St Brigid's Eve.

It may well be, that in this case there occurs a transfer of a
usage from one Feast to another, as sometimes happens. In this
case, it seems most likely that the piece of cloth laid on the

ground to receive the dew belonged primarily to the Feast of
Bealtaine and was later adopted by Imbolc, St Brigid's Eve. We
cannot be sure of this but there are certain indications in the report from Cúil Aodha, Co Cork (IFC 900; 88), maintaining that
the brat was for women and girls and that men were excluded.
The same was true of the parish of Drom Dá Liag close to Cúil
Aodha. This comes close to the cosmetic use of the dew-soaked
cloth at Bealtaine to increase one's beauty. Men, being more or
less content with the face God gave them, tended to leave these
affairs to women. However, if a transfer of usage from Bealtaine
to Imbolc occurred at all, the emphasis was laid on the protective and curative properties of the cloth in the case of Brat Bhríde
rather than on cosmetics.

A similar and curious example of the use of dew is found in
Germany where the dew was gathered at Christmastide and
mixed with the flour in the making of Christmas cakes. Some of
these were given to the cows as it was believed that this would
improve their health and fertility. The Christmas dew was considered to be especially sacred. It is difficult to know if this was
so on account of such a significant date as the winter solstice
(21st December). Both Bealtaine and Imbolc are also significant
dates and one wonders if the position of the sun at these dates
was connected with the collection of the dew for reasons of fertility. On the other hand, the German usage may have a
Christian origin in the remarkable Introit Antiphon of the Mass
on the Fourth Sunday of Advent, very close to Christmas:

'Rorate caeli, desuper, et nubes pluant justum; aperiatur
terra, et germinet Salvatorem' (Isaiah 45:8) (Drop down dew,
O heavens, from above, and let the clouds rain the just: let the
earth be opened and bud forth a Saviour.)

While the fundamental idea is that of dew/rain falling on the
earth to make the vegetation spring up, in this Christian context
it is referred to the earthly birth of Christ from the Virgin Mary
through the heavenly action of the Holy Spirit (Luke 1:26-38).
The part played by the sky is described in the accompanying
Psalm verse: 'Caeli enarrant gloriam Dei; et opera manuum ejus

annuntiat firmamentum' (Psalm 18:2). (The heavens show forth
the glory of God; and the firmament declares the work of his
hands) (cf Miles, 1976, 288-289).

While the Introit Antiphon is based on the ordinary and obvious symbolism of dew as a fertilising agent, it is unlikely that
in Ireland the liturgical text would have played any part in this
particular aspect of the cult of Brigid.

CHAPTER THIRTEEN

Crios Bhríde/Brigid's Belt

Crios Bhríde or St Brigid's Belt consists of a rope made of straw (súgán) or rushes or strong grass, in the form of a ring with one or more crosses on it. It used to be taken around to the various houses on St Brigid's Eve and members of the household passed in and out through it to secure the protection of Brigid for themselves throughout the year.

The crios belongs especially to certain areas of Co Galway, but, perhaps it had a wider circulation at one time.

The following report shows how the Brídeog procession and the crios procession took place together in the Aran Islands:

'La Fhéil' Bríde (ní san oíche) théadh daoine bochta thart ó theach go teach leis an mBrídeog – páistí scoile thuis-mitheoirí anásacha a dhéanadh é. D'fhaighidís fataí (níos minicí ná tada eile), plúr, tae, agus airgead amantaí. Bhíodh an Bhrídeog chomh mór le cailín 6 nó 7 de bhlianta. Éadaí casta timpeall ar mhaide a bhíodh istigh inti agus gúna dearg taobh amuigh díobh. Uaireanta ba fháinnií óir a bhíodh mar shúile inti agus an tsrón, béal agus cluasa daite le peann lu-aidhe.

Ag na cailíní a bhíodh an Bhrídeog agus na buachaillí ag iom-par an chreasa agus na croise. Ag teacht isteach i dteach dóibh 'sé an rann a bhíodh aca:

'Crios, Crios Bríde mo chrios,
crios na ceithre gcros,
Muire a chuaidh ann,
agus Bríd a tháinig as,
Más fearr atá sibh inniu
go mba seacht fearr a bhéas sibh
bliain ó inniu.'

Is as súgán féir a bhíodh an crios Bhríde déanta agus a dhá cheann ceangailte de íochtar na croise. Bhí an crios 12 throigh nó mar sin. Ba ghnás le cuid de na daoine turas a thabhairt:

'sé sin, a dhul isteach faoin gcrios trí uaire. Phógaidís an
chros agus is í an chos dheas a chuiridís amach ar dtús ar a
dhul amach dóibh faoin gcrios. Bhí an chros tuairim 's dhá
throigh ar airde agus troigh ar leithéad. Bhíodh ribíní nó
píosaí éadaigh deasa fuailte don chros.

Ní théann lucht na brídeoige thart le tuairim is 15 bliana
(=1925). Cuireadh suas den ghnás seo' (IFC 902; 3-5; Seán Ó
Maoldomhnaigh, Fearann Choirce, Cill Rónáin, Oileán
Arann, a scríobh).

(On St Brigid's Day (not the night) poor people used to go
around from house to house with the Brídeog – school children of poor parents that used to do it. They would get potatoes (more often than anything else), flour, tea, and sometimes money. The Brídeog used to as big as a girls of 6 or 7
years of age. Clothes, bound around a stick formed the body
with a red dress on the outside. Sometimes, the eyes were
formed of golden rings and the nose, mouth and ears drawn
with a lead pencil. The girls carried the Brídeog while the
boys carried the crios and the cross. When they were entering
a house they used to recite the following 'rann':

'Crios, Brigid's Crios, my crios, crios of the four crosses, it
was Mary that went into it and Brigid who came out. If you
are well off today, may you be seven times better off a year
from today.'

It was from a grass rope that Crios Bhríde was made with its
two ends tied to the foot of the cross. The crios was about 12
feet long. It was the custom for some people to make the
'turas' – the 'pilgrimage / journey' – that is, to go in under the
crios three times. They used to kiss the cross and it is the right
foot they used to put out first when they were coming out of
the crios. The cross was about two feet high and one foot
across. The Brídeog people have not gone around for about
.15 years (=1925). The rite was given up.')

In this account from Inis Mór it is clear that the rites of the
Brídeog procession and the crios procession took place together
– they were combined – and at an unusual time – St Brigid's Day

rather than St Brigid's Eve. The girls carried the Brídeog while the boys carried the Crios. If disguise, such as masks and unusual clothing were worn, it would probably have been mentioned by the Narrator, and the fact that he is able to point out that those who went around were children of needy parents argues that the children were not masked. Nevertheless, this is a fine piece of ritual with a large elaborate Brídeog wearing the red dress of the Aran Islands, and the eyes were probably wedding rings.

The report mentions only one cross on the crios but the 'rann'or ritual verse mentions four crosses – 'crios na ceithre gcros'. A Crios Bhríde from Co Galway in the National Museum, shows three crosses jutting out from the crios and formed from the same material (Danaher, 1972, 36, fig 7).

The entrance 'rann' belongs to the crios procession. The actual ritual appears to be relatively simple. It appears that the person first kissed the cross jutting out from the crios. Then, he lifted the crios over his head, opened it so that it formed a circle and let it fall down around him so that when it fell on the floor he was actually standing inside the crios as at the centre of a circle. Then, putting the right foot first, he stepped out of the crios. This was repeated three times.

It is clear that the 'surrounding' of the person by the crios – above, below and all around (the four points of the compass) – is of supreme importance in this rite. This theme of the 'six directions' is familiar from the episode in *Táin Bó Chuailnge* where the king, Conchubhar Mac Neasa, swears that the cows and women taken from Ulster will be brought back, except the sky fall down on us, or the earth opens up under us, or the surrounding sea invades the land: 'for the sky is above us, the earth beneath us and the sea all around us' (O'Rahilly, 1967, 247). This appears to be a piece of archaic Celtic cosmology in which the world is enclosed between sky, earth and sea. The sky can break its boundaries and invade the land in lightening, the earth can break its boundaries by splitting open in earthquake and volcanic eruption and the sea can invade the land in flooding. To maintain harmony in the universe each of these mighty forces must be kept within its own set boundries.

In a remarkable transition from pre-Christian thought to Celtic Christian *Lúireacha* or protection prayers, God is seen as surrounding the person on the four points of the compass (all around), above and below. A similar formula is found in the Chandogya Upanishad (VII,xxv,1-2):

St Patrick's Breastplate	*Chandogya Upanishad*
Crist issum (Christ below me)	(The Infinite) is below
Crist uasam (Christ above me)	It is above
Crist im degaid (Christ behind me)	It is to the west
Crist reum (Christ before me)	It is to the east
Crist dessum (Christ at my right)	It is to the south
Crist tuathum (Christ at my left)	It is to the north

According to ancient custom, when praying one should face the rising sun in the east. From this, the other directions follow – south to the right, back to the west, left to the north. The monastic communities of the Céilí Dé ritualised this custom by turning to the four points of the compass, up and down, in turn, while reciting: 'O God, come to my aid: O Lord, make haste to help me' along with the Our Father at each point, six times in all (Gwynn, 1927, 68).

The directional key is given in the Lúireach of Mugron:
'Cros Chríst sair frim einech
Cros Chríst síar fri fuinet' (Murphy, 1956, 32-35)
(Christ's cross eastwards facing me; Christ's cross back / west towards the sunset).

Crios Bhríde, with its symbolic overtones of surrounding, protecting, guarding from outside interference, can be seen then within a spectrum of archaic cosmological thought.

When the various examples of the 'Rann' are analysed, six stages can be discerned as the rite evolves:

1. The Presentation of the crios to the household.
'Seo í isteach an crios, crios na gceithre gcros' (Ó Súilleabháin, 1982, 247). (Here enters the crios, the crios of the four crosses.)

2. An Archetype is named: Christ or a saint used the crios long ago.
Crios le ar gineadh Críost, Críostaí a gineadh as' (op. cit., 249)
(A crios by which Christ was conceived; a Christian was conceived from it.)

3. The woman of the house is invited to go through the crios, or to put her child through it.
'Éirigh, a bhean an tí, agus téirigh trínár gcrios' (op. cit., 246).
(Rise up, O woman of the house, and go through our crios.)
'Éirigh suas, a bhean an tí,
Agus gabh trí huaire amach.
In ainm an Athar agus an Mhic
agus an Spioraid Naoimh. Amen' (op. cit., 249).
(Rise up, O woman of the house, and go out (through it) three times. In the name of the Father and of the Son and of the Holy Spirit. Amen.)
'Éirigh suas, a bhean an tí,
Is cuir do pháiste faoin gcrios' (op. cit., 250).

4. A Request for a Gift
'Éirigh suas, a cheann an tí,
Tabhair dúinn ubh na circe buí
Atá thuas i dtóin an tí
Is ná crá Dia do chroí' (op.cit., 250).
(Rise up, O head of the house, give us an egg from the yellow hen that is up at the back of the house and may God not trouble your heart.)

5. The Blessing attached to the Rite
'Pé ar bith cé rachaidh trí mo chrios
Go mba seacht fearr a bhéas sé bliain ó inniu' (op.cit., 249).
(Whoever will go through my crios may he be seven times better off a year from today.)

6. A curse on the householder who will not perform the Rite or give a gift.
'An té nach rachadh tríd an gcrios
Ní móide go mbeidh sé beo bliain ó inniu' (op.cit., 250).
(The person who will not go through the crios, will probably not be alive a year from today)

'An té nach dtabharfadh pingin dom
Go mbrise an diabhal a chos' (op.cit., 250).
(The person who would not give me a penny, may the devil
break his leg)

The same ritual pattern may be seen in other seasonal rites such
as the Rite of Samhain as it is preserved in an account from the
Ring Gaeltacht of Co Waterford (*Saol*, Deireadh Fomhair, 1991, 5).

The children went around to the houses collecting gifts. The
rite was introduced by reminding the householders that this
was the night of Samhain and the ancestral figure,Moingfhionn
was mentioned: 'Anocht Oíche Shamhna Moingfhinne banga.'

A gift was requested and a blessing called down on the generous giver, while a curse was the lot of the stingy.

In the story '*Aidid Crimthainn*' it is told how Moingfhionn
died at Samhain, having being obliged to drink a cup of poison
which she had prepared for her brother. She was a powerful
Bean Sí, well acquainted with magic, and the ordinary people
and women offered prayers to her at Samhain (O'Grady,1892,
332). Here we have two powerful females, Brigid and
Moingfhionn, presiding over two great festivals of the Celtic
Year, Imbolc and Samhain.

The same elements are noticeable in the Scottish Gaelic ritual
'rann' for '*Oiche Challuinn*' (31st December) or 'Hogmanay'. This
explains that the servants of the goddess are outside. The rite
goes back to the ancestors. A collection is made with a blessing
for the generous and a curse for the stingy (*CG* 1, 148ff).

From Donegal comes an account of a parallel practice but
with a medical rather than a protective object. The rite was performed for the purpose of curing hernia in a child. In this case it
was not a straw rope that was used but a very thin growing sally
tree that could be split and the sides held apart so that the child
could be passed through it. Then the split sally was bound so
that the sides came together and in the process of time blended
with each other so that the split was healed. In the same way, it
was believed, the hernia would be cured.

In this particular case a widow and her daughter had care of the child and although they made use of modern medicine they also adhered to the old ways:

> 'On May morning, before sunrise they took 'wee Harry' to the top of the hill behind the house. 'Edlim', I think, where in a 'slough' some willow grew. With the thumbnail – no knife must be used – the old women split a willow-wand sufficiently to allow the child to be passed through the hoop made by pressing the sides apart. These preparations made, they awaited the rising of the sun, and as the golden glory crept upward they passed the child, facing it (the sun), three times 'in the three Holy Names' – through the circle formed by the split willow, which was then carefully bound together with scarlet wool. As the young wood knit together the child's wound would heal – so they firmly believed' (*Béal.* 3, 1932, 332).

In this archaic rite careful attention is given to the rising of the sun on a significant calendrical date, just as in the rites of Brigid. It may be noted also that the use of iron is avoided, a thumbnail is used to split the willow. In the same way, in some places, the rushes used to form the Brídeog were pulled directly out of the ground instead of being cut, and so the use of an iron reaping hook was avoided (IFC 905; 39-40).

In a report from Ros Muc, Co Galway, it is said that it was the custom in that area to make a very large crios and hang it around the door of the cow house so that the animals when going in or out would pass through it and so obtain the protection of Brigid (IFC 902; 32).

CHAPTER FOURTEEN

St Brigid's Holy Wells

A popular part of the cult of Brigid today is the visitation of her wells in different areas throughout the country. Caoimhín Ó Danachair lists 12 Brigidine wells for Co Limerick (*JRSAI*, 1955-1956, 197), and they were probably more numerous at one time than they are today. However, interest in holy wells has increased of late and growing awareness of their historic and religious importance, combined with new prosperity, has resulted in local groups being appointed to repair and embelish the sites and organise local pilgrimages.

Some of St Brigid's wells are well known even beyond the local scene and enjoy considerable popularity. Among these is 'Dabhach Bhríde' in Liscannor, Co Clare, 'Sruth Bhríde' in Faughart near Dundalk, Co Louth, and 'Tobar Bhríde' in Oughtaragh, near Ballinamore, Co Leitrim, which at one time had a very elaborate ritual.

Dabhach Bhríde is found near the Cliffs of Moher in an area of great scenic beauty and behind the well, on a higher level to which steps lead, is an ancient cemetery in which the Uí Bhriain, the Kings of Dál gCais, are buried. There is a large cross here and a circular path around it and part of the Rite of the Holy Well is performed in this area known as the 'Ula Uachtarach' or upper sanctuary.

The Well itself is in the lower ground, the 'Ula Íochtarach' or lower sanctuary, enclosed in a little house full of votive offerings such as holy pictures, rosaries, medals and so forth left by pilgrims. Small items which people carry around with them, such as pens, biros and combs, are commonly found as votive offerings at holy wells.

This site has a peculiar mysterious atmosphere which may be felt at once by the pilgrim as he enters the grove and hears the gentle lapping of the water in the background. Something of the ancient 'Nemeton' (modern Irish *Neimheadh*) – the outdoor Celtic Sanctuary – is, perhaps, to be experienced here.

Many pilgrims from all over Co Clare and from the Aran Islands came to Liscannor. There were four different Pattern Days on which large groups attended: St Brigid's Eve; 'Garland Saturday' and 'Garland Sunday', that is the Saturday and Sunday of Crom Dubh (=the last Sunday of July and its vigil), and on the 15th of August, the Feast of the Assumption of the Blessed Virgin Mary into Heaven (IFC 901; 51). The really great occasion was Domhnach Chrom Dubh and the people of Clare and of Aran spent the whole night at the well. This caused some surprise to a Clare reporter:

'They left home on Saturday, held an all-night vigil at the Blessed Well and arrived home on Sunday. The strange thing about it was that those people didn't mind missing Mass on that Sunday as if the 'round' was more important' (IFC 901; 14; Mícheál De Blaca, Dún Beag). This provides an interesting insight into the native and Roman forms of Catholicism.

Candles blazed around the well (IFC 901; 79) and on St Brigid's Night itself candles were lighted all over the parish and in the surrounding parishes (IFC 901; 54).

Liscannor Well was regarded as a place of healing and crutches were left there as an indication that a pilgrim had been cured through the intercession of Blessed Brigid (IFC 901; 54). A wandering poet describes his visit to the well:

On St Brigid's Eve, as the night fell,
my mother and I went to Saint Brigid's Well,
where the candles do burn and the great walls do shine
on the graves of the dead and the vaults of O'Brien.
(IFC 901; 55-56)

Luckily, there survives an account of the Rite of Dabhach Bhríde Well. Pádraig Mag Fhloinn got the information from people from the parish of Kilfenora, and it is clear from his report that the various parts of the rite were carefully laid out in a well-organised form. In 1993, I saw a notice at the well instructing pilgrims as to how to perform the rite, and clearly only minor differences had taken place throughout the years. A slight reduction had taken place in the number of prayers to be said while performing the rounds – the Our Father, Hail Mary and Glory be to the Father to be said once while walking around the circular path *deiseal* or sunwise, instead of five times as long ago. Nowadays, one Hail Mary is said at each circumambulation of the cross at the Ula Uachtarach instead of the Our Father, Hail Mary and Glory be to the Father said formerly. The prayers to be said while making the 'rounds' vary according to the particular well and this may indicate that these were a late introduction. It is possible that originally the circumambulations were made entirely in silence. When doing the rounds, each pilgrim walks alone, one after the other; they do not proceed two by two as in a procession in the Roman Rite. Generally, nowadays, the pilgrims at Liscannor Well do not perform the rite barefooted as was the custom formerly. The barefooted pilgrim, of course, is in direct contact with the earth.

THE RITE OF ST BRIGID'S WELL AT LISCANNOR, CO CLARE
(IFC 901; 51-53)

INTRODUCTION
Go on your knees in front of the statue of St Brigid and express your intention (e.g. you come to have your headache/arthritis healed). Then say:

    Go mbeannaí Íosa duit, a Bhrighid Naofa,
    go mbeannaí Muire duit is go mbeannaím féin duit;
    Chugat a thána' mé ag gearán mo scéil chugat
    agus d'iarraidh cabhair in onóir Dé ort (IFC 901; 39).
    (May Jesus salute you, O holy Brigid, may Mary salute you
    and may I salute you myself. It it to you I have come making
    my complaint and asking your help for the honour of God.)

SAN ULA ÍOCHTARACH (In the lower sanctuary)
Go on your knees and say 5 Our Fathers, 5 Hail Marys and 5 Glorias.
Stand and proceed to make a round/circumambulation of the Statue of
St Brigid, (sunwise/deiseal – keeping the Statue at your right-hand
side). Recite the Creed while moving.
Do this 5 times.
Go on your knees at the Well.

SAN ULA UACHTARACH (In the upper sanctuary)
Go on your knees and say 5 Our Fathers, 5 Hail Marys and 5 Glorias.
Stand and make a sunwise circumambulation on the long path while
reciting the Creed (I believe ...)
Do this 5 times.

AT THE CROSS
Make a circumambulation (sunwise/deiseal) of the Cross while saying
once the Our Father, the Hail Mary and the Gloria.
Kiss the Cross.
Do this 5 times.

AT THE WELL
Descend the steps to the Ula Íochtarach and go to the Well.
Drink the water 3 times.
Go on your knees and express your intention again.

Presumeably the pilgrims deposited their votive offerings on the
wall before beginning the rounds.

According to tradition there is a fish in Liscannor Well and if
the pilgrim sees the fish he is certain to obtain his request (IFC
901; 53).

This is obviously a very clearly constructed rite along strictly
traditional lines amd worthy of its magnificent setting. As an
Introduction, the pilgrim recites the traditional 'rann' or ritual
verse: 'Go mbeannaí Íosa duit, a Bhrighid Naofa.' This is commonly used at Holy Wells with a change of name according to
the saint venerated at that particular well. The major part of the
rite consists of the *cor deiseal* or sunwise movement around the
statue of St Brigid in the lower sanctuary and around the Cross

in the upper sanctuary. At many holy wells a mug is provided for the pilgrim to drink the water 3 times in the name of the Father, Son and Holy Spirit (Logan, 1980, 34). Often local people will show the pilgrim how to perform the rite.

As with many other holy wells, tradition holds that the water here will not boil. Sometimes the pilgrim will perform the rite for nine consecutive days (IFC 901; 38-39).

If the Rounds are made outside of the four Pattern Days then they must be repeated three times to obtain the same results (IFC 901; 53).

Considering that the first of February is the Feast of St Brigid it may seem surprising that the really big occasion in which large crowds gathered for an all-night Vigil at Liscannor Well was Domhnach Chrom Dubh – the last Saturday-Sunday of July.

Máire Mac Néill, in her great book, *The Festival of Lughnasa*, illustrates the complex tradition of this area regarding the god Crom Dubh, the Lord of the Harvest, known by different names. Donn Duimhche/Donn Mac Cromáin occurs in connection with the coast on the southern side of Liscannor Bay. Another opinion connects him to the Ennistymon area. Moreover, the local saint – Mac Creiche – the interesting remains of his church are still to be seen near Liscannor – is sometimes associated with Donn. Domhnach Chrom Dubh (Garland Sunday) used to be celebrated with great rejoicing on Sliabh Callainn to the southeast of the well. In this way, Dabhach Bhríde at Liscannor occupies a site within a district in which the Festival of Lughnasa was given wide recognition (1982, 198-200, 284-285). It is notable that the second day of August, or the eleventh day according to another view, is the Feast of St Mac Creiche, thus connecting him to Domhnach Chrom Dubh and the Festival of Lughnasa (Mac Néill, 1982, 282).

In other places in Co Clare, apart from Dabhach Bhríde, the 'Turas' or pilgrimage was on the 15th August (the Assumption). It is difficult to know how old this practice is or if the clergy had some influence in attaching Lughnasa to a Christian Feastday, and indeed, the title of the Feast of the Assumption in Irish looks significant – 'Lá Fhéile Muire Mór sa bhFómhar' – the Feast of Great Mary in the Autumn. One suspects that there is a hint here of a Lughnasa background with the idea of the ripening of the corn and the first-fruits of the harvest.

Máire Mac Néill comments: 'The heritage of ancient Lughnasa is to be found in its direct descendants, the assemblies held on certain Sundays in July or on August 12th, but principally on either the Sunday before or the Sunday after August 1st (1982, 25).

There used to be a Pattern at Tobar Bhríde, Castlegar, Co Galway on the first Sunday in August (Mac Néill, 1982, 630) and a Pattern is still held at Tobar Bhríde in Co Roscommon on the last Sunday of July (Logan, 1980, 31).

Difficulty in having children is a great source of anxiety and sorrow to many married couples, and Patrick Logan (a Medical Doctor), speaks of this problem with great sympathy and understanding when discussing holy wells:

'It is quite likely that people prayed for children at many holy wells but did not speak openly about it. Recently (c. 1980) I learned of a statue to Our Lady, which was put on a tree near Tobar Mhuire near Shankill Cross in Co Roscommon. This was done some years ago by a man who had visited the well and prayed for children, and put up a statue in gratitude to Our Lady when his prayer had been answered' (1980, 82).

A remarkable and most valuable account of Well Ritual dealing with this matter comes from Janet and Colin Bord. A man from Aberdeen in Scotland, while he was still quite young, happened by chance to oversee the ritual being performed.

The year was about 1850 and the rite appears simple without any marked Christian element.

Three women were involved as patients, and an old woman conducted the ritual taking complete charge of the proceedings. A somewhat similar situation is known from some Irish wells where a woman distributed the water and gave directions to the pilgrims.

This woman knelt on a flagstone at the edge of the well and gave the signal to the three women to begin the *Cor Deiseal* – the circumambulation of the well following the course of the sun. This meant that the three women, one after the other, walked around the well sunwise, keeping the well at the right hand side. As each one passed in front of her, the old woman, in her role of celebrant in the rite, dipped her hands in the well and sprinkled each woman generously. This was done at each of the three processions around the well. None of the women cried out as the cold water touched her body.

When the ritual had been completed the old woman rose from her kneeling position and all headed for home (1985, 36).

The proceedings were conducted in complete silence, the women obviously knowing what to do and the celebrant merely giving hand-signals. There is a marked difference between this rite and that performed at the ordinary Holy Well. Normally, no special celebrant is required. Each devotee performs the rite for himself/herself. Here, however, the old woman, representing, perhaps, the goddess herself, conducts the ritual action.

This is a particularly valuable account of the use of a holy well for a distinct purpose – the healing of human infertility. It has about it the air of antiquity and authenticity. The *cor deiseal* or sunwise circumambulation of the well is performed in silence with no mention of Christian prayers such as the Our Father, Hail Mary and Gloria being added, as is done at many holy wells. Strangely enough, the drinking of the water is not mentioned but only sprinkling. It is unlikely that the observer would have missed this if it had taken place. It is unfortunate that he didn't indicate the time of the year in which the rite was performed, whether it were an ordinary day or a day of Calendrical significance such as the winter solstice (21 December), summer solstice (21 June), the spring equinox (21 March), the autumn equinox (21 September), or one of the four Insular Celtic Feasts – Samhain (1 November), Imbolg (1 February), Bealtaine (1 May), or Lughnasa (1 August).

At these times one could postulate a certain distinct relationship between the sun and the earth which would be significant in terms of fertility. Presumeably the rite took place early in the morning to avoid publicity and the water of the spring would be extremely cold. This fact gives no real indication of the time of the year.

Taking into account, however, the two great Insular Celtic Feasts associated with fertility, that is Samhain and Bealtaine, it is reasonable to assume that these would be the likely dates for the performance of the rite. If, for instance, the rite took place at Samhain, the woman might hope that conception would take place immediately and that nine months later she would have a child at Lughnasa, the beginning of the corn harvest. Lughnasa is also known at 'Brón Trogain' (the grief of the earth) as at that time the earth is in travail with the harvest. A woman whose child was conceived at Samhain and born at Lughnasa would thus be in harmony with a cosmic pattern, giving birth at the same time as the earth itself, the Great Mother.

Similarly, if the rite took place at Bealtaine, the woman concerned might hope that her child would be born nine months later at Imbolc, the infancy of the year when all nature is awakening from its winter sleep and new life is evident everywhere, the Feast of Brigid, the *bean ghlúine* (midwife) of the Virgin Mary herself, according to Irish and Scottish Gaelic tradition.

An aura of ancient sanctity is evident at St Brigid's Well at Liscannor. The steps leading up from the lower to the upper sanctuary bring the pilgrim into the domain of the dead whose graves surround 'the vaults of O'Brien', the kings of the Dál gCais whose place of Inauguration was the mound of Maigh Adhair, near Tulla, where the *Bainis Rí* took place in which the local king was symbolically married to the goddess of the land to produce the fertility of the soil.

At St Brigid's Well in Liscannor, then, like the other holy wells mentioned in Galway and Roscommon, the Pattern occurred not only at Imbolc but at Lughnasa as well so that Brigid was linked to the sowing of the corn and the reaping of the corn. Indeed, a legend recalls her workmen reaping the corn of her land in brilliant sunshine while torrential rain poured down on the surrounding farms.

A glance at the calendar will show Imbolc and Lughnasa facing across at each other, six months appart. In these particular cases, the site of the cult of Brigid was also used for that of Crom Dubh.

The Feast of Lughnasa celebrated the first-fruits of the earth, both the natural fruits such as the *Fraocháin* or purple whortleberries and the cultivated fruits such as corn and potatoes. This, however, does not correspond to the Anglican Harvest Festival which is celebrated much later when the harvest has been gathered in at 'Harvest Home' and is a heart-felt occasion of thanksgiving to God for the fruits of the earth. In the case of Lughnasa, only a part of the corn is ripe and the Lughnasa Festival is meant to envigorate the earth so that a full ripening will occur and an abundant harvest will emerge.

The Festival of Lughnasa, celebrated in the past in so may areas of the country and still celebrated in Puck Fair, Killorglin, Co Kerry, with a three day holiday of marketing, drinking and entertainment, was one of the great traditional feasts of Ireland going back to a remote past.

It was characterised by climbing certain sacred hills and depositing a sheaf of the newly-ripened corn at the top. The Fraocháins were gathered, games were played, bonfires blazed. It was a time when people from other areas met; flirting took place which often led to eventual marriage six months later at Shrove Tuesday, before Lent began and close to the Feast of Brigid.

Thus two great Feasts, Imbolc and Lughnasa, marked important stages in the social life of the young.

Domhnach Chrom Dubh (the Sunday around the end of July and the beginning of August) got its name from the old harvest god Crom Cróich, associated with Maigh Sléacht near Ballymagauran, Co Cavan. The Rennes *Dindsenchas of Mag Slécht* (No.85) says of him:

'Tis there was the king-idol of Erin, namely the Crom Cróich, and around him twelve idols made of stones; but he was of gold. Until Patrick's advent, he was the god of every folk that colonised Ireland. To him they used to offer the firstlings of every issue and the chief scions of every clan. 'Tis to him that Erin's king, Tigernmas son of Follach, repaired on Hallontide,together with the men and women of Ireland, in order to adore him. And they all prostrated before him, so that the tops of their foreheads and the gristle of their noses and the caps of their knees and the ends of their elbows broke, and three fourths of the men of Erin perished at those prostrations. Whence Mag Slécht – Plain of Prostrations' (*Rev. Celt.* XVI).

This legend suggests a stone circle of twelve monoliths with an outlier or a larger stone in the centre, and Darraugh Rath, overlooking the plain and lakes, has been suggested as the site of Crom Cróich's sanctuary (cf Dalton, J.P., PRI,Vol. XXXVI, Sect. C). The landscape here is indeed quite spectacular and from the hill-top rath one could easily imagine this stingy harvest god looking down with disdain on his worshippers below him on the plain of Maigh Sléacht as they prostrated in the direction of the hill and brought their bags of corn to him as offerings on the Feast of Samhain, in the hope that he would be generous and give them food in plenty.

However, according to the legend, St Patrick came along and hit Crom Cróich with his crozier and overturned him, and his twelve sub-gods disappeared into the ground up to their heads. And St Patrick cursed the demon and expelled him into hell (*Vita Tripartita*).

From Dalton's magnificent survey and detailed map of this area on the boundary of Co Cavan and Co Leitrim, embracing Sliabh an Iarainn, Fenagh Abbey, Maigh Réin, Maigh Sléacht, Lake Garadice, Slieve Russell, the Cuilcagh Mountains, Ballyconnell and Darraugh Rath, it seems certain that this area was a Mecca of ancient religious cults and early Christian church foundations. Perhaps the peculiar landscape of the Cavan area, with its small hills and multitude of lakes, made it difficult of access from outside sources so that local cults flourished undisturbed.

At any rate, Crom Cróich (the Bent One of the Hill) was also known as Crom Dubh and even Morc – Crom spelled backwards – and in the Patrician legend we have a Christianised version of 'Cath Maighe Tuireadh na bhFomhórach', the primordial myth of the conflict of the forces of Light and the forces of Darkness.

The Battle of Maigh Tuireadh, while sited in Maigh Tuireadh in Co Sligo – an area of megaliths – is essentially a supernatural battle between the gods of light, the Tuatha Dé Danann, or Aos Sí, and the gods of darkness, the Fomhóraigh – the primitive but powerful gods of the depths of the sea. A similar division of gods is discernable in Greece – the Olympians and the Titans.

In the myth, the bright gods (TDD) are oppressed by the dark gods (Fomhóraigh) and the Tuatha Dé Danann rebel. Led by the powerful Lugh, they fight a mighty battle at Maigh Tuireadh against the Fomhóraigh who are led by Balar of the Evil Eye. Balar's evil eye spurts a malevolent poisonous fire which destroys everything in front of it. However, Lugh makes a cast with his sling and drives a stone through Balar's evil eye, carrying it out the back of his head to destroy a part of his own followers. After this unforseen disaster, the Fomhóraigh flee and the Tuatha Dé Danann proclaim a mighty victory for themselves and are now free from the onerous burdens imposed on them by the Fomhóraigh.

Nevertheless, the victorious Tuatha Dé Danann realise that Balar, Breas, Crom Cróich, Crom Dubh, Morc or whatever he may be called, knows more about agriculture and has a much greater competence than they themselves, so they allow Crom Dubh to be in charge of corn production – Lord of the Harvest. But his activities are curtailed and he is obliged to distribute the corn generously to all. He is constrained by Lugh and the Tuatha Dé Danann though he is nominally in charge. Perhaps an echo of this situation may be seen in the great Lughnasa Festival of today – Puck Fair. The Puck, apparently representing Crom Dubh, is enthroned on a high scaffolding in the midst of the Fair and as King of the Festival he presides over the proceedings.

He is carried to the site with music and great honour, he is well fed and respected but it will be noticed that he is also well shackled with ropes around his four legs. Now, this may be just a practical measure to prevent the goat from falling off the scaffold. Nevertheless, it may also be symbolic in defining the role of Crom Dubh as agricultural expert but not having entirely a freehand in the distribution of the harvest. This belongs to Lugh alone. A remarkable statue from Puy de Dome in France shows a giant crouching down while a horse ridden by a warrior has his front legs placed firmly on the giant's shoulders. This may be another expression of Lugh's ultimate supremecy over the Lord of the Harvest.

After the Battle of Maigh Tuireadh (cf Gray, E., *Cath Maige Tuired*, Dublin 1982), Lugh and the Tuatha Dé Danann march in a great victory procession to Tailtean, Sliabh na Caillí, the great-megalithic cemetery near Oldcastle in Co Meath. Here the *Bainis Rí* or wedding of the king to the goddess of the land takes place and Lugh is declared king in place of Nuadha, who has been killed in the battle, as seen in the story *Tochmarc Emire*. All this takes place at Samhain. Nine months pass by and Lugh and the goddess have a child at Lughnasa – *Brón Trogain* – the birth-pangs of the earth. The child of course is the new harvest, the wheat, oats and barley. The farmer cuts the first ripened sheaf of the new harvest and takes it up to the top of a Lughnasa hill and lays it there as an offering and acknowledgement to Lugh and indeed Crom Dubh of the gift of the corn. In Co Limerick Domhnach Chrom Dubh was translated as 'Black Stoop Sunday': 'Crom stooped because he carried on his back the first great sheaf of wheat, the inaugural and sacred gift from the Otherworld' (Dames, 1992, 101). In the Lios or great stone circle at Grange, Lough Gur, a huge stone in the circle is called *Rannach Chrom Dubh*, and the goddess Áine of Cnoc Áine and Lough Gur, who is probably the same as Áine of the north of Ireland, is actually linked to Crom in a report from Co Louth where the Sunday is called *Domhnach Aine agus Chroim Duibh* (the Sunday of Áine and Crom Dubh) (Dames, 1992, 101).

Thus Brigid is not the only one to be linked with Crom Dubh or Donn. Within a vast complex of myth and harvest lore, some sites dedicated to Brigid also serve as Lughnasa sites, and Brigid takes her place as Lady of the Corn beside the mighty figures of Lugh and Crom Dubh.

A detailed account of another celebrated St Brigid's Well has come down to us. It is that of Oughteraugh (Uachtar Achaidh), near Ballinamore in Co Leitrim and the pilgrimage to it took place on the first of February. Like the Liscannor Well, the pilgrim was expected to set out on his journey with a firm intention and permit no dawdling on the way (IFC 905; 167).

The Rite to be performed:

1. Say the Rosary 3 times (=15 decades) on your way from your home to the gate of the Cemetery.

2. On the stone stile at the entrance to the old cemetery, go on your knees and and say 5 Our Fathers and 5 Hail Marys for the souls of those buried here.

3. Then perform the *Cor Deiseal* (sunwise circumambulation) around the Rowan Tree while saying the Pater, Ave and Credo once.

4. Do the same thing at the tree at the bottom of the Cemetery.

5. Do the same thing at the tree at the side of the Cemetery.

6. Go to the standing stone on which St Brigid's head is sculptured and say 5 Paters and 5 Aves.

7. Come out of the Cemetery on to the road then and say 5 decades of the Rosary.

8. Go back into the Cemetery again and perform the *Cor Deiseal* around the same 3 trees, exactly as you have done already.

9. Come out of the Cemetery on to the road then and say 5 decades of the Rosary.

10. Go back into the Cemetery again and perform the *Cor Deiseal* around the same 3 trees, exactly as you have done already.

11. Come out of the Cemetery on to the road then and say 5 decades of the Rosary.

12. Go back into the Cemetery again and perform the *Cor Deiseal* around the 3 trees, exactly as you have done already

13. Then go to St Brigid's Well and perform the *Cor Deiseal* around it 3 times while saying a decade of the Rosary or some other prayers (IFC 905; 167-168).

There is obviously a great deal of ritual repetition at this well involving a considerable amount of movement. This may originally have been done in complete silence.

The Rosary in the form we have it today is popularly attributed to St Dominic (died 1221), but may be somewhat later as early paintings of the saint don't show him holding Rosary Beads. At any rate, the ritual is decidedly more archaic than the accompanying prayers.

A cure for toothache is attributed to this Well of Uachtar Achaidh and there is a tradition there that the well was at one time closer to the cemetery but moved to its present position when dishonoured. This is a common tradition (Logan, 1980, 85, 22-23, 67). It is notable that sacred trees and the proximity of an ancient Cemetery are important features of this site.

As regards the offering and use of pebbles or small stones, a fine example is found in St Enda's Well in Bearna. When the number of rounds is large – in many wells 9 rounds are specified – it is difficult for the pilgrim to count the exact number. The custom of taking a handful of pebbles and dropping one after each round solves the problem: 'Rachfá timpeall an tobair seacht n-uaire. Bheadh seacht mearóg i do láimh. Chaithfeá ceann acu isteach sa tobar gach turas' (*Béal.* 48-49, 1980-1981, 149). (You would go around the Well 7 times. You would have 7 pebbles in your hand. You would throw one of them into the Well at each round.) When the pilgrim's hand is empty he has completed the ritual number of rounds.

In Killorglan, Co Kerry, home of the Lughnasa Puck Fair, it was the custom for the woman of the house to stick a pin in the Brídeog (doll) and leave it there when 'Lucht na Brídeoige' visited the house on the Feast of St Brigid (IFC 899; 27). Pins are commonly found at holy wells, presumeably left there as offerings. Some wells are called 'Pin Wells' from this practice (Bord, 1985, 70,170), and the pin was often bent. This may be an echo of bending a sword or breaking a pot before consigning it to a sacred lake or a tomb as an offering. In other words, by bending or breaking the object, it was rendered useless for this world and was transferred to the Otherworld. The pins may also indicate that the well was frequented by pregnant women requesting an easy delivery, as women attending a woman about to give birth were careful to remove knots from their clothing to indicate loosening and freedom (Frazer, 1923,238). The same idea would probably hold for pins which of their nature are constricting.

Pieces of cloth are frequently to be seen hanging on the *Bile* or sacred tree beside the holy well. The wells are sometimes called 'Rag Wells'.

It is not certain if these are votive offerings like the other items – holy pictures, rosary beads, coins, biros, combs, etc. – deposited on a stone shelf at the well. The fact that these pieces of clothing are not placed in the ordinary 'Offertory Table', however, may indicate that they are not of quite the same nature. It seems more likely that, originally, a part of the pilgrim's clothing which was in contact with his/her body was hung on the tree or bush as a means of transferring the disease from the body to the tree. For instance, a woman suffering from headache might hang her headscarf on the tree. The tree would accept her headache and she would go home without it.

Sometimes, the piece of cloth was brought into more direct contact with the well *and* the disease, for in some places a piece of cloth was soaked in the water and then rubbed to the affected limb, the hand or the leg, for example, and then hung up on the *bile* (Logan, 1980, 116). This seems to be in accord with the phrase used by pilgrims to St Gobnat's Well in Baile Bhóirne in

West Cork: 'Ar impí an Tiarna agus Naoimh Ghobnatan mo chuid tinnis d'fhágaint anso' (*JCHAS*, 1952, 60). (After the supplication of the Lord and St Gobnat to leave my sickness here.)

The piece of cloth hanging on the tree may also represent the supplicant's prayer after he has left the shrine in the sense that it remains there praying for him after he has departed, in the same way as a woman entering a church,and saying a prayer before a statue of a saint, lights a candle and then goes off home. The candle continues her prayer after she has gone.

We now turn to another Brigid's Well which is especially associated with the life of the saint herself. This is *Sruth Bhríde*, the Stream of Brigid, at Faughart, a few miles from Dundalk, Co Louth.

This is a place of pilgrimage and a long tradition holds that this area is St Brigid's birthplace (IFC 905; 108). Brigid foretold that this district would produce milk and butter in plenty (IFC 905; 63).

This particular sacred site may be divided in two parts – *An Reilig* (the graveyard) and *Sruth Bhríde* (the Stream).

Nowadays, it is the stream which plays the major part in the pilgrimage but originally much of the ritual took place in the graveyard, almost a mile away on top of Faughart Hill, an Iron Age Hill Fort guarding the pass between Leinster and Ulster. In this ancient graveyard, a stone commemorating the death of Edward Bruce is found. He was killed in the Battle of Faughart in 1318 but is not actually buried here (Meehan, 2002, 292-294).

Within the graveyard, there are the remains of a church known as *Teampall Bhríde na hÁirde Móire* (Brigid's Temple of the Great Height). Near it is St Brigid's Stone. Some meagre remains of an early Christian foundation can be discerned. Near the ruins of the church, within the graveyard, is St Brigid's Well which is visited by pilgrims on the first of February. It is enclosed in a stone beehive hut with steep steps going down to the water. Long ago there used to be a skull at the well from which people drank the water thrice to cure toothache (IFC 905; 57-58).

In the account given by Stanley Howard, it says that pieces of cloth and rosaries were to be seen hanging from the trees at each side of the well (*JRSAI*, 1906, 73).

A description of the rite practised in the graveyard is given by Mary Daly who actually saw the ritual being performed and heard the old people descibe it.

The rite was performed barefoot. The pilgrim went around the monastery (the church) and at each of the four corners of the building he said a decade of the Rosary.

Then he went around the Stone nine times on his bare knees saying a decade of the Rosary at each round. Sometimes, his knees would bleed from the roughness of the stone.

Then the pilgrim went around another stone – *Cloch na bhFaithní* (stone of the warts) – four times saying a decade of the Rosary at each round.

Strangely enough, a visit to the well in the graveyard is not mentioned by the narrator. She says that at this point the pilgrim proceeded to *Sruth Bhríde*, the stream, a considerable distance away, and on his way he said prayers as the actual journey was considered to be part of the pilgrimage.

Having arrived at the Sruth he performed the stations there as they are performed today. In the old days, this pilgrimage in which the graveyard and the stream were both involved, took about four hours. (IFC 905; 54-55).

It does seem, that at the present time, the part of the pilgrimage performed in the graveyard has declined and most of the action takes place at the Sruth.

However, it must be remembered that a great development took place at Faughart from 1933 onwards when the clergy erected an impressive shrine to St Brigid near the stream, with an altar inside and a large statue of her over it.

A flight of steps leads up to the path in front of the shrine and the Stations of the Cross occupy both sides of the path. A Calvary was built and a Lourdes Grotto added and other additions were made at various times.

While purists might well deplore this type of clerical intrusion, with its foreign ways and lack of sensitivity to native tradition, into such a traditional sacred site as Faughart, it may be said that places of pilgrimage try to cater for all comers and many pilgrims are untroubled by strange mixtures of rituals and devotions. The life of St Brigid shows that she followed the gospel closely and the Stations of the Cross are indeed a poignant reminder of the last days of Jesus. The Stations are in themselves a kind of mini-pilgrimage to the Holy Land for those unable to undertake the journey in reality. Similarly, according to an ancient tradition in Ireland and Scotland, Brigid went to Palestine to assist the Blessed Virgin Mary at the birth of Christ.

It is, however, interesting to notice that this clerical development is centred on the stream leaving the hill site with its well, church, graveyard, sacred trees and ritual stones undisturbed. In this connection, Stanley Howard's remarks may be of some significance:

> 'I may add that neither priest nor parson has any control over the churchyard or anything in it; it belongs entirely to the people of the place, and nothing can be touched in it without their sanction. This is probably a curious survival of the tribal system.' (JRSAI 1906, 73)

In the year 1934 Cardinal MacRory chose Faughart as the National Shrine of St Brigid for the whole country and the first-national pilgrimage took place on the first Sunday of July, 1934, with an attendance of 10,000 people from all over Ireland. As well as on this day, many pilgrims came on the first of February and on the Feast of the Assumption (15 August) the ecclesiastical feast close to the Festival of Lughnasa (Carey, 1982, 14-17).

The official directory for the pilgrimage gives the general layout of the ritual. A serious attempt was made to blend together both the native and ecclesiastical traditions:

Preliminaries

On entering the grounds, the Pilgrim says one Our Father, Hail Mary and Creed. The pilgrim may then remove shoes and stockings, if wishing to carry out the Stations barefoot.

a. Say Act of Contrition at foot of steps.

b. Pater, Ave, Creed on the top steps.

c. Say 5 Our Fathers and 5 Hail Marys at Shrine.

TRADITIONAL STATIONS: PART ONE

Descend to Fountain and, making the Sign of the Cross, either drink the water for an internal malady or bathe the part affected for external malady.

1. Say Our Father, Hail Mary, Creed, on near bank.

2. Repeat these prayers on far bank.

3. Repeat again on flat stone in centre of stream.

4. Make ten circuits of mound on which the Cross stands, reciting one decade of the Rosary.

STATIONS OF THE CROSS

Follow the stream to the lower area, making the Stations of the Cross en route.

TRADITIONAL STATIONS: PART TWO

5. Say Our Father, Hail Mary, Creed on near bank.

6. Repeat these prayers at 'Hoof-Marked Stone'.

7. Repeat again at 'Knee Stone'.

8. Repeat again at 'Waist Stone'.

9. Make ten circuits of 'Eye Stone', reciting one decade of the Rosary.

10. Kneel at 'Head Stone' and say one Hail Mary.

BRAT BRÍDE ORAINN

From this Ordo it is clear that different sources have been combined. Some elements are derived from general ecclesiastical practice and some from native tradition. Undoubtedly, clerical influence is very obvious there since it became the National Shrine of St Brigid, but that is not to say that the native traditional element has been obliterated. On the contrary, the native element has been respected and indeed clarified to an extent that possibly was not so obvious before.

The items: a, b, c, and the Stations of the Cross belong to the more clerical side of the rite, though these elements are perfectly well known to native tradition also.

The a, b. c, items look as though they are adaptations of the prayers said by the priest at the foot of the altar, while going up the steps, and when kissing the altar, as in the prescribed ritual of the Mass in the Tridentine Rite in use in the 1930s. Prayers known by heart, such as the Our Father, Hail Mary and I Believe, are substituted for the proper prayers of the Mass. Following the ancient tradition of the Celts, this is an outdoor ritual and no books are in use. In this it varies profoundly from the ecclesiastical tradition which relies so heavily on the book during liturgical functions that it requires a covered space or building to protect the book from rain and storm. This is a rite of movement, not of listening to readings or sermons.

One might well be doubtful about 'Make ten circuits of mound on which Cross stands reciting one decade of the Rosary' (No 4). It is most likely that this was originally nine rounds – a number already in use at 'Cloch na Reilige' in the graveyard (IFC 905; 55) and very common at Holy Wells, being the sacred number 3 multiplied by 3.

> 'The number nine figures so prominently in Celtic tradition that it has been described as the "northern counterpart of the sacred seven of Near Eastern Cultures" '(Rees, 1976, 55).

Nine Rounds are made at 'Turas na Duimhche', at 'Tobar na Croise', at 'Tobar Ghobnait', at 'Tobar Mhichíl', at 'Tobar Mhuire' and at 'Tobar Fhionáin' – all of them in the Kerry Gaeltacht of Corca Dhuibhne (JRSAI, 1960, 71-76). The same nine rounds are found in St Patrick's Well at Lough Gur, Co Limerick.

It does appear, that by prescribing ten rounds there has been a departure from native tradition in this instance. The reason for this innovation was probably an effort at simplification. The author probably decided that as there were 10 Hail Marys in a decade of the Rosary, there should be a round for each Hail Mary, hence 10 rounds. Here, perhaps, a comparatively modern devotional exercise was allowed to interfere with a ritual of extreme antiquity.

In the Ordo page, six stones are mentioned: the Flat Stone (An Chloch Leathan); the Hoof-Marked Stone (Cloch na Crúibe); the Knee Stone (Cloch na nGlún); the Waist Stone (Cloch na Coime); the Eye Stone (Cloch na Súile); and the Head Stone (Cloch an Chinn). The tradition of the area emphasises three of these Stones – Cloch na nGlún, Cloch na Crúibe and Cloch na Súile – as these three stones feature in an episode in the life of Brigid in local lore.

According to the legend, a certain king wanted Brigid to marry him but she refused. He would not accept her refusal, however, and she was forced to flee from him. He followed her furiously on horseback. He caught up with her at Faughart stream. She knelt down on a stone beside the stream and began to pray. The print of her knees can still be seen on the stone – Cloch na nGlún. To disfigure herself and so get rid of him she plucked out one of her eyes and threw it away. The eye fell on a certain stone and left its mark on it. This can be seen to the present day and consequently the stone is called 'Cloch na Súile'. At this point Brigid was so ugly that the king did not recognise her. He turned about quickly and made off, but in turning, the horse left the print of its hoof on a nearby stone and consequently this stone is known as 'Cloch na Crúibe' (IFC 905; 47-48).

The mentality of *Dinnseanchas*, or lore of places, is evident in this type of story. A certain field, or stone, or road or some other feature of the landscape is named after an incident which occurred there. Undoubtedly, this type of ritual landscape appealed enormously to pilgrims as they recalled incidents in Brigid's life which were physically recorded in the landscape.

This phenomenon of a ritual landscape is also recorded in the great shrine of St Gobnat in Baile Bhóirne, West Cork. Here again, certain episodes in St Gobnat's life are recalled in local placenames. Near the sanctuary is 'An Cumar Bodhar' (the Deaf Ravine), an isolated glen where St Gobnat let a sick nun live to avoid the noise of the public road. Another local site is 'Goirtín na Plá' (the little field of the plague). According to tradition, this field marks the spot where Gobnat stopped a deadly plague from entering her own territory of Baile Bhóirne (JCHAS, 1952, 57-59).

Essentially, the legend in Faughart is one of flight from a pursuing enemy and this has international counterparts. In its Brigidine form, it may be considered as a variation of the well-known medieval story 'The Virgin's Grain Miracle' or 'The Instant Harvest'.

The story, which circulated widely in written form in the twelfth century, may have had a much earlier oral form. It was based essentially on 'The Flight into Egypt' story and described King Herod's soldiers pursuing the Holy Family in order to kill the child in accordance with the king's decree (Mt 2:13-15).

On the way to Egypt, according to the story, the Holy family passes by a field in which a farmer is sowing corn. The Virgin Mary instructs the farmer to tell any passing soldiers who may come along pursuing them that he had seen a Mother and Child passing by when he had been sowing the grain. Next morning when the farmer arrives at his field he is astonished to see that the the corn he had sown the day before is now fully grown and ripe for harvesting. He gets his reaping hook and begins to harvest the corn. Then the soldiers arrive and ask him if he as seen a family passing by. He says he saw them pass by when he was sowing the grain. The soldiers naturally conclude that this was months ago and that they are much too late. They return home and the Holy Family arrives safely in Egypt.

This type of adventure and escape from a pursuing enemy is also connected with other saints such as Radegund, Macrine, Walpurga and Milburga (Berger, 1988, 90).

As regards Macrine, she was fleeing from the giant Gargantua who was pursuing her hotly. She rode on a mule whose shoes were turned backwards so that the giant was uncertain if she were coming or going. She passed by a field in which farmers were sowing oats. She instructed them to tell the giant that she passed by when they were sowing the oats. Next morning the oats was fully grown and ripe to the astonishment of the farmers. They began cutting the corn. Then Gargantua came along and asked them if they had seen a woman going by. They said they had when they were sowing the oats. The giant concluded that that was months ago and decided to turn back. Before going home, however, he cleaned his mighty boots and so much mud came off them that they formed two local hills. On one of them a chapel was built in honour of St Macrine and pilgrims flocked to it to invoke her help (Berger, 1988, 60-61).

Similar tales concerning the grain are recorded of St Radegunda, St Walpurga and St Milburga and straw images of the goddess of the corn occur in various kinds of 'Corn Dollies' formed from the Last Sheaf (Berger, 1988, 64), Here in Christianised form the old agricultural goddess of the corn lives on – 'The Goddess Obscured' as Professor Pamela Berger so aptly describes her.

In Faughart, the story of St Brigid's flight from an unwelcome pursuer is still indicated in the stones, and this element unites her to her counterparts in France. The corn element or 'Instant Harvest' theme, however, is absent in the Faughart variant, though Brigid, as Lady of the Harvest is indicated in various ways, as we have seen – in the straw crosses, in the mixing of the corn seed from Brigid's Cross with the seed being sown in springtime, in legends of fine weather for Brigid's havesting operations while it rained in other farms. In Faughart, which may not have been a wheat-growing area, the corn element is absent.

But perhaps the fertility element is actually present but under a different form.

The tradition of this area says that this is the place where Brigid was born (IFC 905; 108). Because of this, it is believed that

she has a special relationship with this district, that it contains
the best grazing-land in Ireland, and that lightening causes no
damage here (IFC 905; 65). Brigid had a garden on the Hill of
Faughart and animals seek out that place to give birth easily
(IFC 905; 52). Brigid made a prophecy that the land here would
be good for milk and butter production (IFC 905; 63). From the
tradition of the country it is clear that cows and milk production
were of enormous importance throughout the centuries.

A man from the area brings together very effectively Brigid's
flight and the fertility of the place from the point of view of milk
production:

> '… And when the man (pursuer) (had) seen her, and her after
> disfiguring herself, he didn't know her at all and left her to
> herself. She brought a blessing on Faughart ever since. I've
> heard it is the best grazing-land in all Ireland' (IFC 905; 64-65;
> Frank Woods, Narrator; M. J. Murphy, Scribe).

The legend of *Glas Ghaibhneann* is widespread in Ireland. She is a
miraculous cow which gives enormous quantities of milk – but
she is not to be insulted (Ó hÓgáin, 1990, 240-241). In Faughart,
however, she belongs to Brigid.

According to the legend, the Glas Ghaibhneann considered it
a mortal insult to place a small milking vessel under her. A certain woman did this. This noble cow filled the vessel courteously
but she was highly insulted and herself and her calf departed
immediately to the sea and there are two rocks still to be seen
there called 'An Bhó agus an Lao' (IFC 906; 16-17).

It does appear that here we have a variation of the 'Instant
Harvest' theme. On account of the different circumstances, it is
not grain which is emphasised here but milk – milk takes the
place of grain and the farmers here attribute the excellent graz-
ing land to Brigid, just as the French farmers attributed their
good harvests to Macrine and Radagunda.

A quaintly topical interpretation is given to the belief that in
the Faughart area lightening does no harm as it does in other
districts. During the 'Troubles', hundreds of local men were
gathered on Faughart Hill while the 'Black and Tans' occupied

the road below. Things looked bleak for those on the hill as the Black and Tans were armed with a plentiful supply of explosives. But, despite all their efforts, the explosives failed to go off and the men on the hill made their escape unharmed (IFC 905; 65).

Brigid's escape from her pursuer was the archetype for the local peoples' escape from lightening and explosives. She had demonstrated her ability to quell the violently destructive power of fire in its natural and artificial forms.

CHAPTER FIFTEEN

Saoire ar Chasaibh
(A Holiday from Turning)

A custom practised on St Brigid's Feast was known as *Saoire ar Chasaibh* and referred to the turning of wheels. Work which involved the turning of wheels such as spinning, ploughing, transport by wheeled vehicles, etc., was forbidden. A report from Co Cork, explains the custom neatly:

'Lá 'le Bríde ina shaoire ar chasaibh agus ní chasaidís aon ní an lá sin. Ní dhéantaí sníomh, ná deilbh, ná treabhadh, agus ní chuirtí capall faoi thrucail' (IFC 900; 12; Nóra Bean Uí Laoghaire, Meall an Mhanaigh, Beantraí, a d'aithris).

(St Brigid's Day used to be a holiday from turning and nothing was turned that day. They used not to weave or spin or plough and they used not to put a horse under a cart.)

Whatever involved turning wheels was forbidden on St Brigid's Day. A report from Co Kerry states that the spinning wheel used to be dismantled on the night before to prevent any violation of the rule (IFC 899; 5).

Another report from Kerry states: '... the people would allow no wheels to be turned on that day, either spinning-wheel, cart-wheels or any other wheels, in honour of the saint' (IFC 899; 17-18; John O'Donoghue, Kilgarvan).

Although the custom was perfectly clear, the people found it difficult to give any satisfactory explanation of its meaning. Seán Segersiúin of Rinnín Dubh, An Coireán, Killarney, maintained that it was Brigid herself who was responsible for the custom. It was she who taught women how to use a sheep's wool to make clothes. Up to then they had no knowledge of this art. On this one day, then, they refrain from spinning out of reverence for Brigid (IFC 899; 52-53) and to express their esteem.

In this theory, Brigid is put forward as a 'culture hero' who brings knowledge and skills to the human race enabling them to advance towards a civilised form of existence.

Another report describes the bad luck which results from a violation of the custom: A certain woman was spinning on St Brigid's Day. She refused to stop when told what day it was. A great storm came that night and swept the roof off her house. It did no harm whatever to the houses of her neighbours (IFC 899; 165-166).

It is likely that the idea began with Brigid and the art of spinning. Since spinning involved a wheel, the presumption is that from the spinning -wheel the concept expanded to cover all kinds of wheels such as those on carts. From this the saying evolved: 'Lá 'le Bríde gan troscadh, gan saoire, gan cead casadh tointe' (IFC 900; 34). (St Brigid's Day without fasting, without holidaying, without permission to turn a shuttle.)

In this context Caesar's statement comes to mind (*De Bello Gallico*, VI, 17, 2) as he discusses the opinion of the Celts that the goddess Minerva (or her Celtic equivalent) originated the Arts: 'Minerva transmitted the beginnings of the arts and crafts' (Tierney, 1960, 244). With regard to this goddess, MacCulloch states: 'The Celtic Minerva, or the goddess equated with her, "taught the elements of industry and the arts", and is thus the equivalent of the Irish Brigid. Her functions are in keeping with the position of women as the first civiliser – discovering agriculture, spinning, the art of poetry, etc.' (1911, 41).

This is an echo of Cormac Mac Cuileannáin's description of Brigid the goddess whom the *filí* or learned class venerated as 'Bé Éigse' (Lady of Poetry). Along with her were her two sisters 'Bé Leighis' (Lady of Medicine) and 'Be Ghaibhneachta' (Lady of Ironwork) – the three daughters of An Daghdha (Stokes, 1862, 8).

In a report from Oileán Cléire, Co Cork, Brigid's curse on those who violated the *geis* or taboo is described as being quite-severe. It could happen that the ploughman broke his hand or his leg or a horse broke a leg or, perhaps, a crop failure occurred. In cases such as these the people believed 'gurbh í Bríd a chuir-

feadh mallacht ar an duine, nó ar an mbeithíoch, nó ar an obair'
(IFC 900; 36). (that it was Brigid that would put a curse on the
person, or on the animal, or on the work.)

The phrase used in the same report, 'B'fhéidir ná fásfadh aon
ní ins an talamh a iompofaí Lá 'le Bríde' (Perhaps nothing would
grow in the land that was turned over (ploughed) on St Brigid's
Day), expresses clearly Brigid's power over the fertility or barrenness of the soil. This feeling is found in other areas and in this
instance the influence of the goddess Brigid on the cult of Brigid
the saint is visible.

A dramatic and spectacular presentation of the power of the
goddess over the fertility or infertility of the land lasted on until
the nineteenth century in the district of Savoy in France. It consisted of a procession from Mache to Bissey, about three kilo-
metres apart, on the Feast of St Valentine (14 February). A
woman, representing the goddess, sat in a cart which was
drawn through the cultivated fields accompanied by large numbers of people and the abbot and monks of the local Benedictine
Monastery of Mache. The woman representing the goddess of
the land carried a horn full of insects injurious to the crops. She
also carried an empty cage. The procession advanced with great
jollity. When the procession finally arrived in Bissey, the church
officials put a live cock into the cage and all those assembled for
the occasion drank wine together. Mass was celebrated and afterwards the people regaled themselves with dancing and good
cheer. Young childless couples brought bouquets of flowers as
an offering. At nightfall, the procession back to Mache began
and the youths gave the cock in the cage to the abbot. By tradition, it was the abbot's duty to feed the cock during the interval
between St Valentine's Day (14 February) and the Feast of St
Peter' Chair at Antioch (22 February). Then the cock was pierced
by a lance and killed.

This ritual gives a very vivid presentation of the power of the
goddess over the fertility of the land. It was held on St
Valentine's Day at the middle of February when preparation of
the land for the sowing of crops was beginning. St Valentine

himself is associated with youth and love in popular tradition but here in Mache and Bissey it was the goddess who presided as a woman, and not in male guise as St Valentine (Berger, 1988, 84-85).

The procession of the Earth-Mother in her carriage through the arable land to give protection to the fields and crops from various destructive insects, with the cock who would eat up the insects and who will later be sacrificed, points to a rite of extreme antiquity. What is remarkable is how strongly the official church was involved in an archaic ritual which quite openly expressed a traditional adherence to the rites of the Great Mother.

It appears that it is within this international context that the prohibition *Saoire ar Chasaibh* is to be evaluated.

This custom, however, was not very widespread. It was to be found in Munster, in Co Galway, in Co Mayo and in a few other areas. Strangely enough, the same prohibition against turning wheels occurs in association with the Feast of St Martin of Tours (11 November) in several places. From Co Kildare comes the account: 'No wheel was allowed to turn, or plough to work, before 12 noon on St Martin's Day. This applied equally to the spinning -wheel as to the cart or mill-wheel' (*Journal of the Kildare Archeological Society*, V, 451). The same prohibition was in force in all of Connacht and in the centre of the country (*Béal* IX, 231, footnote 14).

In this connection, Éinrí Ó Muirgheasa refers to an incident which occurred in the mills in Ballysodare, Co Sligo, when they were first established. The workers refused to work on the Feast of St Martin. The Protestant owners insisted that they work as usual. The mills went on fire that night (Béal IX, 231-232) This closely resembles the curse of Brigid on those who violated the rule *Saoire ar Chasaibh*.

While it must be remembered that St Martin's Day coincided with the great Celtic Feast of Samhain, due to the 10 days correction in the calendar, it does appear that the rule really belonged to Brigid as 'Culture-Hero' and was later transferred to St Martin's Day.

CHAPTER SIXTEEN

Some Localised Cultic Observances

Some areas are marked by observances that deviate somewhat from the more general patterns found throughout the country and, indeed, some of them are known only within a certain very limited territory. In this respect, one thinks especially of Co Leitrim which presents some features largely unknown elsewhere. This gives Co Leitrim a special interest in the study of rituals associated with the cult of Brigid.

An account of the 'Threshold Rite' from Barraduff gives analternative form of the 'Agallamh na Tairsí' or Threshold Dialogue carried on between the person entering the house and the people inside. Apart from this there is the triple circumambulation of the house in which the 'Brat Bhríde' or piece of cloth is carried around instead of the usual bundle of rushes. Obviously, at the period at which the account was given, the Threshold Rite had ceased to be observed and details may have been forgotten or confused:

'Long ago, on St Brigid's Eve, crosses were made from a course grass called '*seisc*' which grows in the bog. The sheaf from which the crosses were made was taken into the house by a member of the family whose name was Brigid. Those inside knelt in prayer. Brigid knocked and said: 'Foscail seo.'
The following was recited three times by those inside:
'Tigeann mo rún,
Tigeann mo shiúil (I don't know what that means)
Tigeann isteach san teach.'
Then 'Cé hé sin amuigh?', three times, and the answer: 'Mise Brighid.'
They all proceeded to make crosses and when finished they

stuck them in the rafters of the house (and) in all the outhouses. They blessed themselves with them at first.

He said it was done to protect themselves and the farm animals from all harm and disease during the year. I asked him if 'Tar' was not the word used instead of 'Tigeann' and he gave me an emphatic 'No.'

The Brat Bhríde was any article of clothing in the house or, strange to say, a meal bag. A girl of the name of Brigid walked around the house three times, knocked at the door and was asked similar questions. The article was then put aside and was supposed to be an infallible cure for cows after calving ...' (IFC 902; 243-245; P. McNulty, Barraduff, Narrator; T. Bean Uí Mhaoláit, Glenade NS, Largdonnell, Co Leitrim, Scribe).

In a further note, the same writer remarks:

'On Brídeog Night, the Eve of St Brigid, they went around with a doll dressed up in a mantle and knocked three times at the door before (being) admitted. None of them knows the rhymes they recited when admitted' (IFC 902; 246).

This latter note clearly refers to the familiar Brídeog process in which a doll, representing Brigid, is carried from house to house. However, the knocking on the door three times and the 'rhymes' would indicate that the same 'Threshold Dialogue' and possibly the three circumambulations of the house, may have been originally attached to the Brídeog circuit from house to-house. If this were so, the Brídeog Circuit Rite would have been quite an elaborate and distinctive affair in which elements of the South and North were united. The rite would involve much walking, in which the doll/Brídeog was brought on a visit to each house in a particular district, and a formal entrance to each house was made, with circumambulations and a threshold dialogue to ensure that Brigid was indeed welcome.

The indications are, however, that the rite as described by P. McNulty was in a confused state as it drew close to its ending. Firstly, a bundle of coarse grass (*seisc*) – the material for making the crosses – was brought into the house by a woman whose name was Brigid. This bringing in of the material was marked by a knocking at the door and a triple 'threshold dialogue'. Then the people inside made the crosses, made the sign of the cross on themselves with them, and then proceeded to put them up on the rafters of the dwelling house and the outhouses to secure Brigid's protection for man and beast. This completed the first part of the ritual.

The second part of the rite involved the 'Brat Bhríde' – a piece of cloth or a meal bag. The meal bag would have been common in farms at that time and had the advantage of being large and sturdy and suitable for laying on the back of a sick cow. A girl whose name was Brigid carried the article of clothing, piece of cloth or meal bag around the house three times, knocking at the door and reciting the same or similar 'threshold dialogue' as when she brought in the bundle of *seisc* for making the crosses.

Some duplication appears evident here. The 'threshold dialogue' occurs twice; something is brought into the house from outside twice; a girl named Brigid is mentioned twice. The impression is given of a rite once unified but now broken up into separate parts.

The available information enables us to postulate three different forms of 'Threshold Rite':

1. A clothed doll, whose 'body' consists of rushes, straw, wood or other materials, represents Brigid and is carried into the house from outside.
2. A bundle of straw or rushes or strong grass represents Brigid and is carried into the house from outside.
3. A piece of clothing or meal bag represents Brigid and is carried into the house from outside.

Numbers 2 and 3 are probably decadent forms of No 1 – a real image of Brigid being the original. One can easily imagine how, with the passage of time, carelessness set in, and in one case the body (straw/rushes) ceased to be clothed, in other words the clothing was neglected, and in the other case the body was neglected, leaving only the clothing (Brat). In this particular example from

Barraduff, Co Leitrim, the 'Brat'/piece of clothing/ bag stands for Brigid, and indeed, as there is so much insistance on the use of a girl called Brigid, the piece of cloth and the girl may coalesce in representing Brigid, the girl being an anthropomorphic figure. However, since, in this area, the health of cattle is of great importance, Brigid may have been thought of as the great physician who takes care of cows, and the bringing in of the 'Brat' – the badge of her profession – may have been seen as a powerful image of the presence of the great healer – the 'Bé Leighis', Lady of Medicine.

The idea of leaving the 'Brat' outside all night to catch the dew is not considered here, though the placing of the entrance of the cloth at the very end of the ritual, after the the crosses had been made and fastened to the rafters may indicate that a distinction was made between the 'Brat' and the material for the crosses.

At any rate, the observances of this particular area suggest that the 'Threshold Rite' and the 'Brídeog Circuit Rite' were once combined to form an elaborate ceremonial unit in honour of Brigid. Gradually, this split into two.

In the South, generally, the Brídeog Circuit Rite was maintained, involving a group of people carrying a doll, dressed in unusual clothing, masked and playing musical instruments. They visited the various houses of an area, sang, danced and made a collection before going on to the next house. Involving the inhabitants of a distinct district as it did, this type of rite had a pronounced social character. The 'Solemn Entrance' to each house with knocking on the door, threshold dialogue and circumambultions disappeared, probably due to practical reasons – it would have caused considerable delay at each house and 'Lucht na Brídeoige' were anxious to visit as many houses as possible on the one night. In this sense, then, the Brídeog Circuit Rite was a truncated version.

Similarly, if the reasoning is correct, the 'Threshold Rite' was maintained in the northern portion of the country while the 'Brídeog Circuit Rite' faded away. Here, the individual family predominated and there was no visiting of other houses in the area. A man or woman, unaccompanied by any group, played the principal part, taking the place of Brigid. As only the family was involved, ritual appurtences such as masks, straw suits, massive straw hats, tall staffs used as walking sticks, musical instruments, a cow's horn blown to announce the group's arrival at a house could all be dispensed with. But the 'Solemn Entrance' was retained, circumambulations of the house, threshold dialogue, entrance with 'Brídeog', festive meal, making of crosses and fastening of crosses to the roofs of the house. The domestic ritual prevailed in the northern areas embracing all that we mean by the term 'Threshold Rite' whereas, in the southern areas, the more gregarious 'Brídeog Circuit Rite' lasted on. The terms 'northern' and 'southern' are used here in a very general way to give some idea of the distribution of the rites and possibly an underlying mentality. But it does appear that in each case, what we actually have is a truncated rite and that at one time the 'Brídeog Circuit Rite' and the 'Threshold Rite' were combined to form a complete ritual unit.

We now turn to another element of this particular version of the 'Threshold Rite' – the actual door dialogue carried on between the representative of Brigid outside and the family members inside. Here again we have a variation from the general pattern: 'Téigí ar bhur nglúine agus oscailigí bhur súile agus ligigí isteach Bríd', with the response from inside the house: "Sé beatha, 'sé beatha, 'sé beatha' (IFC 903; 50-54). (Go on your knees, and open your eyes and let Brigid enter/She is welcome, she is welcome, she is welcome.)

There are similarities between this 'door dialogue' and that found in ancient liturges of the church such as in the Liturgy of Psalm Sunday in the Rite of Braga in Portugal. The celebrant, using the processional cross,raps on the closed door of the church singing the formula: 'Lift up your gates, O Princes, and let the King of Glory enter.' Those inside say: 'Who is this King of Glory?' The priest answers from outside: 'The Lord who is powerful in battle.' This is repeated three times, the doors are

opened from inside and then the priest and his assistants enter
the church to symbolise Christ's ceremonial entrance through
the gates of Jerusalem on the first Palm Sunday.

Again, this traditional formula is found in Psalm 23 (24) and
the plural of 'gates' is used: *'Attollite portas.'* This may explain
the rather puzzling phraseology 'osclaigí bhur súile' – 'súile'
here are not so much 'eyes' as doors – the 'eyes' being the 'doors'
by which one one communicates with the outside world, and
the general formula 'osclaigí bhur súile agus ligigí isteach Bríd'
corresponds quite closely to *'Attollite portas, principes vestras, et
elevamini portae aeternales; et introibit Rex gloriae.'* In a general
way, it means opening the door/doors so that Brigid may enter
the house, in the same way as the gatekeepers are called upon to
open the gates of the city of Jerusalem to let Christ, the King of
Glory, enter as in the Palm Sunday Liturgy in the Rite of Braga.

In some traditional farmhouses, there was both a front door
and a back door. The opening of the back door might have suggested the departure of winter while the entrance of Brigid
through the front door would naturally symbolise the arrival of-
spring.

We now proceed to examine the alternative type of 'door dialogue' presented in the manuscript from Barraduff (IFC 902;
243-245). Brigid knocked on the door and said:

'Foscail seo.' (Open up this.)

Those inside answered: 'Tigeann mo rún,

Tigeann mo shiúil,

Tigeann isteach san teach.'

There appears to be some corruption in this portion of the manuscript and I suggest the following emendation:

'Tagann mo rún,

Tagann mo shiúr,

Tagann isteach sa teach.'

(My beloved one comes, my sister comes, she comes into the
house.) This formula was recited three times by those inside and
is a kind of commentary on the arrival of the beloved visitor.

Then from inside comes the question:

'Cé hé sin amuigh?' and from outside comes the reply: 'Mise Brighid'. (Who is that outside?/I Brigid). This is repeated three times. On entering, the people say: "Sé do bheatha, 'Bhrighid.' (You are welcome, O Brigid.)

Here one is immediately reminded of the elaborate 'door dialogue' of the great Munster love song: 'Éamonn an Chnoic':

'Cé hé sin amuigh,
Go bhfuil faobhar ar a ghuth,
Ag réabadh mo dhorais dhúnta?'
'Mise Éamonn an Chnoic,
Atá báite, fuar, fliuch,
Ó shíorshiúl sléibhte is gleannta.'
(Who is that outside, with an edge to his voice, battering down my closed door?/It is I, Eamonn an Chnoic, who is drowned, cold and wet from ever walking the mountains and the hills.)

It does seem that both of these 'door dialogues' show a similarity to the biblical 'Song of Songs/Canticle of Canticles'. At the beginning of Chapter Five, the male lover comes to the door and knocks. Inside, the female is awakened and thinks: *'Vox dilecti mei pulsantis.'* (The voice of my lover knocking.) He says: *'Aperi mihi, soror mea, amica mea.'* (Open up to me, my sister, my friend.) The similarity of this to the formula: 'Tagann mo rún, tagann mo shiúr, tagann isteach sa teach' is noteworthy.

The phrase *'Quae est ista quae ascendit per desertum'* (3: 6) (Who is she who goes up through the desert) has its counterpart in the formula 'Cé hé sin amuigh?'

It is difficult to know how influence from the 'Song of Songs' crept into a Gaelic Folk Ritual and a Gaelic Love Song. With regard to St Brigid's Feast, however, there may be a clue as to how the usual formula 'Go on your knees, open your eyes (doors) and let Blessed Brigid enter' (Téigí ar bhur nglúine, osclaigí bhur súile agus ligigí Bríd Bheannaithe isteach) came to be part of the ritual. We have seen already that this appears to be an accomodated version of the *'Attollite portas'* phrase of Psalm 23 (24) translated from Latin into Irish.

Now, the Feast of the Presentation of Our Lord in the Temple, or 'Purification' (Candlemas), as it was formerly known, occurs on the second of February and is closely connected with St Brigid's Feast which occurs the day before. Rush candles made from wax and rushes on St Brigid's Eve were brought to the church to be blessed by the priest at Candlemas. A legend connects the two feasts by explaining that the Blessed Virgin Mary, being very shy, feared going to the Temple in the sight of a large crowd of strangers. Brigid intervened, and on the occasion, marched into the Temple of Jerusalem, just ahead of Mary, and bearing on her head a crown of lighted candles. The crowd was so intrigued by this display that all eyes were on Brigid and Mary passed unnoticed. The Blessed Virgin Mary, in token of her gratitude, declared that Brigid's feast would precede her own and ever since. St Brigid's feast is on the first of February while Mary's feast is on the following day, the second of February.

Professor Pamela Berger remarks on the custom of women who had given birth during the year going to the church for a blessing on the Feast of the Presentation and bringing home with them their blessed candles (1988, 115). Like the 'Threshold Rite, 'Churching' as it is often called, contains an Entrance Rite during which Psalm 23 (24) is recited. This psalm declares: 'The earth is the Lord's and the fulness thereof, the world and those who dwell therein; ... Who shall ascend the hill of the Lord? And who shall stand in his holy place? He who has clean hands and a pure heart ... He will receive blessing from the Lord ... Lift up your heads, O gates, ... that the King of glory may come in. Who is the King of glory? The Lord, strong and mighty, the Lord, mighty in battle.' The Psalmist asserts God's control over the world and its fertility. He then proclaims that only those who are pure of heart will enter into God's holy place and receive a blessing. The gates of the sanctuary are asked to open up so that the King of glory may enter. The Jerusalem Bible suggests that perhaps this refers to the Ark of the Covenant – the source of great blessings – being brought into the sanctuary pre-

pared for it by King David. The woman who has come to receive
the postparturition blessing kneels on the steps outside the door
of the church holding a lighted candle. The priest, in surplice
and white stole, sprinkles her with Holy Water, recites the
psalm, and then putting the end of the stole into her out-
stretched hand, leads her into the church, saying: 'Enter into the
temple of God, adore the Son of the Blessed Virgin Mary, who
endowed you with fertility and a child.' She then kneels before
the altar giving thanks to God for the benefits conferred on her
while the priest recites the final prayer: 'Almighty, and eternal
God; through the Virgin Mary's parturition you have made joyful the pains of childbirth for the faithful. Look benevolently on
your servant who comes to your temple with joy and thanksgiving, and grant that after this earthly life is over, she and her
child, through the intercession of the Blessed Virgin Mary, may
enjoy the blessing of eternal life. We ask this through Christ, our
Lord.' There is a further sprinkling with Holy Water, and then
the final blessing: 'May the peace and blessing of almighty God,
the Father, Son and Holy Spirit, descend upon you and remain
with you always.'

An unusual account of the proceedings on St Brigid's Feast
comes from the parish of Baile na gCléireach, Co Leitrim in
which the narrator describes the rituals as he witnessed them
in his youth around 1880. The account may be divided into
two parts:

'The feast of St Brigid was observed in this locality by a visit
of a young girl, specially chosen, to a certain house which
was selected by all the neighbours in the townland. The
neighbours gathered in the appointed house at a given time
and awaited the arrival of the saint's representative who
came and knocked for admission at the back door. The knock
was questioned in the Irish language from inside: 'Who is
there?' The answer from outside was in Irish 'Brighid
Bheannuigh' (Bheannaithe). The door was immediately
opened and the 'saint' was admitted and given the best seat
in the house. The feast then

commenced and any food left by the saint's representative
was carefully left over and divided among the guests who
took their portion home and afterwards busied themselves
making St Brigid's Crosses. These were made of green rushes
and chips of timber and in the making of the cross a piece of
food left by the saint's representative was inserted' (IFC 902;
225-226; Silbheistéir Mac Uidhir, Iorball-Barr, Baile na
gCléireach, Narrator; Peadar S. Mac Fhlannchadha, Scribe)

This unusual procedure presumes a highly developed social
structure in the area, based on the townland and not on the
parish as one might expect. The inhabitants of this townland
had to make two choices each year with regard to the celebration
of the Feast of Brigid. Firstly, they had to select a house in which
they would all meet on the Holy Night. Secondly, they had to
select a girl to represent Brigid in the Rite. Unfortunately, the
manuscript doesn't tell us how these choices were made but it is
obvious that the procedure involves a tightly-knit well-organised local community, socially conscious and probably using de-
mocratic methods of selection. Did they vote on the two issues
or did households take it in turn to supply the house and the
girl? Did some ancient form of social organisation survive here
after it had disappeared elsewhere? In any event, this is not the
usual 'Threshold Rite' in which only one family is involved
within their own home, nor yet the 'Brídeog Circuit Rite' which
involves a visit by 'Lucht na Brídeoige' to a large number of
households in an area.

     In this account also, there is no question of a doll. A girl chosen
by the local community impersonates Brigid. The community
gathered at the chosen house and the girl representing Brigid
knocked at the back door. The 'door dialogue' took place and
this can be reconstructed from the MS IFC 902; 227-228, from the
Ballinagleragh area, also:
     'Cé hé sin?' (Who is that?)
     'Mise Brighid Beannaigh' (Bheannaithe)
     Then someone inside said 'Gabh thart, a Bhrighid
     Bheannaigh.' (Go around / past, O Blessed Brigid.)

The 'Gabh thart' in all probability means that Brigid who is knocking at the back door is told to go around and enter by the front door. Brigid enters, then, by the front door and is given the best seat and the meal begins in which Brigid participates.

The peculiarity is that Brigid leaves certain portions of the meal (bread, meat) aside and this is divided among those present and they take a piece home with them – like dividing the wedding cake nowadays. When the various people who had been present at the central house returned to their own homes they began to make the rush crosses and they inserted the piece of bread/meat they had brought with them into the crosses. Here Brigid was closely associated with food and sustinence for the coming year.

There would not have been space in the selected house to contain all the people of the townland so that probably each family was represented by one or two people. Nevertheless, this must have been a great occasion in which the people of the townland asserted themselves as a distinct community with their own identity. And to this community Brigid made her annual visit to give them hope and confidence for the year ahead.

This was not, however, the only unusual feature in the celebration of the Feast of Brigid emanating from Co Leitrim, as another part of the same account (IFC 902; 225-226) makes clear:

A board about 18 inches long was then procured and on the board was made a representation of the moon and stars constructed from peeled green rushes; in the moon and in each star was also placed a particle of food. The cross and board were then placed over the door which the saint entered and the rosary was recited in honour of St Brigid, and her assistance was invoked for the protection of the family from sickness, sin and scandal for 12 months, at the end of which the same ceremony, as described above took place.'

Another account from the same area confirms this curious use of green peeled rushs to form representations of moon and stars when fastened to a wooden board:

On St Brigid's Night they made moons and stars of peeled

rushes. They were shaped on a board and fastened to it with half-baked potatoes ... A cross of green rushes was put over the board. The board was placed over the front door' (IFC 902; 227-228).

The front door is undoubtedly, as we have seen, the door by which Brigid entered, though she had knocked at the back door.

In an account from Kilcommon, Iorras, Co Mayo, the usage was the same – the 'door-dialogue' took place at the back door, but the man bearing the image entered by the front door (IFC 903; 50-54). The board was put above this front door and the cross above the board again.

It is clear that these descriptions of the wooden board to which rush figures of moon and stars were fastened and put up-over the front door on the inside of the house, caused consider-able surprise to Seán Ó Súilleabháin, the Cláraitheoir of Coimisiún Béaloideasa Éireann at the time, as he had not come across this usage before. He wrote to Peadar Mac Fhlannchadha who had taken down the account from Silbheistéir Mac Uidhir asking for more details. Mac Fhlannchadha was equally sur-prised at receiving this letter as he had naturally assumed that this was a well-known usage throughout the country and not just limited to parts of Co Leitrim. In his return letter he wrote:

Bhíos ag lorg a thuilleadh eolais ó shin i dtaobh na samh-laoidí ceanna agus chomh fada agus is féidir liom a dhéanamh amach – mar is beag duine is féidir leis iad a dhéanamh anois – bhí dhá shaghas samhlaoid ann mar leanas:

a. Ceann nach raibh air ach an ghealach agus na réiltíní thart timpeall uirthi, agus

b. Ceann ar a raibh an ghealach agus na réiltíní, leath na gealaí faoi sin agus dréimire trí runga faoi sin arís. Bhí na samhlaoidí seo go léir greamaithe do phíosa adhmaid tim-peall le hocht déag n-orlaí ar fhaid agus sé horlaí ar leithead' (IFC 902; 229).

(I was looking for more information on these figures / repres-entations and as far as I can see – as few are capable of making them now – two kinds of figure were available:

a. A type which had only the moon and stars around it.

b. A type which had the moon and the stars, a half-moon below these, and a ladder with three rungs below the half-moon again. These figures were all glued to a piece of wood about 18 inches long and 6 inches wide.)

The glue for fastening the figures to the board came from half-baked potatoes, and a crumb of food – bacon generally – left aside by Brigid's representative at the festive meal was inserted into the figures on the board. Due to hurry and carelessness, the figures were sometimes simply drawn on the board with chalk. Kevin Danaher, gives a fine illustration of a board with figures from the National Museum (1972, 24). At the top portion of the board there is a large circle of rushes. This is surrounded by four stars – each star having seven spokes. Directly below the circle is the 'Half-Moon'. The 'corrán' or crescent is to the left, denoting the waning moon. Then below the half-moon is a ladder with three rungs.

The figures on the board are very carefully arranged with mathematical precision, and winding the rushes to form the sun (moon?) and the half-moon in particular, would demand considerable skill and patience. However, Kevin Danaher remarks rather grandly:

> In a few places in County Leitrim, children practised a custom which does not seem to be known elsewhere. They got a small piece of a flat wooden board about 30cms by 15cms and with the viscous exudation of a partly boiled or roasted potato fixed peeled rushes upon it in figures representing 'the sun, the moon and the stars'; this was then hung up with the cross' (1972, 23).

This unique custom, involving a beautifully constructed artistic object, gives rise to many questions regarding its meaning which remains obscure. Firstly, as regards the figures themselves; there seems to be no doubt about the identity of the half-moon and the stars. But what of the full circular figure? Is it the

sun, or is it the full moon? The ladder with its three rungs seems
to be clear enough. Again, Peadar Mac Fhlannchadha stated in
his letter to Seán Ó Súilleabháin:

> Maidir leis an gciall a bhí leis na samhlaoidí, níor éirigh liom
> aon eolas cruinn a fháil ina diaidh. Dúirt bean liom, áfach,
> gur chuala sí bean, a raibh na samhlaoidí á ndéanamh aici
> oíche Fhéile Bríde, á rá go gciallaíonn trí rungaí an dréimire
> creideamh, dóchas agus carthanacht' (IFC 902; 230).
>
> (As regards the meaning of the figures I did not succeed in
> finding any precise information about them. One woman
> told me that she heard a woman, who was actually engaged
> in making the figures on St Brigid's Eve, saying that the three
> rungs of the ladder symbolised faith, hope and charity.)

Theologically, this explanation makes perfect sense; the three
great virtues of faith, hope and charity do indeed lead to God,
traditionally thought to abide in the heavenly realm of sun
moon and stars. The ladder naturally carries with it the idea of
ascent. While the symbolism is perfectly valid, it is difficult to
understand why it was connected specifically with the Feast of
St. Brigid.

    However, the ladder comes to the fore again in another con-
text, in a report from Carrickmore, Co Tyrone (IFC 905; 146-147)
and this account, coming from quite a different part of the country, may throw some light on the usage:

> It is another custom for a young girl to make a spinning
> wheel from rushes and give it to a young man to put under
> his pillow that night (St Brigid's Eve) and he is supposed to
> see or dream about the girl whom he is going to be married
> to. The young man makes a ladder from rushes for the girl
> and people say that she dreams about the man who is to be
> married to her.

Here perhaps, we have the key to a different interpretation of the
board and its figures. Supposing that the circular figure, normally
thought to be either the sun or the full moon, is neither of these,
but instead a spinning wheel, much of the problem is solved.

As the report from Carrickmore says, a young woman puts a rush figure of a ladder under her pillow on St Brigid's Eve so that she will see in a dream the man she will marry. Thatching and repairing roofs, being characteristically a man's work, is symbolised by the ladder. The ladder symbolises the man. Similarly, a young man puts a rush spinning wheel under his pillow to dream of the girl he will marry. Spinning, being the characterisic work of a woman at that period, the spinning wheel naturally stood for the woman. What of the remaining figures – the half-moon and stars? I suggest that these simply represent the period of night, the nocturnal sky, the time of dreaming in which the revealing will take place.

As we have seen, St. Brigid's Eve, like Samhain, is a time for prognostication, for foretelling the future, and we have a report from another part of Co Leitrim (IFC 902; 239) describing how the candles made from rushes on the Holy Night were used for this very purpose. Each member of the family present received a candle and the person whose candle went out first would be the first to die.

What we have here, on the otherhand, is a method of prognostication concerned with marriage and it may be that the person, man or woman who actually made the object was looking forward to marriage in the near future, for many marriages took place on the Sunday before Lent or on Shrove Tuesday, the day before Ash Wednesday. Depending on the calculation of the Easter Cycle for that particular year, this would be quite close to St Brigid's Day. On this year, 2005, for instance, the Sunday before the First Sunday of Lent is on the 6th February and Shrove Tuesday is on the 8th February – just a few days after St Brigid's Feast.

An Toirtín

In other areas, and especially in Co Mayo, the 'Toirtín' was well known. The Toirtín was a cake, often quite large and closely associated with St Brigid's Feast. The usage is described in a report from Ballycastle, Co Sligo:

There used to be an oatmeal cake laid on the window (out-
side) for St Brigid's Night. One in the (Brídeog) procession
would sing the following rhyme in Irish:
Oíche Bríde Bricín,
Bain an chluas den toirtín,
Lig isteach an Bhainríon,
Is tabhair a shaith don dailtín (IFC 903; 190).
(On the night of freckled Brigid, take the ear (a piece) off the
cake. Let the Queen enter , and give the servant-boy his due
measure of food.)

In this *rann*, Brigid is referred to as 'the Queen' and her entrance
to the house is part of the Brídeog procession. As regards 'bricín'
(speckled): '… tradition says that St Brigid was either pockpitted
or very much freckled. In some of the old sayings she is referred
to as "Bríd Bhreac" or "Bríd Bhricín". She was a lowsized or
stockilly built woman, with somewhat coarse features – not per-
sonally handsome, but in charity and character she had few
equals' (IFC 903; 57).

The phrase 'Tabhair a sháith don dailtín' is difficult to understand. However, it may be related to the social conditions of the
time. The 'dailtín' is, perhaps, a farm-worker. During the winter
period there wasn't a great deal to do but with the arrival of
spring, with St Brigid's Day, farmwork increased enormously.
The phrase 'Is tabhair a shaith don dailtín' enshrined in the
Brídeog *rann*, gave a gentle hint to the inhabitants of the house
to increase the food supply to their workman. A report from
Rathmore, Co Cork, states that a third meal per day was provided from Féile Bríde on (IFC 900; 124-125).

The phrase 'Bain an chluas den toirtín' is again difficult and it
probably means 'Take a bit/bite of the cake'. A report from
Clare illustrates the practice: 'A sheaf of wheat and a loaf of
bread used to be left on the doorstep on the vigil of the feast so
that St Brigid would divide same among the poor' (IFC 901; 19).
Here, it is taken for granted that St Brigid will return from the
Otherworld on the Holy Night and will distribute largesse
throughout the land. The loaf and sheaf of corn, left on the

threshold to symbolise the opening up of this world to the Otherworld, show the desire of the humans to contribute their small share which will be magnified by Brigid's supernatural power during the course of the year, as in the gospel story the people's insignificant contribution of five loaves and two fishes was magnified to feed five thousand (Jn 6:5-15), or indeed, when the faithful, in the early church, brought their little loaves of bread and flasks of wine to the altar at the Offertory procession, to be transformed into something vital for the destiny of mankind.

An account from Co Offaly describes a big sweet cake being baked for the occasion. This was kept on the dresser and was eaten by 'Lucht na Brídeoige' when they arrived. In this case, the 'Brídeog' was not a doll but a girl dressed in white with a green cloak (IFC 907; 11).

Echoes of an ancient observance of an offering made to the Tuatha Dé Danann, or Aos Sí, who had gone underground into the 'Sí' – the sacred hollow hills – but still controlled the fertility of the land may be seen in an account from Socker, Co Donegal: 'A sheaf of corn and an oaten cake used to be placed on the doorstep on St Brigid's Eve for the "wee folk" (fairies), and also as a thanksgiving for a plenteous grain crop and for good luck during the following year' (IFC 904; 178).

Here, St Brigid's Eve, the Feast of Imbolg, is ranked among the other great Feasts of the Old Calendar – Samhain, Bealtaine, Lughnasa, when it was appropriate to make an offering to the Old Divinities. In a great cycle of reciprocity, one made one's offerings joyfully to the 'déithe dúileacha' – the elemental gods, and they in return, provided an abundant harvest.

In some places in Co Mayo, a little house was made of straw and a large cake put inside it at the back door (IFC 903; 117). This may have been to accomodate a group of Brídeoga arriving very late after the household had gone to bed.

This tradition of a special cake was also found in Gaelic Scotland in connection with the four great Feasts. There was an especially made cake for Samhain (Bonnach Samhthain), for

Bealtaine (Bonnach Bealltain), for Lughnasa (Bonnach
Luanastain) and for Imbolg (Bonnach Bride). Along with these
there was the large ornamental cake, 'Struan Micheil', for the
Feast of St Michael the Archangel (29 September). Alexander
Carmichael, in his magnificent study of the rites and customs of
the Islands and Highlands, *Carmina Gadelica*, describes the use of
these ritual cakes at the beginning of each of the four seasons (I,
208-209).

The use made of them, however, seems to differ from that of
Ireland, and the ancient sacrificial principle *'Do ut abeas'* seems
to prevail; that is, an offering of part of the cake to various inimical animal spirits is made to induce them to go away and leave
his property in peace according to the 'I give so that you may go
away' principle:

'The people repaired to the fields, glens and corries to eat
their quarter cakes. When eating them, they threw a piece over
each shoulder alternately, saying:
   "Here to thee, wolf, spare my sheep;
   there to thee, fox, spare my lambs;
   here to thee, eagle, spare my goats;
   there to thee, raven, spare my kids;
   here to thee, marten, spare my fowls;
   there to thee, harrier, spare my chickens".'

Likewise, the Toirtín carried the idea of banishing the spirit of
hunger from the house for the year that was to follow. The
'Bairín Breac', with its ring to foretell a coming marriage, seems
to be the lone survivor of the Seasonal Cakes in Ireland, apart
from the Christmas Cake.

An interesting report from the Ordinance Survey in Co
Derry, c. 1830, shows a different use for the Toirtín (strone).
Here the normal 'Threshold Rite' takes place, the rushes are
brought into the house and spread on the floor. In this case,
however, it is not a pot of mashed potatoes (Brúitín) that is
placed on the rushes, as was frequently the case, but the large
cake itself:

'A strone or large cake of oatbread is made in the shape of a cross. The rushes are thrown on the floor, and the strone placed on the rushes. All kneel round the rushes and the bread, and at the end of each short prayer a piece is taken off the strone by each person and eaten. When all is eaten the crosses are made, and when blessed by the priest or sprinkled with holy water, are placed over the door, usually by the third day after the Feast in the hope that the family may have a plentiful supply of bread until that time twelve months, and in honour of St Brigid' (*Ulster Journal of Archeology*, 1945, 64).

In this particular example, the family meal over the rushes, consists of the Toirtín. The celebration takes a highly Christianised form with the Toirtín in the form of a cross, the family kneeling, and eating punctuated by prayers. The detail of the crosses being blessed by a priest and the three days delay probably aligns St Brigid's Feast with Candlemas on 2 February. The people probably brought St Brigid's crosses to the church to be blessed along with the candles. Three days would have passed by the time the crosses were finally hung up on the walls. Many people may have gone to the church on the next day also (3 February) for the Blessing of the Throat on the Feast of St Blaise. Thus the first three days of February must have been a period of serious religious observance at the beginning of the agricultural year.

In some of the accounts, the 'Loine' or churn-dash is mentioned as being used to support the cake at the doorway: 'A cake was placed by the *bean a' tighe* on the top of the churn dash and the dash planked in the doorway. Everyone that passed along was supposed to take a piece of the cake in honour of the generosity of St Brigid to the poor' (IFC 903; 76-77).

The churn-dash was readily available as it was used for butter-making and consisted of a long handle, like a sweeping-brush, with a large circular wooden top. It was often used as the foundation for the body of the doll or Brídeog, straw, rushes or clothing being wrapped around the handle. The advantage of this was that when brought into the house the Brídeog/doll could stand without being supported while 'lucht na Brídeoige' danced around it:

> They (lucht na Brídeoige) went into every house, stood the brídeog on the floor (as shown – the illustration shows a very large brídeog, with a cross-bar tied to the handle of the churn-dash to form arms. The effigy is well padded and clothed, and in this case, the base of the dash is in the form of a cross), danced around it and sang some rhymes. According to old Seán a Búrca this was the rhyme he knew:
> 'Éirigh suas, a bhean a' tighe,
> Ná cráidh Dia do chroidhe,
> Is tabhair rud éicint don Bhrídeoig' (IFC 903; 113).
> (Get up, O woman of the house, let not God trouble your

heart, and give something to the Brídeog people.)
In other cases the churn-dash was turned the other way. A hole was made in the ground and the handle put in it so that the top formed a platform on which the cake rested. This system was also used in areas of Co Sligo where the Easter Sunday Cake-Dance was in vogue. The cake rested on the up-turned dash, while the people danced out of doors. The cake was given to a young man who gave it to his girlfriend. She cut it up and divided it among those present. It was expected that the wedding would follow (Béal. XI, 1947, 137-138).

Apart from the Toirtín, another custom is alluded to in the rhyme:

> 'fhéil' Bríde bricín,
> Bainigí an chluas den toirtín,
> Agus ligigí isteach an moiltín' (IFC 903; 59).
> (Let in the little sheep)

This is excplained by a report from Eachleim, Co Mayo: 'Ba ghnách, chomh maith, an oíche sin, molt (caora) a mharú in onóir Naomh Bríd mar a mharaítear gé Oíche l' Mhartain' (IFC 903; 71-72). (It was customary, too, on that night to kill a small sheep in honour of St Brigid just as a goose is killed on St Martin's Eve.) St Martin's Eve (10 November), due to calendrical dislocation corresponds to Samhain (31 October) and it may be that St Brigid's Feast has borrowed the custom from St Martin.

The custom is clearly explained in a report from Co. Mayo:

'... it was the custom among townlands or communities to kill a young fatted wether, which was divided among the neighbours on St Brigid's night. One house in the place in turn killed a sheep, usually a wether or 'Moiltín' on this particular night and, when delivering the individual portions of meat at each door, the messengers would say:

'Fhéile Brighde Bricín,

Bainigí an chluas dhen toirtín,

Agus leigí isteach an moiltín' (903; 58-59).

This custom of the 'Moiltín' does not appear to be widespread, and in this Mayo case, as in the case of the Baile na gCléireach area in Co Leitrim, it involves a well-organised community and makes of St Brigid's Feast a social occasion in which the local people are conscious of their solidarity.

The use of rushes in the Rites of Brigid
We have seen the widespread use of rushes as a basic material for the making of St Brigid's cross and the Brídeog. It was also used in some places for making rush candles which were blessed by the priest at Candlemas on the second of February and so, intimately connected with the Feast of Brigid, the candles having been made on St Brigid's Eve along with the crosses.

There is, however, another use made of the rushes in connection with the feast and this is as a carpet. The rushes were laid down on the threshold for Brigid to kneel on or to walk on, at her return from the Otherworld for her annual visit to her people on the Holy Night: 'On the Feast of St Brigid green rushes were placed on the doorstep and outside the door in her honour' (IFC 907; 245).

A similar report from Rath Eoghain, Co Westmeath, stresses the physical contact of Brigid with the rushes spread as a carpet on the floor: 'Rushes are also shaken in the house on St Brigid's Eve, as it is said that St Brigid walks on them on the eve of the feast (IFC 906; 99). From Delvin, in Westmeath also, the message was the same: 'It was customary, too, to spread green rushes on the floor on St Brigid's Eve' (IFC 906;156).

Another report from Knockbride, Bailieboro, Co Cavan, stresses the importance of due preparation for Brigid's visit, and in this case a bundle of rushes was placed on the threshold to be used as a cushion by her when she knelt to pray:

> The man of the house also prepared a sheaf of green rushes to be placed outside the door for St Brigid to pray on going by. If these preparations were not made for the saint, it was believed that the house had not her blessing' (IFC 905; 209).

The same idea occurs in a report from the other end of the country, from Co Cork: 'Rushes were strewn on the doorstep and the door was left unlatched as it was thought the saint did visit homes where a welcome was made ready' (IFC 900; 159).

In all of this, it is clear that the people were preparing a carpet for Brigid to walk on, in much the same way as today a red carpet is spread to welcome some distinguished visitor to the country. The practice is ancient and is described by Joyce:

> It was a common practice in the better class of houses to strew the floor with rushes; and when distinguished visitors were expected, the old rushes were removed and fresh ones supplied. The use of rushes for this purpose was so well understood that there was a special knife for cutting them; and such a knife is enumerated among the household articles in the house of a brewy (1908, 305).

The ancient story *'Altram Tige da Medar'* recalls how Ealcmar, lord of Brú na Bóinne (Newgrange) had rushes strewn on the floor of the Sí in preparation for the visit of Manannan Mac Lir, god of the sea (Ériu, XI, 1932, 189)

It is likely that the Isle of Mann is named from Manannan, and indeed, Frazer traces an ancient bond between Brigid and the island in so far as legend has it that she went there to receive the nun's veil from its patron saint, Bishop Mac Goill.

On the Holy Night, it was the practice for the householder to gather a bundle of rushes, stand at the door and, in Manx Gaelic, invite Brigid to come in:

'Brede, Brede,

tar gys my thie,

tar dyn thie ayms noght.

Foshil-jee yn dorrys da Brede,

as lhig da Brede e heet staigh'

(Brede, Brede, come to my house, come to my house tonight. Open the door for Brede and let Brede come in.)

Then the rushes were spread on the floor for Brigid to walk on them (1923, 133-135).

The use of rushes in the rites shows considerable variety. They could be used for St Brigid's Cross; Crios Bhríde (rope girdle); Leaba Bhríde (bed); Brídeog/image/doll; carpet; kneeler; candles (rush-lights); St Brigid's Board (with rush-figures of sun, moon, stars, spinning wheel and ladder); a little rush basket and riddle used to contain some seed potatoes and corn to be mixed with the main supply of seed at sowing-time (IFC 905; 139); the Buathrach – a rush spancel for bad-tempered cows with a habit of kicking over the milk bucket, or for that matter of kicking the milkmaid. All of these matters were connected to the Feast of Brigid through the use of rushes.

Professor Ogilvie draws attention to elements of ancient Roman sacrificial practices such as the triple procession of the victims (bull, sheep, pig) around the altar or area to be enclosed as a protected space:

'The accepted ritual – which still survives in Britain in the custom of beating the bounds during Ascension-tide in May – was to lead a procession of a bull, sheep and pig, three times round the fields and then to sacrifice them to Ceres, the goddess of growth' (1969, 88).

Certain echoes of this type of procedure may be felt to be present in the Brídeog and Threshold Rites of Brigid. The encircling of a space is seen as providing those within with a shelterd habitat free from danger from harmful forces outside.

Rush-puppets come to the fore in a 'substitute' sacrifice in ancient Rome. Throughout the city there were 27 small shrines called *'sacra Argeorum,'* and on 17 March, rush-puppets, resembling men bound hand and foot, were deposited in these shrines and were collected after a long delay, two months later, on 15 May, during a magnificent procession, and brought to the oldest bridge in Rome, the Pons Sublicius where they were thrown into the Tiber. It is thought that 'the rush-puppets were a substitute for old men who used to be thrown into the river in times of acute famine as a human sacrifice. There is a record of such a sacrifice being performed in 440 BC and the custom had given rise to a proverb which was common in the time of Cicero – 'off the bridge with the sixty-year-olds' (Ogilvie, 1969, 87-88).

At a period when life-expectancy was low, it was felt that they had outstayed their welcome.

In Brigid's case, the theory was that the rush-puppet representing her was sacrificed, dismembered, after it had been taken around the house three times – the house, in this instance, being the space to be protected from the evils of the year coming from outside. The various elements such as the cross, *crios, leaba, buarthach* and so forth, deriving from the fragmented body, in the tradition of the Purusa Myth, bring about the safety, health and prosperity of the household. The fact that the Irish word *'Luachair'* (rush) is in all probability connected with the Latin *'Lux'* (light), and that rush candles are made on the Holy Night and that the blessing of candles and a candle-light procession is part of the liturgy of the Roman Rite on 2 February, is suggestive of Brigid as 'Light-Bringer' and the ritual ensemble as a mode of assisting the growing power of the sun and the lengthening of the day.

The ancient custom of Rush-Bearing is retained in some places in England such as Ambleside and Grasmere in Westmoreland. It recalls the days in which the stone floors of churches were periodically strewn with rushes. Large bundles of rushes were brought to the church with much music and dancing on the way. The rushes were woven into various shapes such as harps, crosses and pillars and placed on the walls (Hole, 1978, 259-261). The popular hymn, 'Hymn for the Rush-Bearers', was long in use in Grasmere:

Our fathers to the house of God,
As yet a building rude,
Bore offerings from the flowery sod,
And fragrant rushes strew'd.
May we, their children, ne'er forget
The pious lesson given.
But honour still, together met,
The Lord of earth and heaven (Hazzlitt, 1995, 529).

New Year Rituals

As we attempt to situate the major rituals of the Feast of Brigid – the Brídeog Procession and the Threshold Rite – within a pattern of annual celebrations, we look at the various dates at which the year began according to different computations throughout the centuries.

The first of January, New Year's Day, (Lá Caille) is our present mode of calculating the beginning of the year. This is the system in vogue since 1751 when the new calendar was introduced into Ireland. Before that, the year began, according to law, on 25 March (Spring Equinox 21 March). This traditional date was obviously based on the Spring Equinox, the period of equal day and equal night when the sun rises exactly in the east.

However, our modern New Year's Day is very close to the Winter Solstice (21 December), the shortest day of the year and the day on which a ray from the rising sun penetrates to the interior of the great megalithic monument at the bend of the Boyne, Newgrange (Brú na Bóinne).

The rituals performed on or around these dates, then , may be seen as New Year celebrations or new beginnings. They mark a definite stage in the progress of the sun around the earth and so bring about an awareness of mankind's connection to the cosmos.

As regards Oíche Shamhna (Halloween) at the beginning of the dark half of the year (1 November) and Oíche Bhealtaine (May Eve) at the beginning of the bright half of the year, they too are markers of a definite period of time defined by the progress of the sun along its prescribed path. Of these, Professor Rees remarks: 'The customs of both Eves have characteristics of New

Year celebrations generally; for example, the practice of divination and the re-lighting of household fires from a ceremonial
bonfire' (1961, 89). The same may be said of Midsummer (21
June) which marks the start of the sun's decline. Imbolg, the
Feast of St Brigid is the beginning of spring and the start of the
farmer's year. Lughnasa, around the first of August, is the beginning of the authumn season and the start of the harvest.

The seasonal rituals, then, may be seen largely as Rites of the
Beginnings. It is understandable, as we have seen, that seasonal
rituals have a tendency to borrow elements from each other.

On the Feast of St Martin (corresponding to Samhain) it was
customary to sacrifice a chicken, or a goose or some animal 'in
onóir Dé agus Naomh Máirtín' (in honour of God and St
Martin). Éinrí Ó Muirgheasa gives an account of the practice:

'In Ballina, Co Mayo, there is a special market called 'St
Martin's Market' , where fowl – geese especially – are sold
for the feast.

About a week before the festival the bird or animal is segreg-
ated from the rest of its kind. This was apparently the 'dedication' as thenceforth it was specially fed in preparation for
the sacrifice. The killing was a formal affair, generally done
by the head of the house, and its blood was spilled in the four
corners of the house inside and was sprinkled or daubed on
the door posts. This was done 'in onóir Dé agus Naomh
Máirtín'. As far as I have been able to find out, the daub on
the door posts was not a cross. Sometimes the blood was
sprinkled on the threshold also' (Béal IX, 230).

The account goes on to say that the performance of this rite
would protect the household from all misfortune throughout
the year. This was the people's belief. The goose was cooked
then and eaten and the quills given to the children. It was
thought that the use of such a quill would improve the child's
handwriting.

In another report from Co Mayo it is stated that on St Brigid's
Feast, every woman of the house killed a chicken or hen and
'Níor mhaith leo rotha an túirne a chur thart an lá sin' (IFC

903;72). (They didn't want to turn the spinning-wheel that day.)
It would appear that in this case the Feast of Brigid had borrowed the sacrifice from St Martin's Feast while his feast had
borrowed the *Saoire ar Chasaibh* from St Brigid. This type of parallel is noticed in another report from Co Mayo: 'Ba ghnáthach
chomh maith, an oíche sin, molt a mharú in onóir Naomh Bríd,
mar a mharaítear gé oíche Fhéile Mhártan' (IFC 903;72). (It was
customary also, on that night, to kill a wether in honour of St
Brigid as a goose is killed on the eve of St Martin's Feast.)

Another small item of information from Co Sligo, links the
two feasts together: 'In Co Sligo a piece of flannel was left outside the house on St Martin's night (10 November) and was preserved for curing persons or animals' (Béal IX, 234). This is obviously parallel to the *Brat Bhríde* usage on St Brigid's Eve. It is also
connected with the Feast of Bealtaine, as we have seen, and from
which it is probably ultimately derived. The tendency of big
feasts to borrow elements from each other is obvious in this case.

In the case of the well-known practice of stopping the clock
during wakes and funerals, it can first be remarked that this
must have been a relatively late custom. Its attendent custom of
turning the mirror to the wall may, perhaps, be explained by a
desire to safeguard the living at a dangerous time when angels
and demons gathered to dispute over the destiny of the soul of
the dead. It might have been felt that a person seeing himself in a
mirror at such a time was, as it were, handing over something
essential of himself to the mirror, exposing his soul, which in the
circumstances could be easily grabbed by demons.

It is more difficult to explain the stopping of the clock, but
again, a wake is a very solemn occasion, in which a very definite
encounter with the Otherworld takes place. What could be more
natural than to take some element such as *Saoire ar Chasaibh* from
the Feast of Brigid and transfer it the wake. The wake was very
largely an indoor affair and the stopped clock hanging on the
wall would remind the mourners that this was a sacred and
mysterious time when the 'prohibition on turning' was to be observed.

A parallel exists between the Mache-Bissey rite of sacrificing a cock on 22 February and the Ballina custom of sacrificing a goose on the 10 November in the matter of segregation. In the case of Mache-Bissey, the sacrificial cock was aquired on the day of the feast itself – St Valentine's Day, 14 February – and the segregation process, with feeding and fattening, lasted until 22 February when the cock was sacrificed. In the case of Ballina, Co Mayo, the sacrificial goose was bought at Ballina Fair a short time before St Martin's Feast. In 1989, for instance, the Fair was held on Monday 6 November. This was the first Monday in November (*Old Moore's Almanac*, 1989). This left just a few days for the segregation process before the sacrifice took place on 10 November. By separating the intended victim from his companions and giving him special honourable treatment, his separation from the profane world became evident as he was prepared for his journey into the Otherworld.

It does not appear that the first of January, or the night before it, had any great significance as the beginning of the year untili recent centuries. The Roman custom, however, had been in vogue in Scotland for a long time and the Scottish connection may have influenced its later popularity in Ireland (Danaher, 1972, 258-259).

Strangely enough it is from the south of the country, from Gleann Eatharla in Co Kerry, that an account emerges of a New Year's Ritual (1 January) which embraces elements of the St Brigid's Eve 'Threshold Rite' (Gnás na Táirsí) and the Scottish custom of 'First Footing'.

It was the first person in the house to get up who was in charge of the rite. He went out and circumambulated the house three times (*deiseal*, undoubtedly) and when he arrived at the door each time he shouted: 'Go mbeannaí Dia anso, agus go dtuga Dia bliain nua mhaith daoibh.' (May God bless all here and may God give you a good new year.) He only entered the house after the third round (as in the Threshold Rite) The people inside, or at least those who were awake, apparently gave the ordinary reply: 'Dé bheathasa chugainn.' (You are welcome.) He replied: 'Go maire sibh slán (agus bhur ndotháin agaibh).' (May you be healthy and have plenty.) When the woman of the house got up she gave him a fine breakfast (An Seabhac, 1932, 318).

In Scottish tradition, the 'First-Footer' is the person who first comes into the house early on New Year's Day, the first of January. The 'Luck of the Year' was dependent on the 'First-Footer' and so householders were anxious that a fine, hand-some, wealthy person would present himself at dawn of day rather than some beggarman. The First-Footer had a present for the family and he/she had his/her breakfast with them. In Yorkshire he was called the 'Lucky Bird' and in the Isle of Man the 'Quaaltagh'. Elsewhere in Europe he has other names (Hole, 1978, 104-107).

The gifts the First-Footer brought were often symbolic of health and prosperity for the New Year – gifts such as fuel, money, food and salt, and a branch of evergreen to denote the continuation of life. Christina Hole suggests that there may have been an earlier form of the rite as it is recorded that in some areas the First-Footer entered the house in complete silence and laid a coal or a peat on the fire – the life-centre of the household. In another account, the First-Footer entered in silence carrying an evergreen branch and a branch of mistletoe. He laid the green branch on the fire and placed the mistletoe on the mantelpiece above. He then turned and wished the family a happy New Year, and it was with this that the ritual silence was broken (Hole, 1978, 105).

First-Footing was widespread in Scotland, England and Wales and though at times performed at Christmas it belonged to the New Year at its first of January date. The Quaaltagh in the Isle of Man might be a woman and similarly in Scotland. 'But in England a female First Foot is a disaster almost everywhere' (Hole, 1978, 105).

The First of January may be considered to be a kind of com-promise between two considered dates for the Winter Solstice, 21 December and 6 January. The Winter Solstice marks the time when the sun recovers slowly from its decline and turns round to give new hope to mankind with its increasing heat and length of day. It is on the Feast of Imbolg, St Brigid's Day, the first of February, that this recovery of the sun becomes obvious to the people of Ireland in the greening of the grass, the lambing season, the new growth of vegetation, the singing of the birds. This is the farmers' New Year and St Brigid's Day stands half way between two significant stations of the sun – the Winter Solstice and the Spring Equinox (21 March).

The Brídeog Procession, in which Brigid is believed to visit each house at the beginning of the agricultural year may be considered as an ancient and elaborate form of First-Footing which Brigid undertakes to bring her people the 'Luck of the Year'.

One of the most dramatic and primitive of the New Year rites celebrated on the first of January must certainly have been the 'Hogmanay' of the Western Isles of Scotland. Its primitive character would suggest that it belonged originally to Samhain and that it was transferred to the first of January with the introduction of the new calendar.

Hogmanay was the visit of a 'Bull-Man' and his companions to the various houses of the area around midnight on the first of January. A man was clothed in a bull's hide still maintaining horns, hooves and tail. The hide was preserved in the rafters of a house throughout the year and taken down when needed. At midnight the Bull-Man set out to visit all the houses of the area followed by his team. They carried hurley-sticks and pounded the hide as if they were beating a drum as they marched about. They chanted a special *Rann* or ritual song:

Calluinn a bhuilg,
Calluing a bhuilg,
Buail am boicionn.
Buail am boicionn.
(McNeill, 1961, 3, 89-90, 155)

Now, the walls of old houses in the Hebrides used to be very thick as they needed to be against the storms. They were from five to eight feet in width and the thatched roof rose from the inside of the walls at the top so that there was actually a pathway

on top of the walls going all around the house. This was an extremely clever arrangement as it made thatching and repairs to
the roof very convenient, making steep ladders to ground level
unneccessary. Permanent steps led to this platform-path so that
one could ascend and descend easily. This arrangement is referred to in a *Rann*. When the Bull-Man and his team the 'Gillean
Callaig' (servants of the Kalends) arrived at a house, they climed
up the steps to this path on top of the walls. They circumambulated the house from this position once or three times, *deiseal* or
sunwise (McNeill, 1961, 3,118). As they walked, they beat the
Bull-Man and the walls with their hurley sticks with great en-
thusiasm. They proceeded in single file, following the course of
the sun, as at Holy Wells. When the proper number of rounds
was completed they descended the steps to ground level and
chanted a *Rann* before the door:

'Nist (anois) o thaine sinn dh'an duthaich,
Dh'urachadh dhuibh na Callaig,
Cha ruig uine dhuinn bhi 'g innse,
Bha i ann ri linn ar seanar (sinsear)' (CG 1, 152).
(Now,since we have come to your area to make new for you
the Kalends (New Year), there is no need to tell you of it, it
was there in the time of our ancestors.)

The Rann then describes what will happen inside the house
when they enter. This part is complex as there were different
modes of presentation.

One method in use was for the Bull-Man to put a corner of
the hide into the fire (which was in the middle of the room) and
singe it. Then he went around the room with the burning piece
and each member of the household smelled it. The smelling of
the hide of the sacrificed bull was believed undoubtedly to bring
health and prosperity to the household. This is obviously a form
of communion. The sacrificed bull had gone over to the
Otherworld, to Tír na nÓg, the land of youth and health and
prosperity. But it still had links with this human world because
its hide still existed and was actually being worn by the Bull-
Man. The hide served as a bridge between the two worlds. The

singeing of the hide created a smell which each of the participants could experience in a personal way. The Bull-Man was especially identified with the Bull – for the duration of the rite, he
was the Bull. But the Bull was in the Otherworld where all perfection lay and when the humans participated in the being of the
Bull something of the perfection of the Otherworld was con-
veyed to them in terms of health, fertility, prosperity – the 'Luck
of the Year'.

An alternative method, though less direct, was for the leader
to have in his pocket the 'Caisein Callaig' – this was a piece of
hide from what was probably an animal sacrificed at Samhain at
some time in the past and preserved, as in the case of the hide
from year to year, to be used at the Hogmanay Rite. Again, this
was singed in the fire and the participants smelled the smoke
and thus communed with the sacrificed animal in the
Otherworld in order to procure for themselves the blessings of
the Otherworld existence for the coming year. A Rann chanted
during the ceremony describes what happened:

Caisein Callaig 'na mo phocaid,
Is mor an ceo thig as an fhear ud,
Chan 'eil aon a gheobh de aile,
Nach bi gu brath de fallain'

Gheobh fear an taigh 'na dhorn e,
Cuiridh e shron anns an teallach;
Theid e deiseil air na paisdean,
Is seachd araid bean an taighe.

Gheobh a bhean e, is i 's t-fhiach e,
Lamh a riarachadh na Callaig,
Lamh a bhairig cais is im duinn,
Lamh gun spiocaireachd, gun ghainne (CG 1. 152).

(Caisein Callaig in my pocket, great is the smoke which will
come from it, nobody who smells it will be without health
forever. The man of the house will take it in his fist, he will
put its nose in the fire; he will go around the children sunwise, and very specially the woman of the house. His wife

will get it and it is she who deserves it, hers is the hand that
will distribute the Hogmanay presents; hers is the hand that
will give us cheese and butter, the hand without stinginess or
scarcity.)

In this alternative use, it appears that while the Bull-Man and his
team brought the Caisein Callaig around to each house, it was
the man of the house who actually singed it in the fire, walked
around his wife, *deiseal*, then held out the Caisein for her to
smell. Then he carried out the same procedure for each of the
children. The two methods are essentially the same.

A clever hint is given in the Rann that *Bean a' Tí* (woman of
the house) is expected to reward them generously for their 'luck-
bringing' visit.

While this extraordinarily archaic rite was practised until recent centuries, and the Rann is in modern Gaidhlig or Scottish
Gaelic, a prototype of it may be seen in the *Tarbhfheis* of ancient
Ireland as described in the tale, *Togail Bruidne Da Derga* – a tale
bristling with the supernatural and dating from probably the
11th century, while another written form of it may have gone
back to the 9th century (Knott, E., (Ed.), *Togail Bruidne Da Derga*,
(Dublin 1936).

The text describes the scene when the king, Eterscelae, had
died:

'Con-grenar tairbfheis la firu Hérenn .i. nomarbad tarb leó
ocus no ithead oenfhear a sháith de ocus no ibead a enbruithi
ocus no chanta ór firindi fair ina ligiu. Fer at-chichead ina
chotlad is é bad rí (Sec .11). (The men of Éire gathered together at a 'Tarbhfheis' – 'Bull-Sleeping'; a bull was killed by
them, and one man ate his fill of him, and drank his broth,
and a spell of truth was chanted over him while he was lying
down. The man he saw in his sleep – it was he who would be
king.)

By this method of divination, the man who had eaten the flesh of
the sacrificed bull and drank his soup had become identified
with the bull itself. The bull was now in the Otherworld, the

Land of the Ancestors, where knowledge abounded. The bull made known the knowledge of a suitable candidate for kingship to the seer in a dream. In the morning, the seer described the man he had seen in his dream to the druids and then they sought out a man of this description.

While a thousand years may separate them , the description of the New Year's Bull Rite in the Hebrides closely resembles the Irish Tarbhfheis. In both cases the bull is in the Otherworld. This is the place of health, prosperity, eternal youth and knowledge. In the Isles, the people want health and prosperity during the New Year now beginning, and they obtain health and prosperity by communion with the bull by smelling his burning hide.

In the Irish example of the Tarbhfheis, the purpose of the rite was more specific, related to a distinct occasion, the choosing of a new king on the death of the old one. This too was connected with beginnings. In this case, the search was for knowledge, a light from the Beyond to direct them towards the selection of the right man for the kingship. This too was connected to health and prosperity for the successful marriage of a good king to the goddess of the land would guarantee the welfare of the kingdom.

In a similar way, in the well-known story of how Fionn Mac Cumhaill acquired his supernatural knowledge, a fish is caught and boiled. The fish has supernatural knowledge already as it has eaten the hazel berries of wisdom, and in any case, when killed it has entered into the Otherworld. Fionn burns his finger when boiling the fish and puts his finger in his mouth to relieve the pain. In doing so he eats a little of the fish. After this, he has only to chew his thumb, that is, indulge in the symbolic eating of the fish, to acquire hidden knowledge (Sutcliff, 1972, 15-17).

Sometimes an effort was made to give a more Christian tone to Hogmany as when the Leader from outside called on Bean a' Tí to open the door:

Mise gille Mhic De air Chollaig,

Eirich fein is fosgail dorus.

Callain seo. Callain seo. (CG 1, 154).

(I am the servant of the Son of God, at Hogmanay; get up

yourself and open the door. This is Kalends. This is Kalends.)

In houses where they were well treated and generous gifts were placed in the *Bolg* or bag carried around for that purpose, the group marched around the fire, *deiseal*, chanting a Rann of blessing on the house itself and on all who lived there, indeed a kind of consecration of the house at the start of the new year:

Gum beannachaidh Dia an t-ardrach,

Eadar chlach, is chuaille is chrann,

Eadar bhithe, bhliochd, is aodach,

Slainte dhaoin bhi daonnan ann (CG 1, 156).

(May God bless the dwelling house, both stone and beam and stave; both food and drink and clothing; May healthy people be always there.)

Seasonal Rites containing ideas of animal sacrifice building bridges to another world, communing in the sacrifice by various means such as eating and drinking, smelling, wrapping oneself in the hide of the sacrificed animal and so forth will strike many modern people as lacking respectibily and out of sympathy with prevalent ideas. Nevertheless, at the heart of Catholic Christianity is the figure of Christ on the Cross and the rich materials used to depict the scene, combined with the artistic competence of the artist or sculptor, do not hide the shocking reality of the original happening. Nor does the strict teaching of the church regarding the Body and Blood of Christ in the Sacrifice of the Mass lessen the archaic character of the Eucharist and its links to ancient tradition in the religious history of mankind.

The problem is not new as is clear from the Jews' reaction to Our Lord's statement: 'I am the living bread which has come down from heaven. Anyone who eats this bread will live for ever; and the bread that I shall give is my flesh, for the life of the world.' Then the Jews started arguing with one another: 'How can this man give us his flesh to eat?' they said. Jesus replied: 'I tell you most solemnly, if you do not eat the flesh of the Son of Man and drink his blood, you will not have life in you' (John 6: 51-53).

The Winter Solstice (21 December) in Ireland is marked by another observance apart from the entrance of the sun into the megalithic tumulus of Newgrange. This is the 'Hunting of the Wren' *(An Dreoilín)*, well known in Ireland and certainly one of the few places left where the rite is practised today. It centres around the Winter Solstice, St Stephen's Day (26 December) being the usual date for the Wren Boys/Girls to go around collecting, carrying a dead wren tied to a holly bush. The rite is associated with transition – with the turning of the year as the sun recovers from its downward path and is just recovering its strength for the half-year ahead of growing light and heat.

While the Wren Rite takes place six weeks (half the sum of the quarter days) before St Brigid's Day, they both mark the beginning of the year from different points of view, and in folklore accounts the two rites are often compared as they resemble each other closely.

The wren is one of the tiniest of birds, sings loudly even in cold weather and is very prolific. He cannot fly very well and lives mostly in hedges. Anciently it was believed that it was unlucky to kill a wren – outside of the ritual killing at the Winter Solstice. He was known as 'King of All Birds' as an international tale tells of the bird's desire to have a king over them. They decide that whoever flies the highest will be chosen. When nobody is looking, the puny wren climbs up on the eagle's back. The eagle soars up in the air above the other birds. The wren takes off from there and the other birds declare that he is king. The ritual, however, makes it clear that there is a price to be paid for his kingship.

For the Rite itself a wren is killed and tied to a holly bush with berries and decorated with ribbons. The Wren Boys/Girls are masked, use extravagant dress, men often wear womens' clothes, and on St Stephen's Day – not the night before – they proceed from house to house, playing music on the way. Sometimes the 'Láir Bhán' or Hobby Horse is carried around. They stop at each house and recite the Rann:

'The wran, the wran, the king of all birds,

on St Stephen's Day he was caught in the furze.
Although he is little, his family is great,
Put your hand in your pocket and give us a trate (treat).
So, up with the kettle and down with the pan,
give us some money to bury the wran.
We wish you a merry Christmas and a happy new year,
with your pockets full of money and your cellar full of beer.'

The Rann refers to significant aspects of the observance when it mentions the king; St Stephen's Day (Winter Solstice period); the wren's notable fertility (his family is great); the burial of the wren (the householders are paying the expenses of the funeral); and the prosperity which will come as a result of faithfully carrying out the Rite – 'the luck of the year.'

This Rann or an alternative version is chanted outside each house visited. The householders are expected to make a donation, and in this way they participate in what is ritually the funeral of the king. In some areas, especially in Wales, a small bier in which the dead wren was enclosed was carried on the shoulders of two men. Sometimes they pretended that they were carrying a very heavy weight – as if they were carrying a real human king. The wren was buried in the local graveyard. The suggestion is that this is the funeral procession of a dead king.

Whatever the antiquity of this rite – and Eward Armstrong in his *Folklore of Birds* (1958) concludes that it derives from a very ancient Wren Cult carried by megalithic builders and reaching Britain during the Bronze Age. Its essentially profound meaning has been established by Dr Sylvie Muller in 'The Irish Wren Tales and Ritual – To Pay or Not to Pay the Debt of Nature' (Béal. Iml. 64-65, 1996-1997, pp. 131-169).

What we have comes essentially from nature – we are in debt to nature for its gifts of life and food. This debt to nature has to be acknowledged and if this is done willingly and gladly then nature, in its turn, will be magnanimous and will deal generously with the human race in the way of food and prosperity.

The King is the representative of his people. When the period of his reign is over and his successor is ready to succeed him, he is expected to go willingly to his death – as representative of his people to give himself back to nature as an acknowledgement that both he and they have received everything from her. Because of this gesture of self-sacrifice on behalf of his people, nature, in turn, will be generous to his successor and give him a prosperous reign. 'The King is Dead, Long Live the King.'

In Carcassone, in France, where a very elaborate form of Wren Rite was performed, the phrase 'Vive le Roi' with the date of the New Year about to begin was written in chalk on the door of each house visited (Frazer, 1923, 536-538).

A notable detail in the performance of the Rite in Ireland was that a household in which a death had occurred during the year was left unvisited by the Wren Boys. In the normal way, it would be considered an insult to the householders to pass them by, but this was the exception. The reason is clear. The people of this house, in losing one of their members, had already paid their debt to nature for this year. They were not required to do so again by making a donation, as the others in the area did. For in making a donation 'to bury the Wren/King' they had shown their solidarity with the King in his willing surrender of himself to death, on his own and on their account. They too, in a small way, had acknowledged their debt to nature.

Given that the wren stands for man, what of the wren-boys or wren-killlers? From the stories collected in Ireland connecting the wren with the fox, the mouse,the eagle and female birds, as well as the vegetable and animal masks, suggest that they stand for nature. If the wren is man and the animals/birds/vegetation is nature, then nature is taking back from man what she has given him, and he has willingly given it back to her as an ac-knowledgement of his debt and in the belief that she will give back life generously.

Dr Muller, discusses the findings of a French anthropologist, Roberte Hamayon, concerning some Siberian hunters and food collectors and their attitude to nature which they regard as their supplier of food.

'For these people, human flesh is given back to nature in return for all the animal flesh which has been taken from nature. After death, the hunter's body is thus exposed in the forest to be eaten by wild beasts. Therefore nature feeds man as long as it can feed on him in return. In other words, death, his own death (and his diseases), is the price man has to pay to nature for enjoying life (and health). Furthermore, this means that man can induce nature to feed him even better by symbolically and ritually feeding it in advance with human flesh' (Béal. 64-65, 149).

This then, seems to be the ideology behind the Rite of Hunting the Wren – an ideology that goes to the heart of mankind's relations with nature.

In a hunter-gatherer society, this link with nature, as the great supplier of food and health-giving herbs, was close and immediate. A change of ideology must have come about gradually at the advent of the Megalithic Period when a new and more distant attitude to nature occurred.

At this period, stock-breeding and cultivation of the land for the growing of corn developed, combined, no doubt for a considerable period, by hunting and gathering – until recently one could see people picking blackberries from the hedges of country roads. But now, with this development, man was becoming more independant of nature. The cows were there in the field close to his house. They provided milk on a daily basis. If necessary, cattle could be killed for meat and for leather clothing. Similarly, while cropping was precarious, grain could be stored to provide a relatively reliable source of food for most of the year, and this was renewable, as some of the grain could be set aside as seed for next year's crop. From this new independence a more distant relationship with nature could develope. Man could become more self-reliant and the old 'give and take' relationship with nature weakened. Man was very gradually approaching modern man's isolation from the sources of life and food, and an ideology of domination of nature rather than a relationship of participation was developing. The 'Hunting of the Wren' seems to point to a very early stratum of society in which man was very aware of his true position in the universe.

Often, the performers of the rite have little knowledge of its meaning but still it is important that the actual performance takes place as the meaning can always be supplied. In some places, a carved effigy of the wren is used. In other places there is no wren at all. This is like a Tea Party with no tea and all that remains is a kind of pageant. This ritual is a treasured heritage from the remote past and the myth behind the ritual contains an ever-valid doctrine of the relations between man and nature.

The 'Mumming Play' tradition, as it is known in Britain and in the southeast of Ireland, is closely allied to the beginning of the year and particularly the Christmas Season. In many ways the Mummers resemble the Brídeog as they go from house to house to perform a miniature drama and collect some money. As the Mummers' Plays deal essentially with the victory of good over evil, of light over darkness, they are particularly appropriate to the period of the Winter Solstice with the turning of the sun and the increase in the length of daylight. It would seem that in origin the Mummers' Play was a rite of magic, a death and resurrection scene enacted by humans to produce a similar effect in nature – the death of the old season and the birth of the crops in the new year.

The mummers traditionally wear greenery or straw as a disguise, with the idea of new life emerging from the dead year. Sometimes one of the characters is even called 'Jack Straw'. Alan Gailey suggests that a straw effigy may have once been carried around by the Mummers to personify vegetation and the bounty of nature (1969, 75).

In a typical kitchen scene the characters enter:
Turkish Knight: 'Here come I, a Turkish Knight,
Who learned in Turkish land to fight;
I'll fight this man with courage bold.
If his blood's hot I'll make it cold' (Hardy, 1974, 138)
St George: 'Here come I, Saint George, the valiant man,
With naked sword and spear in hand,
Who fought the dragon and brought him to the slaughter,
And by this won fair Sabra, the King of Egypt's daughter;

What mortal man would dare to stand
Before me with my sword in hand?
If then thou art that Turkish Knight,
Draw out thy sword, and let us fight' (Hardy, 1974, 138)

Usually it is the great Hero (St George) who is defeated and sinks down on the earth mortally wounded. His mother or wife enters and weeps floods of tears with great lamentation. A Doctor is summoned and, with many humorous remarks as to his medical qualifications and his fee, he succeeds in reviving the dead Hero by means of some magical brew. There is great rejoicing and the revived Hero is taken away amidst much shouting and noisy cheering.

In the fallen Hero one can see the corn seed ploughed into the earth. Then the rain and moisture and heat come – the tears and medicine of the wife and doctor standing for the processes of nature which have the effect of making the seed sprout and rise up above the ground. The Hero is not really resurrected as he was before, in his human form (though in the actual Mummers' Play this is how it has to be shown) but as the soul of vegetation. He comes back to life in the growing corn. A wonderful relief from Philae in Egypt, reproduced by R. T. Rundle Clarke (*Myth and Symbol in Ancient Egypt*, London 1959, 101) shows the cow-headed goddess Hathor pouring water from a jug into a channel filled with earth – a symbol of irrigated land. Corn springs up, and out of the midst of the corn rises a soul-bird, a bird with a human head. This is the god Osiris. 'When Osiris rises in his soul-form the plants begin to grow. In fact they are really the same thing' (Ibid 102). In Egypt, the period close to the Summer Solstice (21 June) marks the rising of the Nile, the rising of the corn, the rising of the soul of Osiris, the rising of Sothis (Sirius), the Dog Star and the rising of Orion.

While the Hero-Combat did not form part of the Brídeog or the Threshold Rite, nevertheless, the death and resurrection theme is found, as we have seen, in the Rites of Brigid in the very direct form of taking grains of corn from St Brigid's Cross and mixing them with the seed being sown in the spring.

Again, the suggestion has been made, that the 'Purusa Myth' was involved as a background to certain pracices such as the 'dismemberment' of the effigy of Brigid and using the parts as a means to health, prosperity and protection in the Threshold Rite.

In speaking of the Purusa Myth – the myth of the primordial man being sacrificed by the gods and dismembered so that his head formed the sky, his hair the vegetation, his blood the seas, his flesh the earth, and so on – in relation to Brigid's Threshold Rite, it may be remarked that a popular English Mummers' Play may also have this Myth as a background to the ritual.

This is the play known as 'The Little Tup' and centred round the song of 'The Derby Ram'. The Tup Play was usually performed around Christmastide. About six men took part and their arrival was eagarly awaited by the household. The tup or ram was represented by an artificial ram's head with a large cloth representing the body in much the same style as the 'Láir Bhán'. The ram had a rope around his neck held by one of the characters and he pranced around to the great amusement of the onlookers. The play began as in so many other Circuit Rites by the recitation of a formula outside the door:

> There is a little tup,
> And he's standing at your door;
> And if you'll have 'im in, Sir,
> He'll please you more and more.

Those inside the house shout: 'Bring 'im in, bring 'im in.'
> The Mummers and Tup enter and the rhyme continues:
> The very first day that tup was born,
> He cut some funny capers.
> He ate a field of turnip tops,
> And fourteen tons o' taters. (potatoes)
> Bailey, Bailey, laddie-fer-lairey-aye.

> The wool that grew (up) on his back, Sir,
> It grew so mighty long,
> The eagles built their nests in it,

I heard the young ones' song.
Bailey, Bailey, laddie-fer-lairey-aye.

The horns that grew up on his head,
They grew so mighty high,
That every time he shook 'is head,
They rattled against the sky.
Bailey, Bailey, laddie-fer-lairey-aye.

The Leader calles for a butcher to kill the Tup and a butcher called Jack enters. He draws his knife and goes through the motions of killing the ram. The Tup falls to the ground. All sing an unusual song depicting the various uses made of different parts of the body of the Tup:

All the women in Derby
Came begging for his hide,
To make some leather 'approns'
To last them all their lives.
Bailey, Bailey, laddie-fer-lairey-aye.

All the young lads in Derby
Came begging for his eyes
To kick them up and down the street
For footballs and bulls-eyes.
Bailey, Bailey, laddie-fer-lairey-aye.

All the (ringers) in Derby
Came begging for his tail,
To ring the Derby passing-bell
That hangs upon the wall.
Bailey, Bailey, laddie-fer lairey-aye.

This concluded the Old Tup Mummers' Play. Cakes and alewere distributed and a collection was made (Abrahams, R., 'Folk Drama' 355-357 in Dorson, R., (Ed.), *Folklore and Folklife, An Introduction* (Chicago 1972).

In some versions of the play a doctor is called and the Tup revived. This brings it into conformity with the death and resurrection theme of other Mummers' Plays (Pennick, 1998, 107).

It appers, however, from the unusual content of this play, that its theme is quite different – that it is a Creation Theme that is involved, based on the Purusa Myth of a great giant from whose dismembered body the universe was formed.

According to the Derby Ram Song, the ram is so huge that he covers an acre of land with each stride. He is finally slain and several onlookers drown in the torrent of his blood. His gall-stones are rolled away like boulders. As Quentin Cooper and Paul Sullivan (1994, 356) point out there is a distinct similarity between this and the Germanic gigantic god Ymir.

He was slain and the rush of his blood drowned all the Frost Giants and formed the oceans of the world. His flesh became the earth, his teeth became the rocks, his skull the sky. His bones became the mountains and his hair became the trees (vegetation). Other versions add that Purusa's (the primordial man) mind became the clouds and his breath became the wind. Ymir (or Purusa) 'inhabited a primordial realm, rich in potential but as yet unformed' (Lincoln, 1986,1-2)

The general thesis of this widespread Creation Myth, so different from that of the Book of Genesis, is that a primordial being is killed and dismembered , and that from that being's body, the cosmos is created. There are many variations of this general theme.

It does appear, that in the English Midland Tupping Play, the Purusa Creation Myth is 'the Myth behind the Ritual' and in this humble, unsophisticated drama, preserved by farmers and villagers of the English Countryside, we have a presentation of the Purusa Myth of the Indian 'Rg Veda' dating back to 900BC. We have seen that the dismemberment of the Brídeog and the appropriation of the different parts for different purposes on St Brigid's Eve appears to be a variation of the same Creation Narrative acted out in ritual.

This study began with a short account of the life of Brigid as it is found in the literary sources. We saw the mystical statement about her in the Leabhar Breac where she is envisioned as a sun shining down on the angels in heaven, in the presence of the

Holy Trinity. This vision of Brigid belongs to the Otherworld, the world beyond, but the author does not forget those who are still inhabitants of this world here below, and he sends up a fervent prayer to Brigid, that she assist us in reaching that Eternal City which she adorns by her presence. The widespread Cult of Brigid in all its varied and complicated forms represents this prayer and embodies the hopes and longings of her many devotees. We have seen that accounts of her hospitality, her charity and care for the poor have influenced people down through the ages. The various rituals and customs which have accumulated around her feastday on the first of February, the ancient Celtic Feast of Imbolc, are a testimony to the honour in which she is held.

She is the great link between pagan past and Christian present. Her life embraced a period of transition and this is reflected in the form taken by various elements of her cult. The saint stands in the shadow of Brigit the Celtic Goddess, daughter of An Daghda Mór. Central to her cult is the idea of her annual return to bring a blessing on the household who welcomes her.

Apart from the domestic cult of Brigid there are pilgrimages to her Holy Wells. Here, local communities gather to show their collective veneration of the saint. She is associated with the beginning of the the farmer's year, with the new life and vigour which springtime brings. At her annual return from the Otherworld, she visits her people with a message of hope for a new beginning.

Bibliography

Almquist, B., Ó Catháin, S., Ó Héalaí, P., (eds.), *The Heroic Process* (Dún Laoghaire 1997)

'An Seabhac', *An Seanchaidhe Muimhneach* (Baile Atha Cliath 1932)

Archdall, M., *Monasticon Hibernicum* (Dublin 1886)

Baildini, U., *Primavera* (London 1986)

Barrington, T. J., *Discovering Kerry* (Dublin 1976)

Berger, P., *The Goddess Obscured* (London 1988)

Bergin, O., *How the Dagda got his Magic Staff* (New York 1927)

Best, R. and Lawlor, H., *The Martyrology of Tallaght* (London 1931)

Bord, J. and C., *Earth Rites* (London 1982)

Bord, J. and C., *Sacred Waters* (London 1985)

Bowen, E. G., 'The Cult of St Brigit', *Studia Celtica* 8-9 (1973-1974) 33-47

Breathnach, D., *Chugat an Púca* (Baile Atha Cliath 1993)

Burl, A., *Rings of Stone* (London 1979)

Burl, A., *Prehistoric Stone Circles* (Aylesbury 1983)

Butler, A., *Butler's Lives of the Saints* (London 1956)

Calendarium Romanum (Roma 1969)

Campbell, J., *Occidental Mythology* (London 1976)

Cammaerts, E., *Flemish Painting* (London 1945)

Carey, E., *Faughart of Saint Brigid* (Dublin 1982)

Carmichael, A., *Carmina Gadelica* (Edinburgh 1972) = (CG)

Cawley, A. C., (Ed.), *Everyman and Medieval Miracle Plays* (London 1974)

Chemery, P., 'Vegetation', Eliade, M., *The Encyclopedia of Religion* (New York 1987)

Compte, P., *The Wordsworth Dictionary of Mythology* (Ware 1994)

Connolly, S., 'Cogitosus's Life of St Brigit', *JRSAI* 117 (1987)

Cooper, Q. and Sullivan, P., *Maypoles, Martyrs and Mayhem* (London 1994)

Crepin, J., *Guide du Pelerin a la Chapelle de Sainte Brigide d'Irlande en la ville de Fosses, au Diocese de Namur* (Fosses 1924)

Croker, T. C., *Researches in the South of Ireland* (London 1824)

Dames, M., *The Avebury Cicle* (London 1977)

Dames, M., *Mythic Ireland* (London 1992)

Danaher, K., *The Year in Ireland* (Cork 1972)

Davidson, H., *Myths and Symbols in Pagan Europe* (Manchester 1988)

De Bhaldraithe, T., (Eag.), *Cin Lae Amhlaoidh* (Baile Atha Cliath 1976)

Delaney, J., 'Fieldwork in South Roscommon', Ó Danachair, C., (Ed.), *Folk and Farm* (Dublin 1976)

De Smedt, C., et De Backer, J., *Acta Sanctorum Hiberniae* (Edinburgh 1888)

de Vries, *La Religion des Celtes* (Paris 1977)

Dillon, M. and Chadwick, N., *The Celtic Realms* (London 1967)

Dinneen, P., (Eag.), *Foras Feasa ar Éirinn* (London 1908)

Duchesne, L., *Christian Worship: Its Origin and Evolution* (London 1931)

Elworthy, P., *The Evil Eye* (New York 1989)

Eogan, G., *Knowth and the Passage Tombs of Ireland* (London 1986)

Evans, E. E., (Ed.); *Harvest Home* (Armagh1975)

Evans-Wents, W. Y., *The Fairy Faith in Celtic Countries* (Gerrards Cross 1977)

Farmer, D. H., *The Oxford Dictionary of Saints* (Oxford 1978)

Farrar, J. and S., *Eight Sabbaths for Witches* (London 1981)

Fortescue, A., *The Divine Liturgy of Our Father among the Saints: John Chrysostom* (London 1908)

Fraser, J., 'The First Battle of Moytura', *Ériu* VIII (1915), 1-63

Frazer, G., *The Golden Bough* (London 1923)

Gailey, A., *Irish Folk Drama* (Cork 1969)

Gimbutas, M., *The Goddesses and Gods of Olf Europe* (London 1989)

Gougaud, L., *Gaelic Pioneers of Christianity* (Dublin 1923)

Gray, E., *Cath Muige Tuired* (Dublin 1982)

Green, M., *Dictionary of Celtic Myth and Legend* (London 1992)

Guerber, H., *Greece and Rome* (New York 1986)

Gwynn, A. and Hadcock, R., *Medieval Religious Houses, Ireland* (London 1970)

Gwynn, E., *The Metrical Dindshenchus* (Dublin 1906)

Gwynn, E., (Ed.); *The Rule of Tallaght, Hermathena* No. XLIV, Second Supplement. Vol. (Dublin 1927)

Happe, P., *English Mystery Plays* (Penguin Books 1975)

Hardy, T., *The Return of the Native* (London 1974)

Harrison, J., *Themis: A Study of the Social Origins of Greek Religion* (London 1989)

Hastings, J., *Encyclopedia of Religion and Ethics* (Edinburgh 1909)

Hazlitt, W., *Dictionary of Faiths and Folklore* (London 1995)

Henderson, C., *Survival of belief among the Celts* (Glasgow 1911)

Hennessey, W. and Kelly, D., (Eds.), *The Book of Fenagh* (Dublin 1875)

Henry, F., *La Sculpture Irlandaise pendant les douze premiers siècles de l'Ere Chretienne* (Paris 1933)

Henry, F., *Irish Art in the Early Christian Period to 800 AD* (London 1965)

Hole, C., *A Dictionary of British Folk Customs* (London 1978)

IFC = Irish Folklore Commission collection of manuscripts.

James, E., *Seasonal Feasts and Festivals* (London 1961)

Johns, C. A., *Flowers of the Field* (London 1916)

Jones, G. and T., *The Mabinogion* (London 1949)

Joyce, P., *A Smaller History of Ancient Ireland* (Dublin 1908)

Kenney, J. P., *The Sources for the Early History of Ireland* (New York 1929)

Killanin, Lord, and Duignan,M., *The Shell Guide to Ireland* (London 1976)

Killip, M., *The Folklore of the Isle of Man* (London 1986)

Knott, E., (Ed.), *Togail Bruidne Da Derga* (Dublin 1936)

Knowles, D., *The Monastic Constitutions of Lanfranc* (London 1951)

Lang, A., *The Maid of France* (London 1908)

Leask, H. G., *Glendalough, National Monuments* (Dublin)

Lempriere, J., *A Classical Dictionary* (London 1886)

Le Roux, F., et Guyonvarch, C., *Les Druides* (Rennes 1982)

Lietzmann, H., *Liturgishche Texte, Ordo Missae Romanus et Gallicanus* (Berlin 1935)

Lincoln, B., *Death, War and Sacrifice* (Chicago 1991)

Logan, P., *The Holy Wells of Ireland* (Gerrards Cross 1980)

Lucas, A. T., *Penal Crucifixes* (Dublin 1958)

Macalister, R., (Ed.), Lebor Gabala Erenn, Part III, (Dublin 1940)

MacCana, P., *Celtic Mythology* (London 1970)

MacCulloch, J. A., *The Religion of the Ancient Celts* (London 1991)

MacDonald, K., *Saint Bride* (Edinburgh 1992)

Mac Giolla Chomhaill, A., *Naomh Bríd, Muire na nGael* (Baile Átha Cliath 1984)

MacKillop, J., *Dictionary of Celtic Mythology* (Oxford 1998)

MacLysaght, E., *Irish Life in the Seventeenth Century* (Dublin 1939)

MacNeill, M., *The Festival of Lughnasa* (Dublin 1982)

Mac Philibín, L., *Mise Pádraig* (Baile Átha Cliath 1960)

Mann, N., *Glastonbury Tor* (Annenterprise Publications 1986)

Martene, E., *Tractatus de Antiqua Ecclesiae Disciplina in Divinis Celebrandis Officiis* (Lugduni MDCCVI)

McCone, K., 'Bríd Chill Dara', *Léachtaí Cholm Cille* XII (1982) 30-92

McCone, K., *Pagan Past and Christian Present in Early Irish Literature* (Maynooth 1990)

McNeill, M., *The Silver Bough, A Calendar of Scottish National Festivals* (Glasgow 1959/1961)

Martimort, A., *L'Eglise en Priére* (Tournai 1961)

Martyrologium Romanum (Roma 1930)

Mason, T. H., 'St Brigid's Crosses', *JRSAI* LXXV (1945) 160-166

Meehan, C., *Sacred Ireland* (Glastonbury 2002)

Meyer, K., *Fianaigecht* (Dublin 1910)

Michell, J., *New Light on the Ancient Mystery of Glastonbury* (Glastonbury 1990)

Migne, J. P., *Patrologiae Latinae Cursus Completus* (Petit-Moutrouge 1849)

Miles, C., *Christmas Customs and Traditions* (New York 1976)

Missale Romanum (1970)

Murphy, G., *Duaniare Finn*, Vol.3 (Dublin 1953)

Murphy, G., *Early Irish Lyrics* (Oxford 1956)

Mueller, M., *St Caesarius of Arles, Sermons* (Catholic University of America Press 1973)

Nic Dhonnchadha, L., (Ed.), *Aided Muircheartaig Meic Erca* (Dublin 1964)

Ní Shéaghdha, N., agus Ní Mhuirgheasa, M., *Trí Bruidne* (Baile Átha Cliath 1941)

Nutall, P., *A Classical and Archaeological Dictionary* (London 1840)

O'Brien, M., 'The Old Irish Life of St Brigid', *Irish Historical Studies*, Vol I (1938)

Ó Catháin, S., *The Festival of Brigit* (Baile Atha Cliath 1995)

Ó Céileachair, D., *Sgéal mo Bheatha* (Baile Atha Cliath 1948)

Ó Corráin, D., and Maguire, F., *Gaelic Personal Names* (Dublin 1981)

O'Curry, E., *Lectures on the Manuscript Materials of Ancient Irish History* (Dublin 1878)

O'Curry, E., *On the Manners and Customs of the Ancient Irish* (Dublin 1878)

Ó Danachair, C., (Ed.), *Folk and Farm* (Dublin 1976)

O'Donovan, J., *Annala Ríoghachta Éireann: Annals of the Kingdom of Ireland by the Four Masters* (Dublin 1856)

O'Donovan, J., (Ed.), *Leabhar na gCeart or The Book of Rights* (Dublin 1847)

Ó Duilearga, S., (Eag.); *Leabhar Sheáin Í Chonaill* (Baile Átha Cliath 1978)

Ó Duinn, S., *Forbhais Droma Dámhgháire* (Corcaigh 1992)

Ó Duinn, S., *Orthaí Cosanta sa Chráifeacht Cheilteach* (Maigh Nuad 1990)

Ó Fiaich, T., *Gaelscrínte i gcéin* (Baile Átha Cliath 1960)

O'Flaherty, W., *The Rig Veda* (Penguin 1981)

Ó Floinn, T. agus Mac Cana, P., *Scéalaíocht na Ríthe* (Baile Átha Cliath 1956)

Ogilvie, R., *The Romans and their Gods* (London 1969)

O'Grady, S., *Silva Gadelica* (London 1892)

O'Hanlon, J., *Lives of the Irish Saints* (Dublin 1875)

Ó hAodha, D., (Ed.), *Bethu Brigte* (Dublin 1978)

Ó hÓgáin, D., *Myth, Legend and Romance: An Encyclopedia of Irish Folk Traditions* (New York 1991)

Ó Laoghaire, D., *Ár bPaidreacha Dúchais* (Baile Átha Cliath 1975)

O'Meara, J., *Topography of Ireland: Giraldus Cambrensis* (Dundalk 1951)

Ó Muirgheasa, E., 'The Holy Wells of Donegal', *Béaloideas* (Nodlaig 1936) 143-162

Ó Nualláin, S., *A Survey of the Stone Circles of Cork and Kerry* (Dublin 1984)

Opie, I. and Tatem, M., (Eds.), *A Dictionary of Superstitions* (Oxford 1992)

Opie, I., *The Singing Game* (Oxford 1988)

O'Rahilly, C., *Táin Bó Cualgne* (Dublin 1967) (=TBC)

O'Rahilly, T., *Early Irish History and Mythology* (Dublin 1946)

Ó Riain, P., (Eag.), *Cath Almaine* (Dublin 1978)

Orpen, G., 'Aenach Carmen: its Site', *JRSAI* XXXVI (1906)

O'Sullivan, J. C., 'St Brigid's Crosses', *Folk Life* XI (1973)

Ó Súilleabháin, S., *A Handbook of Irish Folklore* (Dublin 1942)

Ó Súilleabháin, S., 'An Crios Bríde', Gailey, A. and Ó hÓgáin, D., (Eds.), *Gold under the Furze* (Dublin 1982)

Penfick, N., *Practical Magic in the Northern Tradition* (Wellingborough 1989)
Plummer, C., *Bethada Naem nErenn: Lives of Irish Saints* (Oxford 1922)
Plummer, C., *Irish Litanies* (London 1925)
Porteous, C., *The Ancient Customs of Derbyshire* (Derby)
Powers Coe, P., 'The Severed Head in Fenian Tradition', *Folklore and Mythology*, 13 (1989) 17-41
Puhvel, J., *Comparative Mythology* (Baltimore 1989)
Rawlinson, G., (Ed.), *Herodotus: Persian Wars* (New York 1942)
Raya, J., *Byzantine Missal* (Alabama 1958)
Rees, A. and B., *Celtic Heritage* (London 1976)
Ross, A., *Everyday Life of the Pagan Celts* (London 1972)
Ryan, E., *New Catholic Encyclopedia* (Washington 1966)
The Sarum Missal in English (London 1868)
Schilling, R., 'Vesta', *The Encyclopedia of Religion* (New York 1987)
Schulte, A., *Consecranda* (New York 1906)
Shah, I., *Oriental Magic* (St Albans 1973)
Smith, W., *A Smaller Dictionary of Greek and Roman Antiquities* (London 1953)
Smyth, A., *Celtic Leinster* (Irish Academic Press 1982)
Southern, R., *The Seven Ages of the Theatre* (London 1985)
Spence, L., *British Fairy Origins* (Wellingborough 1981)
Stercks, C., 'Une Formule Paienne dans des Textes Chretien de l'Irlande Ancienne', *Etudes Celtiques* XIV (1974-1975) 229-233
Stewart, R., *The Waters of the Gap* (Bath 1989)
Stevenson, K., 'The Origins and Development of Candlemas: a Struggle for Identity and Coherence', *Ephemerides Liturgicae* 102 (1988) 316-346
Stokes, S. and Windisch, E., *Agallamh na Senorach* (Leipzig 1900)
Stokes, W., *The Martyrology of Oengus the Culdee* (London 1905)
Stokes, W., *The Tripartite Life of Patrick* (London 1887)
Stokes, W., *Three Irish Glossaries* (London 1862)
Stokes, W., (Ed.), *Three Middle Irish Homilies on the Lives of Saints Patrick, Brigit and Columba* (Calcutta 1877)
Stokes, W. and Strachan, J., *Thesaurus Palaeohibernicus* (Cambridge 1903)
Streit, J., *Sun and Cross* (Edinburgh 1984)
Stutley, M. and J., *A Dictionary of Hinduism* (London 1977)
Sutcliff, R., *The High Deeds of Finn Mac Cool* (Penguin 1972)
Swaddling, J., *The Ancient Olympic Games* (London 2004)
Taylor, D., *Singing Rhymes* (Loughborough 1979)
Taylor, I., *The Giant of Penhill* (Dunnington 1987)
Thurneysen, R., (Ed.), *Scéala Mucce Meic Dathó* (Dublin 1935)
Tierney, J., *The Celtic Ethnography of Posidonius* (Dublin 1984)
Tommasini, A., *Irish Saints in Italy* (London 1937)
Ua Muirgheasa, E., *Seanfhocla Uladh* (Baile Atha Cliath 1907)
Ua Murchadha, D., *Sean-Aimsearacht* (Baile Átha Cliath 1939)
Vallency, Col., *Essay on the Antiquity of the Irish Language* (Dublin 1781)

Van Hamel, A.G., *Compert Con Culainn* (Dublin 1933)
Varagnac, A., et Chollot-Varagnac, M., *Les Traditions Populaires* (Paris 1978)
Vendreyes, I., (Ed.), *Airne Fíngein* (Dublin 1953)
Whitlock, R., *A Calendar of Country Customs* (London 1978)
Wormald, F., *English Kalendars before AD 1100* (London 1934)
Wright, T., *The Historical Works of Giraldus Cambrensis* (London 1887)

Journals:

Béaloideas
Éigse
Ephemerides Liturgicae
Ériu
Joournal of the Cork Historical and Archaeological Society (=JCHAS)
Journal of the Royal Society of Antiquaries of Ireland (=JRSAI)
La Maison Dieu (=LMD)
Proceedings of the Royal Irish Academy (=PRIA)
Revue Celtique (=RC)

(LU = *Lebor na hUidre/Leabhar na hUidhre*)

Index